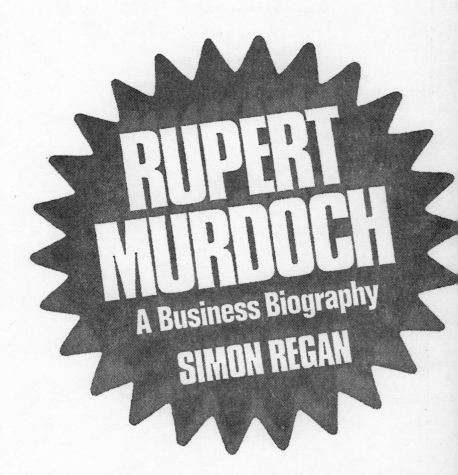

RUPERT MURDOCH

A Business Biography

SIMON REGAN

Angus and Robertson · Publishers

Angus & Robertson · Publishers
London · Sydney · Melbourne
Singapore · Manila

First published by Angus and Robertson (U.K.) Ltd. 1976

Copyright © Simon Regan 1976

ISBN 0 207 95509 3

Made and printed in Great Britain by
Northumberland Press Limited, Gateshead

CONTENTS

Preface

There were many ways this book could have been written. But, for two reasons it could only end as half a book. Rupert Murdoch has, I am asssured by many of his friends, only just started. This is by way of a half-term report. Murdoch's life has been so full of events, surprises, tales and anecdotes, that to do the job properly would take several volumes. And a little longer than the year it took me. I felt the whole purpose of this book was to explain an enigma.

In order to introduce this man and explain who he is and what he is doing, I have therefore presented a series of pen-portraits of him, his habits and complexes, his friends, way of life, his enemies and the environments he dominates. It is not a definitive biography and does not attempt to delve far into the chronology of events. Rather, it attempts to introduce a man and his surroundings at a significant point in his own history.

Rupert Murdoch was far from keen for this book to be written. In fact he cooperated with me only after a rather dubious piece of blackmail on my part as I said I had accepted a commission and was going to write a book anyway. In the past he has always turned down all light-hearted or serious attempts to write his life story. A definitive study of his father has been held back by him, even though it has won two literary prizes in manuscript form. Murdoch did not want me to write the book for two reasons. He felt the time was wrong and he felt if he ever did have a book written about him he had several friends in journalism who he would like to do the job. Murdoch also made it plain to me he did not share many of the views I have put forward and, in fact, vigorously argued against some of them. This is therefore neither an official nor even a semi-official book.

This said, after Mr Murdoch had seen the inevitability of the book, he was very helpful and at no time tried to stop me seeing anyone in his organization or prevent me from seeing any papers or cuttings. He never tried to influence me. But constantly advised on the occasions we met that I should try to write an honest book, even if he disapproved of it. We did go over the manuscript together and certain errors of fact were corrected. He expressed doubts on the book only in areas where he thought I had been too kind to him and said his critics would become my critics. To him and to them I say that I have tried to write a fair and honest book about a controversial person. It is inevitable that his numerous friends and enemies will both say I have been biased towards the other.

Simon Regan 1975

Chapter 1

Battle for the News of the World

I

At a little after seven o'clock Sydney time on the evening of Tuesday October 15th, 1968, Rupert Murdoch was sitting in his spacious but windowless office on the fifth floor of the Holt Street headquarters of his News Limited of Australia. Predictably he was on the telephone; he was, as usual, doodling rapidly on the corner of an envelope as he spoke. Although the paper was scored and rescored, underlined, boxed in, and then embroidered with circles and lines the name 'Maxwell' could be seen quite clearly amid the squiggles. His stylish secretary Dorothy came in and delivered another sheaf of telex messages. She had taken it for granted she would be working late that evening and had already called her husband to warn him.

On the other side of the world the deputy London editor of News Limited, Frank O'Neill, was nursing a hangover in their London headquarters in Red Lion Court, just off Fleet Street. He kept a coffee percolator constantly on the boil as he telephoned everyone he could think of who might help him gain further information about the short Press Association announcement earlier that morning. Robert Maxwell, publisher, old adversary of Murdoch's and millionaire socialist MP, had offered a cool twenty-six million pounds in a takeover bid for the News of the World Organization which published the world's largest circulation Sunday newspaper.

The clock above O'Neill's typewriter showed it was creeping up to ten o'clock London time, on a rather dismal Wednesday morning. It would be a full hour before the first editions of the evening papers hit the street. O'Neill's instructions were very simple. He had to feed into the telex a non-stop running commentary of the latest news concerning the takeover bid until Murdoch had decided, one way or the other, if a counter-bid was feasible or not.

A few hundred yards on the other side of St Paul's Cathedral Lord Catto, Chairman of Morgan Grenfell, the Queen's merchant bankers, had called a hurried conference with his chief advisers and they had all joined in the immediate flurry of speculation and gossip which only a major takeover bid can bring to the City of London.

Catto spent an hour on the telephone before he decided Murdoch might be interested and booked a call to Sydney. The lights were burning late that night in the gaunt Surrey Hills building, a stone's throw from Sydney's city centre, where a constant stream of newspapers surge off the Murdoch presses. Dorothy was calling London. Somewhere across Asia the lines crossed and Murdoch's call to Catto rang shrilly in the City office a few minutes before Catto's call was finally cancelled by Dorothy in Sydney. To this day they both claim they were the first to call each other.

It was unclear at this stage exactly what Murdoch could do about the bid. He had been flirting with Fleet Street for some time. He wanted a foot in the door and this might be it, but at first glance it looked as if Maxwell was on very strong ground. It would be hard to oust him. He had already assured himself of about one third of the shares and was valuing the company higher than its actual share-worth. He was brimming with confidence and for months had been courting the City press, who at this stage were behind him to a man.

The only conceivable plan which the banker and the thirty-seven-year-old millionaire newspaperman could think of at that stage was the very one which would eventually make him the new prince of Fleet Street. Catto was despatched for a mid-morning conference with Hambros, the financial advisers to the News of the World Organization (NOWO) board under the chairmanship of Sir William Carr. It was immediately obvious to Catto, and Murdoch agreed with him, that neither News Limited of Australia (NLA), or the NOWO, could beat Maxwell on their own.

But, with some clever foreplay, much gambling, tough negotiation and a lot of candle-burning with his team of aides,
Murdoch saw a way of joining forces with Carr so that both
sides could wage successful jungle warfare with the bristlingly
confident Robert Maxwell.

In 1968 Fleet Street was divided up among seven concerns—
six of them family orientated. Northcliffe's Associated Press
owned the *Daily Mail, Daily Sketch* and *Evening News*; Aitken's Beaverbrook Organization owned the *Daily* and *Sunday
Express* and the *Evening Standard*. The International Publishing Corporation (IPC) owned the *Sunday People*, the *Daily Mirror*
—the world's largest-selling popular tabloid—the *Sunday Mirror*,
the then ill-fated *Sun* and a huge proportion of the country's
magazines. Lord Thomson had *The Times* and the *Sunday
Times*; *The Observer* was held in trust by the Astor family;
Lord Hartwell's *Daily* and *Sunday Telegraph* were safely
guarded. All that was left to a potential buyer, apart from the
Financial Times, was the *News of the World.*

At first sight the Maxwell bid looked very attractive to the
City desks of every Fleet Street paper. The NOWO had a highly
lucrative chain of provincial newspapers in Bemrose; book and
directory publishing interests; and the papermaking firm of
Townsend Hook. Maxwell's Pergamon already had a vast publishing and printing outfit which, according to the published
figures, showed neat figures with healthy profits.

For several years Murdoch had been flirting with Fleet Street
through the back door of the City of London. He had shrewdly
been sifting away profits from News Limited and putting them
into Fleet Street.

Sir Norman Young had introduced him to Lord Catto. Catto
is one of the shrewdest financial takeover operators. Young and
Lord Catto were old friends. After various turmoils in the past,
Sir Norman and Rupert are now reconciled and share a healthy
respect for each other.

Catto had been instructed by Murdoch to find out the
feasibility of a Fleet Street takeover. In between times Murdoch

had, against most advice, gone for the big stuff. He eventually bought two million pounds of IPC shares with a view to getting an equity of ten per cent. He had been finally convinced the task would be difficult. But Catto was also looking at the takeover vulnerability of the rest of London's papers. They were all, as he eventually pointed out, a difficult proposition to get into.

Catto and Murdoch had disagreed in a general way about IPC. Catto was convinced Murdoch was wasting his time. 'He would never have got a large enough share to hold the board meetings,' he said. But Murdoch had hatched a plan. He could see the company was failing and was probably going to bust up. He felt it was obvious that Cecil King was riding for a fall and there was no one else to run the company. He knew, when King left, the bankers would be looking for an alternative solution. They eventually found it, of course, in Reed International. But if Murdoch had been there at that time—sitting there with ten per cent and possibly with a partner with another ten per cent—he feels he could have probably stopped the Reed group very easily. 'I don't think it would have been a terribly good financial deal, but it would have been a question of getting in and playing it from there.'

Had Morgan Grenfell looked at the NOWO a little closer and earlier they would have discovered what the bankers, Hill, Samuel, discovered for Robert Maxwell: that the organization was ripe for a strong bid and that, with the agreement of only one major shareholder, the paper could be wrested from the Carr family. But it took a shrewd bit of talking by Maxwell to get a promise of twenty-five per cent of the shares from Professor Dereck Jackson, Sir William's cousin, before the NOWO woke up one morning to find itself so vulnerable. In fact, Jackson had decided for some time before the takeover that he wanted to get rid of his shares. Rothschilds had been casting around for a possible buyer and had heard Maxwell could be their man. Hill, Samuel and Rothschilds finally got down to working out a takeover formula before anyone else had a look in.

The telephone in the spacious air-conditioned area of Holt Street the journalists call Mahogany Row, was never on its hook that Tuesday night. Murdoch called round every one of consequence to and in his Australian empire, kept the telex machine jingling all night and spoke several times to Catto in London. By the time Catto was being ushered in to meet Harry Sporborg of Hambros, Murdoch had a fairly good idea of where he stood. He called all his advisers and spelt out instructions to underlings the breadth of the continent and immediately succumbed to the excitement and recharge of adrenalin which he admits only the possibility of a big takeover can bring him.

II

The reaction to Maxwell's bid flooded across Fleet Street, spreading tentacles of speculation and that peculiar brand of gossip found only between the Strand and Ludgate Circus. Hambros found themselves not a little bewildered. The bank's Harry Sporborg, one of the best City infighters in the game, had first heard of Maxwell's bid on the eight o'clock news that morning. At eleven he welcomed Catto amid the constant jangling of telephones and an endless stream of banking executives scurried in and out of his office like rabbits. Hambros had been taken clearly off guard and a sense of panic had invaded the normally sedate atmosphere of their lushly carpeted offices.

Amid this confusion Catto spelt out Murdoch's plan. At first Sporborg thanked him very kindly and told him they would certainly keep it in mind. By the end of the week Sporborg was begging Catto to bring the Australian tycoon over on the first available flight.

Immediately after that first meeting Sporborg taxied to the NOWO building in Bouverie Street where a hurriedly convened board meeting was trying to assess the situation. Sir William Carr, who was not well at the time, sat listening dispassionately as the immediate situation was spelled out to him. The then editor, Stafford Somerfield, was amazed to find the company was so vulnerable. Sporborg pointed out what some of the board members had known for some time but had been loath to accept: the company was in one hell of a mess. A convincing argument to this effect, plus the sale of the Jackson shares, could swing the vote quite clearly Maxwell's way.

By now the evening papers had splashed the story of the bid all over London and a retinue of journalists and City philosophers ate up every word with avaricious delight. Maxwell was a controversial and 'newsy' character and takeover bids of this magnitude were always big news. But this was no normal takeover. The world's largest-selling Sunday was on the market and few working journalists can ever resist an incestuous interest in the intrigues, politics and high finance of Fleet Street.

Politically speaking the Maxwell bid was also highly interesting. The *News of the World* was then as true-blue as you could find. It was right-wing, reactionary to the point of being almost fascist, and Enoch Powell was its political darling. Maxwell was a flamboyant socialist. The opposing policies of the old *News of the World* and its potential new owner were as far apart as two things could be. No one believed Maxwell's claim that the paper would carry on in its traditional way. Most people still believe a *News of the World* under Maxwell would have become a socialist newspaper and Maxwell did admit later on, 'Harold [Wilson] wanted me to have it.'

By midnight in Holt Street, Murdoch and Mervyn Rich, his chief financial adviser, had sketched out a possible takeover formula. They spent most of the night drinking coffee and Murdoch smoked several packs of cigarettes. (He subsequently gave up smoking when he came to London and now has quite an aversion to cigarettes.) It was a rough and ready plan at that stage, but it was the beginnings of a remarkable coup. On his eventual return from meeting Carr in London, the two businessmen were to turn it into a working set of military tactics which would put Murdoch firmly in the seat of power in Bouverie Street.

At that stage Murdoch could never have found the thirty million pounds cash needed to better Maxwell's bid, even with the highly sympathetic resources of the Commonwealth Bank of Australia behind him. Rupert Murdoch also had no intention of giving up large slices of his Australian empire, even for a newspaper which then had more than eighteen million readers.

But Sir William Carr's NOWO was in a terrible financial state. Without a newcomer with both formidable experience and hard cash to join their flagging team, they would not only lose the company but their pride as well. Catto, Rich and Murdoch included this 'face-saving' as a major factor in the power game they were about to play.

As the midnight oil was burning in Surrey Hills, Maxwell was enjoying a late lunch at the Savoy with a handful of important City editors. Jackson, then living in Paris, had 'gone fishing for the weekend' and was unobtainable. The NOWO board had gone their separate ways for various lunches with key City personnel and Catto was preparing his office for a major confrontation.

Jackson had offered his shares to Sir William weeks earlier, but the chairman had been unable or unwilling to find enough cash to buy his cousin out. It is interesting to speculate on whether Sir William, had he taken note of the warning signal of a large block of shares becoming available, might have been able to avert the impending crisis. It seems difficult to believe he could ignore Jackson's move and be so surprised when another bidder showed up.

All that week and into the next, Maxwell kept up a terrific campaign of public and press propaganda. The City geared up for the battle to come with relish. The NOWO board, with a great deal of arrogance and fury, consolidated their rather weak defences, which seemed in the main, to be a personal attack on Maxwell.

III

On the following day, Thursday October 17th, 1968, Sir William and Stafford Somerfield thrashed out a message to their readers for the following Sunday. Maxwell kept his ears glued to the ground and found that things seemed to be going his way very satisfactorily. It was now the Wednesday evening in Sydney, and Murdoch and Rich had the whole of Holt Street bubbling with activity. There is one thing no journalist who works for Murdoch ever feels surprise at—their chairman's new activities.

By Friday morning Hambros had calmed down somewhat. Sporborg called Catto and told him that, although they felt the heat was off for a while, could he keep Murdoch standing by. It was not, they added calmly, necessary for Murdoch to come over just yet. Catto informed Murdoch and Rupert prepared to shelve his takeover dossier for the weekend and go to the Caulfield Cup races in Melbourne.

But Maxwell had also noted the situation seemed to be cooling down. The City pages were taking a closer look at both Pergamon and the bid. Some were asking some pertinent questions. Maxwell decided the situation needed hotting up again. Through his public relations man, Tim Travers-Healey, it was leaked very effectively that he was going to up his bid to around the thirty million pound mark. Fleet Street snatched it up and Friday's evening papers were devoted to the Maxwell-orientated rumours.

Hambros and the NOWO board quickly returned to a state of panic. Catto was called and they asked him to bring Murdoch over on the first available flight. Late on Friday night Catto was still in his office at Great Winchester Street trying to get hold of Murdoch. He was nowhere to be found.

As Catto tried to call him, Murdoch was on his way to Melbourne. It was unusual of him to have told no one where he was going, and the entire Murdoch organization was mobilized trying to find him. Secretaries spent all day at home 'phoning round every conceivable place he might be and junior reporters were sent to restaurants where Murdoch was known to lunch occasionally.

In fact, Rupert was indulging in one of his happiest pastimes —gambling. As he flew the five hundred and fifty miles from Sydney to Melbourne he had good reason to think his luck was in. He had walked away from the previous year's Cup with a tidy few thousand dollars profit. On arriving in Melbourne, his home town, he went to a hotel for a few hours rest before the big race and was fast asleep at the time everyone was trying to find him.

Eventually Catto decided to call his old friend Sir Norman Young. Sir Norman hesitated for a minute and then said, 'Rupert hasn't missed the Caulfield Cup for years.' He told

Catto he would ring back. He then got Murdoch's secretary to ring round all the top Melbourne hotels. At first the hotel where Murdoch was staying made a mistake and said he was not there, but a second check brought a sleepy-eyed Murdoch to the 'phone. Within four hours he was on a Europe-bound Boeing with an attaché case full of memoranda and a small overnight bag of clothes.

Those four hours must have been among the most active in Murdoch's life. In that time he called his wife to pack his belongings; got Dorothy to rush to Sydney airport with the dossier; and flew from Melbourne to Sydney to catch the Sydney–London flight. His office persuaded the Lufthansa plane to delay for a while as Murdoch was sped across the tarmac from the incoming flight.

Murdoch is a bad traveller who dislikes planes and finds it takes him several days to get over long flights. He must, in his way, have been excited at the prospect of going for the biggest newspaper in the world. He knew nothing of the battle ahead. He was a virtually unknown figure outside Australia and he was plunging into a situation completely cold. He was also going to a place where he had few friends and he would be completely on his own against two gigantic forces which were both to look on him at first as merely a pawn in the game.

By good chance the flight ended at Frankfurt and this enabled Murdoch to get a European flight to the European terminal at London Airport which helped him enter the country unnoticed. Lord Catto was there to meet him.

After a long discussion with Catto that night, Murdoch was determined not only to join the battle—but to win it. He was to enter into an arena far larger and more important than anything which had gone before in his flamboyant and controversial history—a fight which would not only be a three-way war between three big publishers, but would involve the expertise of four of the City's most important banks. It would take up thousands of column inches of news space. It would have large political implications. It would be the forerunner of boardroom tactics which had never been seen before in half a century of newspaper publishing. And, more important, it would be the opening of a completely new era of British journalism.

Murdoch had arrived about mid-morning on Sunday, only five days after the announcement of the Maxwell bid. As Catto and Murdoch sped through the outskirts of London in the chauffeur-driven Rolls Royce, they stopped to pick up that morning's copy of the *News of the World*.

It was the morning of Stafford Somerfield's famous front-page editorial attacking Maxwell and calling the *News of the World* and the Carrs 'as English as roast beef and Yorkshire pudding'. In passing they mentioned Maxwell's original name—Jan Ludwig Hoch. The whole article was a clear appeal to the supposed British nationalism of their readers and most journalists viewed it as a monument of bad taste.

Murdoch and Catto went to the Savoy and immediately got down to business. They had been introduced to each other some time before by Sir Norman Young and had met two or three times. But they did not know each other well, so Murdoch was virtually friendless on the eve of battle. His London editor, Peter Gladwyn, a good friend and trusted aide, was in hospital. Frank O'Neill, Gladwyn's deputy, knew Murdoch, but not well. It was, at that time, imperative that Murdoch should keep his presence secret, so he could not even look up any of his old Fleet Street acquaintances.

Murdoch slept well that night but had still not completely adjusted to the time-lag when he awoke to find himself faced with a very heavy day. By chance he met his old Adelaide chum Alex McKay in the lobby of the Savoy and invited him up to his suite for a bottle of champagne. He admitted he was in town for the NOWO takeover bid but pledged McKay to secrecy.

Soon after, he was taken by Catto to see Sporborg and the Hambros banker arranged a meeting that evening with Clive Carr, Sir William's director son. He met up with Clive and Sir William's nephew and their wives at the Mirabelle restaurant. During the dinner it was confirmed Maxwell had upped his bid from 37/6 (£1.87½) to 50/- (£2.50) a share. Clive Carr and Murdoch got on well from the beginning and they still do. The younger Carr made it plain to both Murdoch and Sir William that he felt Murdoch's inclusion in the family firm was a very healthy thing for the company. Murdoch urged Clive Carr that they must have a breakfast conference with Sir William first thing in the morning. By coincidence Catto was having dinner in another part of the restaurant and while he and Murdoch decided on their tactics for the crucial meeting, Clive Carr was persuading his father by telephone that they must all meet by eight next morning.

According to Murdoch later Sir William almost fainted when he heard he would have to start talking business at the crack of dawn. He argued vehemently at the early hour and persuaded Murdoch to make it half-past eight, although the meeting did not finally get under way until nine.

IV

Murdoch and Catto arrived for the meeting by car and parked outside Sir William's London home a little after eight. They sat and waited for the others to arrive. Catto pointed out each personality as they walked up the steps and knocked on the door. It was the first time Murdoch had seen most of them. When Catto told him he thought they had all arrived the two men went in themselves.

Sir William had been visibly shaken by the events of the past two weeks. Throughout the takeover, in fact, his health declined until eventually he was rushed to hospital. He was certainly in no physical or mental condition to face up to the rigours of a takeover bid featuring such adversaries as Maxwell and Murdoch. At that breakfast conference he appeared to be suffering from depression and a sort of hopelessness.

Murdoch, with his slight nervous twitch covered by his brashness, immediately got down to business, almost before they had finished shaking hands. Coffee was produced as Murdoch carefully spelled out his offer. He insisted, before anything, they could not even begin to talk business unless he was offered full executive control of the company on the day he took office— that is, he would be managing director in every sense of the word. Sir William saw the last vestiges of his power fading away. He hesitated and made vain attempts to fight the inevitable. Murdoch listened for a little while and then, suddenly, using the natural powers of theatre inherent in all true gamblers, he said quietly, 'Gentlemen, either you concede to my wishes or I catch the next 'plane home. I've come here at my own expense. It has cost you nothing. I'll cut my losses and go home if we can't agree right now.'

Murdoch even started heading towards the door. Sporborg leapt to his feet and, while trying to calm Sir William down on the one hand, urged Murdoch to give them five minutes on their own to talk it over. Murdoch and Catto then went to another room.

This five minutes of activity sums up a great deal of Murdoch's general character. He *meant* everything he said. But it was a gambler's statement, and it has to be open to some doubt, of course, whether he really would have caught the next 'plane home. He insists he would have done and certainly everyone in the room thought so too. While they were thrashing it out, Murdoch was on the 'phone upstairs to Prime Minister Gorton, asking about the possibility of getting some millions of dollars out of Australia. It was characteristic of Murdoch that he had made his bet without even being sure he could get the money out to pay for it.

Bankers in Britain were not used to such outrageous brashness. Nor was Sir William. After all, they had not even finished coffee before Murdoch had launched his ultimatum. He had foregone all the traditional niceties and preliminaries in which even bitter enemies participate on such occasions. He had said, in effect, before getting anywhere near the company, that he would oust Carr from the top position of executive control—or he would let Maxwell have it. This was all a little too much so early in the morning.

When Murdoch made his gamble, two things happened. Firstly Sporborg pointed out that Carr did not really have an alternative. Secondly Carr *believed* Murdoch. He was totally unused to people creating such situations. I think, too, that Murdoch was so unused to the particular vulnerability of Carr's situation, he did not really believe it when the old chairman gave in so easily.

Sir William and his aides discussed the position for thirty-five minutes. Then Murdoch and Catto were ushered back in.

'But we knew before we went back in that we had got it,' said Murdoch later. 'When Sporborg jumped up and tried to calm Sir William, I knew we had won. As we left the room Catto winked at me. He knew we'd won too.'

What few people in Britain then realized was that Murdoch had done it all before, often with adversaries far more cunning than anything Britain had to offer. What was Fleet Street, after all, compared to those early days in Sydney when newspaper proprietors literally punched each other on the nose at the races and set fire to each others' buildings? What could the Carrs and Cudlipps do to Rupert that hadn't been tried before by such people as Sir Frank Packer? What game could be played against Murdoch, what chicanery, what intrigue, which he hadn't left far behind? Compared to those early days Murdoch found in London mumblers and bumblers who he was eventually to twist around his little finger.

While the Carrs thought they were adding Australia's News Limited to the NOWO stable, Murdoch was busily doing the opposite. When the day was done, he had lost the equity in one weekly paper, one glossy woman's magazine and a few bits and pieces, and acquired the *News of the World* for his family firm.

Murdoch and Catto that morning had indeed won the first battle in a long and bitter war. They were told that, if they did business together, Murdoch would go in as chief executive. They asked if he would mind if Sir William became joint managing director. Murdoch bluntly retorted he would indeed mind. Sir William could have the title of chairman but Murdoch was to have the 'chief executive' tag. Sir William, who looked completely shattered, nodded lamely and the two sides got down to thrashing out the details of their consortium.

V

Later that day, while Murdoch was visiting McKay in the *Daily Mirror* offices, Hugh Cudlipp, then IPC's chairman, walked into the room. He immediately recognized Rupert and so was brought into the secret too. He also pledged he would not say a word.

However, the following morning's *Daily Express* carried a full report of Murdoch's presence in the country. The cat had got out of the bag. The afternoon London papers carried wildly speculative reports about the new and intriguing situation of the takeover battle now that Murdoch was reported to be in town.

Frank O'Neill made desperate attempts to put off all inquiries. He denied everything. But Catto and Murdoch eventually realized the situation was absurd, and both agreed they would have to issue a statement soon.

On the following day, Wednesday, Murdoch found Frank O'Neill in his favourite public house opposite what was then News Limited's London headquarters. O'Neill, who has that typically Australian phobia about sycophancy, tried his hardest to greet Murdoch as casually as he could.

During the time they had a few drinks together it became obvious to O'Neill that Murdoch had something special on his mind. Although Murdoch was obviously enjoying the company of a fellow Australian, and especially one within the organization, O'Neill detected that his chief executive wanted something more from him. In fact, Murdoch was going through one of his intense periods which are characteristic of his mental approach to anything big. He was slightly withdrawn, abstracted in most of his conversation and seemingly miles away from his surroundings. But O'Neill remembers he suddenly came round and began being conversational and buoyant again. He asked Frank if he would come back to the Savoy for dinner with him.

O'Neill explained he had promised his wife he would be back early that night and Murdoch offered to ring her and explain the situation. Back at the Savoy he did this in what O'Neill describes as 'the politest fashion you have ever heard from a living mortal'.

During dinner Murdoch explained the situation, then afterwards they went up to Murdoch's suite where Murdoch got

down to writing a short statement admitting he was in London
to contend in the NOWO bid. Sitting on the carpet O'Neill phoned
it over to the Press Association. When the world woke up the
following day it was to find that the man they once called
Adelaide's 'Boy Publisher' had, indeed, come to town.

VI

The old-boy network of British banking began humming
through the City the very day after Murdoch and O'Neill made
the announcement from the Savoy Hotel. Hambros for the
NOWO board and Sir William Carr, Rothschilds for Professor
Dereck Jackson, Morgan Grenfell for Murdoch and Hill, Samuel
and Flemings for Maxwell. Big bankers in this sense are rather
like top QCs. They advise their clients and represent them at
various meetings and hearings—but more than that, they 'jockey
for position' out of court.

A huge 'sounding out' process began that week. All unofficial,
of course, and very tentative. But a series of 'phone calls to old
friends and the odd City lunch gave each bank a rough idea
of where their clients stood long before any shareholders'
meeting. Maxwell at first had scoffed when he heard Murdoch
was attempting guerilla warfare with him. His bankers very
quickly told him the threat was real. But in fact, having been
assured of Jackson's twenty-five per cent block of shares, Maxwell
appeared to be fighting from a formidable position.

Murdoch and Maxwell soon emerged as the two real adversaries of the game which was steadily unfolding. Hambros and
Sir William Carr played hard and the bank showed a determined
toughness which amazed the City. But in the public eye it
became a war of personalities and only two of the gladiators
could live up to the image the public, and Fleet Street in particular, wanted of them.

On the one hand Murdoch was an almost unknown quantity.
To this day he is something of an enigma and in those days he
seemed to have emerged from nowhere. In terms of the media
he was soon to have a great influence on the people of Britain.
Yet, even now, to many he is a mythical figure and is more

often than not misunderstood by most of the people who profess a knowledge of him. He was the antithesis of Maxwell, and the clash of personalities, in their almost daily appearance on the front pages of the British national press over the next few months, made one of the best running stories of 1968.

When Murdoch is in the middle of a takeover battle he is a bundle of nervous energy. His strength is his confidence and his reputation. He has a well-trained organization behind him whose whole life has been to watch the boss get into something new. During takeovers Murdoch will work an eighteen-to-twenty-hour day, relentlessly exploring ever inch of the battle-field.

'I once watched him when he heard a newspaper might come on to the market,' an Australian executive remembers. 'He had two telephones working at once. He called lawyers, bankers, the whole board, executives, family and so on. In a matter of hours he had found out the situation, confirmed the rumours, assessed his own position and set the whole thing in motion. He knew what he could spare from the kitty, how much more he could borrow, what the price might be, who his competitors were, and when and how he should make the bid. It was an amazing sight to watch. He had heard of the chance at around eleven in the morning and by dusk that evening the whole organization was geared up to get weaving. By eleven the following morning Murdoch had made his bid.'

Another of Murdoch's strong points is the confidence that the Commonwealth Bank of Australia has in him. He knows when he makes an offer he can often rely on the backing of the bank just by picking up the 'phone and telling them what he is doing. This dates back to the very early days when the bank was inaugurated and Murdoch was one of its first big clients. They wanted to look after him. His relationship with them is more than just business, so that he had personal friends there who were free with their advice about his finances. It also happens that Murdoch rarely lost money on any of the deals he initiated through them, which must help bolster the confidence of any big bank.

It is customary for Murdoch to go for a firm which is top-heavy and losing money. He makes his bid mainly on short-term credit loans, then, in most cases, he sells off all assets which do not directly affect the main product—the newspaper. With the sale of these he pays back most of the loan. Then he smacks the product into shape—and repays the balance with profits. It is a formula which has rarely failed.

On the other hand Maxwell is an equally interesting man. He is an experienced in-fighter who is not prepared to give up without a fight. He is a loud giant of a man, given to wearing American-style suits with loud ties. He is not everyone's cup of tea, but despite almost overwhelmingly hostile publicity he retains great loyalty from those who like him. Before losing three campaigns he was an ambitious MP and, constituents remember, a very good one for them. Nothing was too small for him to take an interest in. His huge PR camp was quick to point out how he carried coals to a cold old-aged pensioner and so on. He had geared himself up to the oncoming fight and was prepared with a massive onslaught against any rivals. By every rule in the book he should have won. He still thinks so and is very bitter about his failure.

His view on Murdoch is quite simple. He thinks Murdoch is dishonest and capable of almost any kind of knavery to get his own way. He said Murdoch broke every rule in the book to get the *News of the World* and led other, 'more serious people, like bankers' into breaking the rules with him. His view is that Murdoch has been responsible in one fell swoop for obliterating all the good things about the popular press in this country. He accuses Murdoch of being uncouth and lowering all journalistic standards, and condemns the takeover with one of his favourite phrases, 'never has a bigger whale been caught by a smaller fish'.

But all through the crucial stages various ex-Maxwell aides who had become disenchanted with their previous boss were offering their services to the NOWO. Depending on their former level within the Maxwell organization they were treated with various degrees of seriousness. Many lunches were held between journalists, management executives and former Maxwell employees, several of them in a private room at the Cheshire Cheese public house opposite Bouverie Street.

Information on Maxwell's business activities, past and present, was collected and passed on to Stafford Somerfield who in turn passed them on to Carr. Much of this information was hostile to Maxwell and came from deep within his organization. Chapter and verse on all of these activities within his organization were collected. It is difficult to know exactly how much of the information gathered was accurate. Some of it was clearly sour grapes from sacked executives who made no bones about the fact they bore a grudge.

It is difficult to plot the exact course the information took on its journey from the Cheshire Cheese to the City pages of various newspapers, but Carr, Murdoch and John Addey, Murdoch's takeover PR, were all aware of its existence as was Lord Catto, Murdoch's financial adviser for the takeover.

Some of the facts thrown up during the Murdoch–Maxwell battle for the *News of the World* clearly caused Maxwell a lot of embarrassment in the City. After he had lost control of Pergamon to the American firm of Leasco, the Board of Trade started an inquiry into his handling of the publishing company. It was not, however, until November 1973 that the Board of Trade published its findings.

I feel it true to say that, had Maxwell never gone for the NOWO, he probably could have continued operating as he had always done in the past—very definitely in the top seat. In 1974, of course, Maxwell regained control of Pergamon.

Underneath the takeover battle itself a shrewd battle of wits was going on between two PR consultants. Public relations in this sense means not only promoting your own client, but going out of your way not to give credit to the other side. On the one side Murdoch had John Addey, a suave ex-lawyer who happily admits to having a weakness for champagne. On the other Maxwell enjoyed the talents of Tim Travers-Healey, equally suave and equally versed in the manoeuvres demanded by City politics during battles of this nature.

Their respective tasks were very simple. They were to collect, in the form of sworn affidavits, as much information about the other man's client as they could. They had roughly two months to do it and both of them did it within the time allotted to them. When the day was done, John Addey, for Murdoch, appeared to be somewhat ahead on points.

Travers-Healey's job was to attempt to find evidence that Murdoch was, as Maxwell put it, 'ruthlessly breaking all the rules of the Stock Exchange with tricks of deception and mis-information.'

Addey's job was to prove that Maxwell's generalship of Pergamon showed that he was not capable of handling an operation like the *News of the World*.

Addey arranged, through his contacts in Fleet Street, for the information he had gathered to be fed to those papers where it would be certain to have the greatest coverage.

The professional public relations man constitutes a side of takeover bids that the general public rarely sees. Journalists are aware, for instance, that someone somewhere is arranging press conferences, information releases and television appearances. But the Addeys and Travers-Healeys of this world do a little bit more than that, and they remain in a unique position of power because, almost inevitably during the course of their duties, they find the skeletons in the cupboards of their clients.

VII

When the day was done the two PR men had prepared the stage for each of their clients and skilfully helped them to sharpen their performances, while making sure there was enough rotten fruit to throw at their respective rivals.

Between the end of October 1968 and January 2nd, 1969, each day held new surprises for both camps. Some of them far more entertaining and intriguing than even the PRO's fertile brains could muster up.

On Friday October 25th, three days after the Tuesday morning conference with Carr, Murdoch had bought up three and a half per cent of the available NOWO shares. He had promised Hambros and Sir William Carr that he would eventually buy up nine per cent. Meanwhile, Lord Catto had gone along to the Takeover Panel and explained Murdoch's point of view to this august body. Murdoch claims he was very careful all through the negotiations to ensure that the Takeover Panel had the situation explained to them in full. He was surprised when the Panel suddenly stopped all dealings in NOWO shares on the Stock Exchange before Murdoch could buy up his full quota. In theory the Panel had accepted Murdoch's intervention even though he had told a press conference that week, 'I can't make a full bid for the *News of the World*. I haven't got enough money.' But at the same time the highly attractive fifty shilling Pergamon offer could not be matched by anyone else, including Murdoch, and valued the company at an astonishing thirty-four million pounds. The Takeover Panel's decision to stop dealings had come after one of the most frantic share-buying bonanzas in Stock Exchange history.

One of the most interesting aspects of this period was the direct confrontation between Hill, Samuel and Hambros. It was a piece of City politics of the first order. For almost the whole of the previous year Hill, Samuel had been the doyen of the City press. They had been written up as the new takeover force in the City and they were enjoying a golden heyday of excellent publicity. They were building a huge reputation as the 'go-go' bank and Hambros felt they could not be allowed to win another takeover battle—whatever the price, they had to be stopped. Hambros went in with their own money—a very rare occurrence in the City. They spent over two million pounds in the market buying shares. Whatever Maxwell offered, they offered considerably more. 'We took some of the shares from them, but later on they sold at a loss,' said Murdoch. 'They didn't mind, they had done the job.'

When Hambros had gone in and upped the market price, the big shareholding institutions in the City realized what was going on and had decided to take the cash while the share price looked good. This was the best thing for Murdoch because they were likely to have been influenced by the City press which was all for Maxwell. When they sold, Maxwell lost a lot of support which he could otherwise have counted on at the shareholders' meeting. In this way the Murdoch camp neutralized a million opposition votes and because of this it became one of the toughest takeover battles ever fought up to that time. 'It was probably the noisiest public brawl ever,' said Murdoch later.

At another stage Maxwell persuaded three trustees of the NOWO pension fund to try and get a court order to prevent the fund as a whole voting for the Carr–Murdoch platform. Personally groomed by Maxwell they duly appeared in court. It was a highly crucial move which could have tipped the balance firmly his way.

He and his aides attended court and sat next to editor Stafford Somerfield and Michael Gabbert—then *News of the World* assistant editor. The two journalists remember that during the final summing up they were convinced Maxwell had won the day. 'Maxwell started to puff up with confidence and we looked at each other and raised our eyebrows,' Gabbert recalls. 'We thought we'd lost it. Then, just as we were about to leave, the judge said, "On the other hand . . ." and Maxwell saw the whole thing, in one quiet phrase, go right out of the window. As the judge went on we got steadily puffed up with confidence ourselves as Maxwell got deflated. When the judge's vote finally went against Maxwell, Maxwell stumbled from the court looking furious.'

Later on, Murdoch was returning from the country and, as he left Victoria Station, he bought a copy of the evening paper and saw his picture on the front page along with most of the directors of the *News of the World*. It said in huge headlines that they were being sued for conspiracy by the Public Trustee. 'We certainly got a bit of a shock,' said Murdoch. 'But these were the sort of things that were going on throughout the takeover. It's what made it exciting.'

Later, Murdoch decided to fly home to gear the Australian side of his business up for battle and to thrash out the final details of the consortium with Mervyn Rich. He also had to make sure his organization would remain stable as he planned to spend most of his time in London. Consequently many of his executives got switched around.

As Murdoch got to the airport he heard the Takeover Panel had made a public announcement banning him from voting any of the shares he had already bought. This meant Murdoch could not vote his crucial three and a half per cent at the forthcoming shareholders' meeting which would decide the fate of the two other main contenders.

Murdoch was hopping mad. He had got to the airport feeling he was winning and the announcement was a serious blow. 'I thought the game was up,' he said.

It did not mean that Carr could not vote, just anyone who had bought shares since the takeover offer. But Catto assured Murdoch that they were still in with a winning chance. 'I thought,' said Murdoch later, 'to hell with it, I'll vote them. Lord Catto told me I shouldn't do anything, or make a statement until I'd thought about it. But he said I was entitled to vote them if I wanted to.'

Murdoch felt they had been stabbed in the back, with the Takeover Panel giving in to public opinion. It took him a long time to calm down. He called London from every airport he stopped at on the way back to Sydney.

Murdoch argued that he had kept in close contact with the Takeover Panel throughout. He had gone to see the chairman Sir Humphrey Mynors two or three times to show him they were a substantial company and so on. Mynors had assured him that Murdoch was playing the game according to the rules. Now he felt they were being unfair to him.

Maxwell maintains that the Takeover Panel managed to turn a blind eye to the Carr–Murdoch marriage. He says the two were able to plough through the Takeover Code—and that no one did a thing about it. In straight figures, Carr's board created a further thirty per cent of equity which they sold to News Limited, for Australian assets, bringing Murdoch's total voting power to thirty-three per cent. The NOWO board's shares added to Murdoch's ensured they had their fifty-one per cent between them. They were, in effect, then able to tell the rest of the shareholders, 'You can take it or leave it, the battle is won.'

But not everyone was so optimistic on their behalf. Anthony Bambridge, the respected City editor of *The Observer*, pointed out that their arithmetic was devastatingly simple. The cash alternative Maxwell was offering valued the *News of the World* at thirty million pounds. The Murdoch deal increased the company's capital by forty per cent. So, to outbid Maxwell, the company should be worth forty-two million pounds. Murdoch's News Limited was then capitalized at twenty million pounds on the Australian market. The *News of the World* was capitalized at just over twenty million pounds and Murdoch certainly had no intention of feeding all his Australian assets into Sir William's pot. 'No one has ever made two and two make five. How can Hambros and Morgan Grenfell think it's possible?'

The short-term answer is that it was possible for two reasons. They had their fifty-one per cent of the shares—come what may. And they were able, before the fascinating shareholders' meeting, on January 2nd, to reduce Maxwell's chance of success.

Since then Bambridge is on public record several times admitting he was wrong about the Murdoch bid. Maxwell's City campaign had been planned for two years before. He had carefully nursed his very numerous City newspaper contacts. So, whereas while it is true to say that news desks could not resist the cavalier drama Murdoch added to the scene, the City desks came out to a man behind Maxwell. Six years later, with profits soaring every year and the company on the healthiest footing it has been for a half a century, the City journalists have no alternative but to agree that their original opinions were misplaced.

VIII

Murdoch and Maxwell finally came face to face at the Connaught Rooms on January 2nd, 1969. Maxwell got up first and threw everything he could at Murdoch. His speech was half about what a great guy *he* was and what he could do with the company; the other half was a direct attack on Murdoch. It was a skilful speech. But I think it indicated Maxwell's lack of knowledge about his adversary—and his own legendary self-confidence. He was smiling throughout. He talked of Murdoch in indulgent terms, dismissing him as an upstart colonial boy.

When Murdoch's time came he made a speech which was the exact opposite. Whereas Maxwell had been full of fire and oratory, Murdoch was diffident, nervous, cool and to the point. He explained rather quietly, and within a few minutes, that he had had a great deal of experience making a lot of money for people out of newspapers which had been losing money. He said he was very confident he could turn the NOWO losses into large profits within two years. He invited anyone who was interested to read his records. Then he sat down.

Murdoch assesses he won that meeting because most shareholders are more influenced by their High Street bank managers than they are by the City press, 'and the High Street bank managers did not like Maxwell'.

Maxwell accuses, 'He won that meeting because he had unfairly stacked it with hundreds of employees from the *News of the World.*'

'Maxwell accused us of stacking the meeting,' admitted Murdoch, 'which was half true. What happened was that I had been reading the Articles of Association [of the *News of the World* Ltd] very carefully and saw a loophole in it, which, to my surprise, Maxwell hadn't seen. We knew we had the numbers if we went to the vote, but if anyone had asked for an adjournment for a month it would have to have been decided on a show of hands of those there. I thought Maxwell would see that if it went to the vote he was beaten, but if he could get an adjournment, it would be another whole month of fighting for all sides, which would have meant more time for the whole deal to get unstuck. So I made sure that the hall was full of our people. We didn't turn anyone away but we had our numbers there in case it came to a show of votes. There were several people there who had had one hundred votes or so put in their name a few days before. As it happened the vote was very fair and absolutely overwhelmingly for us. Which goes to show that City journalists don't have that much influence with the small shareholder. The ordinary shareholder came down with us. They had obviously had acres of material sent to them, but they didn't take much notice of it.'

Even secretaries at the NOWO had been given shares for a few days—and had to sign a contract they would return them when the meeting was over. The Murdoch camp claims it was all the name of the game and points out that nothing illegal was ever done on their side.

At the end of the day, Murdoch and Carr carried the company and Maxwell retired to brood about his near-miss. A small celebratory champagne party was held for the victors and Murdoch allowed himself to relax for the first time in several months.

It was not the first or last time the two men would meet on opposing sides of the fence. But from then onwards, even though he disliked Murdoch, Maxwell never forgot that the young Australian had been brought to adulthood in a training ground as heavy-fisted as anything he himself could arrange.

When the deal was done Murdoch moved in with a vengeance. He was impatient to get cracking. He had carved up Maxwell. Now he sent his knife away to be cleaned and resharpened for the other battles to come.

Chapter 2

Foundations of an empire

I

The Rupert Murdoch saga started in 1903 when his father, Sir Keith Murdoch, joined the *Melbourne Age* and eventually became the doyen of the Australian press. The dynasty had started humbly enough, but Sir Keith was to leave his son a heritage and a reputation which the young Murdoch was to build up to a world-wide empire. The *News of the World* bid was, at that stage, the culmination of his personal life-style, and the launching of the *Sun* and its huge success quickly showed he meant business. But even this is only a halfway stage to the ultimate empire he has in mind.

Murdoch's paternal grandfather had been minister of the tiny kirk at West Cruden Bay in Scotland. He arrived in Melbourne a year before Sir Keith was born. The family were integrated rapidly into the new community although they were, according to Murdoch, pretty poor. They may have had a little money, but the family of eight was brought up on four pounds a week. All the children had to get scholarships to go to school. They never starved but it was what Murdoch called a 'poor church existence'.

On the maternal side Rupert's grandparents, Mr and Mrs Rupert Greene, had both been born in Australia. They lived in Toorak, the most famous and fashionable of Melbourne's countless suburbs. His grandmother was a strong, strange woman of very high principles. His grandfather, an expert engineer in the wool trade, was always thought to be a very attractive sportsman, and he was a highly competent cricketer who nearly played for Australia. He enjoyed gambling and drinking and was said to be very popular, with hundreds of friends.

Sir Keith, with his presbyterian upbringing, often seemed to disapprove of his father-in-law. On both sides they sometimes look at Rupert and tell him he takes after Rupert Greene rather than his father.

Sir Keith's father, P. J. Murdoch, was a preacher of immense moral principle. People still talk about his sermons at Kew, just outside Melbourne.

Sir Keith's wife, Dame Elisabeth, was born in 1909, the year in which Sir Keith started an economics course at the London School of Economics. Keith Murdoch and Elisabeth Greene married in Melbourne on June 6th, 1928, just one year before he was made managing director of the *Herald* and *Weekly Times*. It was an exciting time to be in Australia and both families were forging their lives in a virtually new world. Both were good old British stock, tough and resilient, respectable and industrious. The seeds of Australian nationalism which were to motivate both Keith Murdoch and his son in later years were sown then.

Sir Keith and Dame Elisabeth were devoted to each other for the whole of their lives together. It would be difficult perhaps to find a man and a woman so admirably suited. They both lived by high moral principle, by devotion to each other and by a deep sense of family union. Murdoch is very much the son of both of them. Born in March 1931 he has the toughness and resilience of his father coupled with the down-to-earth sense and energy of his mother. Both parents managed to forge in the young Rupert the sense of family which is the single most important factor of Murdoch's motivation.

Murdoch's father soon became an important part of the destiny of Australia, while his mother brought up the family. Both of them seem to have been extremely sensible parents, discussing together family matters and showing a sense of love for each other which was the mainstay of childhood security.

II

Sir Keith Murdoch started his newspaper life as a suburban correspondent on the *Melbourne Age*. Seven years later, in 1910, after a trip to London, he was taken on to the regular staff at four pounds a week. When World War I broke out he had already become recognized as a thorough newsman and was made Melbourne correspondent to the *Sydney Sun*. (Melbourne was then the capital of Australia.) The following year, when he was twenty-eight, a nation-wide ballot of journalists voted him as an official Australian war correspondent. It was during this war that he established himself, not only as a first-class newspaperman, but as a political and authoritative younger statesman in the affairs of Australia.

The most famous single piece of writing to emanate from the steadfastly prolific pen of Keith Murdoch was his now famous letter from Gallipoli. It changed the course of the war, caused ferment in the British Cabinet and eventually brought Keith Murdoch into contact with some of the most important people in Britain.

As an official Australian war correspondent he had been asked by the then prime minister, Andrew Fisher, to look over Australian troops in Egypt, especially their postal arrangements. While he was there, he had asked General Sir Ian Hamilton, commander-in-chief of the Gallipoli operation, if he might visit the campaign where there were many Australians and New Zealanders 'locked in deadly struggle with the Turks'. This permission was eventually granted although Sir Ian was later to regret it hugely.

'My father's letter from Gallipoli to Fisher,' said Murdoch, 'was a highly emotional, important and nationalistic piece of reporting. He described in graphic detail how British officers were sitting five miles behind the lines drinking iced gins and directing our Australian boys down in the thick of the fighting without even a lump of ice for their wounds.'

Murdoch senior was extremely impressed and—eventually—depressed by what he found. His conversations with officers and men shocked him. A better-known British journalist called

Ellis Ashmean-Bartlett asked Murdoch to help him defy the censor and deliver his personal report to the British government.

But another correspondent, Henry Nevinson, warned Hamilton, and Murdoch was picked up in Marseilles and refused access to Britain unless he handed over Ashmean-Bartlett's letter. This quickly disappeared into the bowels of the War Office and was only released in 1973.

Murdoch, however, had seen enough to compose his own letter which he addressed to Fisher. I quote the *Melbourne Herald* which recently published the text in full,

It was an astonishing document, a compound of truth and error, fact and prejudice, serious charges against Hamilton and the British general staff, talked of low morale amongst the troops and predicted disastrous consequences if the campaign was continued. This sort of thing, of course, was grist to the mill of the critics of Britain's War Minister, Lord Kitchener, and of the Gallipoli campaign. One of the foremost of those critics was the Minister for Munitions, Lloyd George. Lloyd George also saw Murdoch's letter, and at his urging, Murdoch sent a copy of it to the British prime minister, Mr Asquith. Asquith, without consulting Kitchener or Hamilton, had it printed as a state paper and circulated it to the members of the Dardanelles Committee. They decided that Hamilton, who was strongly opposed to the evacuation of Gallipoli, would have to go. His successor, Lieutenant General Sir Charles Monroe, immediately recommended evacuation.

It was, and still is, a highly controversial document which still enjoys the interest of many World War I historians. Sir Ian later retorted that the report was full of 'untruths and exaggerations'. Nevertheless, when Keith Murdoch stayed on in London he was not merely an Australian war correspondent, but a man of influence and prestige. He took over the United Cable Service for Australian newspapers and built up a fruitful friendship with Lord Northcliffe—then the most prestigious proprietor in London with his respectable *Times* and popular *Daily Mail*. Through Murdoch, Northcliffe was to influence the whole course of Australian journalism, its style and its concept.

After many reports from the Western Front—and a tour with the Prince of Wales in 1920—Keith Murdoch was asked home to take over editorial control of the *Melbourne Herald*. So started an era of journalism which is still having repercussions all round the world.

The *Herald* he joined was not a bad paper but merely plodding along with little zest or influence. Keith Murdoch brought a young, keen and skilled hand to the editorial helm. The ensuing thirty years, in which he built the daily paper into a huge multi-million-pound publishing concern and established himself as one of the 'Fathers' of journalism of his generation, are part of Australia's history.

Murdoch recalled that his father did several important things when he took over control of the *Herald*. He popularized the paper and immediately caused a huge uproar, by staging the first beauty contest ever held in Australia. People tut-tutted and said many of the things they say about Rupert Murdoch today. But people were walking to the last block in Melbourne to buy the last edition with the result in it.

More importantly, he realized the time differential in Australia and knew that the buying public was fascinated by world news. He astutely reckoned that the afternoon papers could steal all the major foreign news stories by quickening the cable service.

Melbourne was very 'establishment' in those days and the *Argus* and the *Age* had all the esteem and prestige, and the *Herald* found it difficult to get a look in. Murdoch printed acres of almost unreadable stories alongside the foreign news and the popular pages so that gradually doors started to be opened to prestige advertisers and board-rooms. He broadened it out and eventually the *Argus* started an evening paper to rival him. Murdoch fought hard—and eventually wiped the floor with them. The *Argus* never did recover and much later sold out to the London *Daily Mirror*.

But Sir Keith Murdoch was not just publishing newspapers.

He was also pioneering in every direction. A tribute to him on his death said, 'Never, surely, has so wide a range of expansion in journalism been so boldly guided by one man. While his interstate interests were forging ahead, he was equipping Flinders Street [the old home of the *Herald*] with the first fifty thousand copies-an-hour printing machinery to reach Australia. The *Herald* was pioneering picturegram services in 1933, publishing Australia's first radioed photograph from overseas in 1934, mastering the rivalry of the *Star* and raising its own circulation to a new record of 195,000 in 1935.'

Describing the board-room battles in which his father got involved in those days, Murdoch said it came to a climax when his father had a heart attack in the thirties. The Melbourne family which owned a large share block began to feel the destiny of the paper was getting indelibly linked to Sir Keith. They were deeply involved with trying to oust Murdoch senior. But they never succeeded and eventually gave up the fight.

Sir Keith went on to create the Australian Associated Press and brought together the two cable services operating from abroad. He was the first newsman in Australia to see the impending world crisis when he went abroad in 1936. He called for additional drive in building up the Australian press's foreign coverage.

At the same time this remarkable man was piling up newsprint in case of war. But, more important, by the time war broke out he had realized his dreams of an Australian national newsprint industry, and by 1941 mills amongst two hundred square miles of Tasmanian forest were churning out newsprint.

Sir Keith was an anti-communist of the old school. He saw nothing but evil in communism and was capable of quite formidable tirades of abuse against those who spoke for communist principles. But according to Murdoch his father was able to forgive him his radicalism at school and Oxford. Murdoch is also quick to point out that, for most of his life, his father was a strenuous supporter of the Labour party. 'You've got to remember it was in the middle of the cold war and people had very strong feelings about Russia. My father shared them, but he was not a Conservative. Quite the contrary, in many ways.'

Contemporaries remember him as essentially someone who took a great interest in people. Sir 'Jack' Williams recalls an incident when a man was caught for petty pilfering. Sir Keith inquired about his family and wages, and decided the man was not being paid enough, and he got a rise. There are countless stories of this kind.

The short book published on his death by the *Herald* indicates several facets which his son has clearly inherited.

'While he was generous as well as shrewd in the bestowal of confidence on others, it can be said that delegation of authority was never complete with him. The ventures he launched were so much a part of him that it would have been impossible to stand aside when executive detail had passed to other hands. To the end, his character impelled him, often with a disarming diffidence and always with good sense, to be the working journalist among his lieutenants.'

There are many quotes from Sir Keith in the book to indicate his editorial opinions. Nearly all of them show the influence British popular journalism had had on him. Many of them might have been said by Northcliffe or Beaverbrook: 'The desk habit is, of course, one of the curses of journalism,' being a typical example, along with directions like: 'Always the need will be for condensation—all the news pointed, clear, terse— never an unnecessary word.'

It was all sound advice for working journalists and the rules laid down by the older Murdoch were studied and utilized when his son returned to Adelaide to take over.

Keith Murdoch did, during the course of his rumbustious career, make some enemies. It is doubtful whether anyone in his position could have avoided it. Certainly there were a handful of board-room wrangles, which he managed to survive, and there were times when his tough views caused controversy (he was never one to mince words), and some people in Australia

(as they still do) argued with him about the general popularization of newspapers. But it was generally considered unwise
to disagree with him, as often he was a lot more right than he
was wrong. He enjoyed great influence and he had a command
of language which made it difficult to debate with him on any
public issue and win.

Sir Keith eventually built the *Herald* into an influential and
much-read newspaper, turned the *Weekly Times* into Victoria's
most important rural journal and started new newspapers right,
left and centre. He introduced popular magazines into the
country and proved himself to be a shrewd business investor,
giving the *Herald* group strong assets and a sound economic
basis. He also became an immensely tough circulation battler.
When the *Evening Star* appeared, he battled from a huge
circulation loss of twenty-two thousand to the *Star*'s oblivion
only two years later.

III

As children, Murdoch and his three sisters held their father
in some awe. They were aware that he was more important than
other men. They had a healthy respect for him but a sincere
love too. He was awe-inspiring as a father and at a very early
age he would go over newspapers with his son advising him to
learn all he could as fast as he could.

Dame Elisabeth recalls, 'I would often find Keith and Rupert
poring over papers. I would say to my husband, "Don't you
think it is a little too early to be talking business?" I mean,
Rupert was only about nine or ten at the time. He would
say, "It is never too early, my dear." And I suppose he was
right. Rupert is very good at figures.'

Murdoch can remember how his father tried to leave the
Melbourne Herald and concentrate on his new acquisitions.
But he could not leave the paper alone. He would quit for a
while but two months later he would start looking at the paper
and the opposition, and, feeling it was going downhill, he
would get back in harder than ever. It was probably very hard
for the people under him. He was, of course, one of the major

shareholders. But he took no salary in the last few years so he could be free to get on with his own business. It must have been very difficult for people like Sir John Williams who was his most influential aide.

But, in fact, 'Jack' Williams has nothing but absolute praise for Sir Keith. A picture of 'The Boss' still stands above his desk and he refers to the *Herald* and Murdoch as one in London refers to the *Express* and Beaverbrook. But at the time, according to Murdoch, Williams and Murdoch senior were bitter in-fighters. 'He has always been completely loyal to my father. He would never let anyone criticize him at all and would always support his name and reputation. But at the time they often came to verbal blows. In fact the day before he died my father sacked Williams after a long wrangle. It was a board-room fight as much as anything and eventually my father became convinced, or persuaded, that 'Jack' Williams was not the man to succeed him. He went to the board on the Friday and got an agreement that Williams should be sacked. He died on the Saturday and the board asked Williams to come back while they considered the position. Jack, of course, is still there.'

Even in semi-retirement, Sir Keith could not leave the newspaper itself alone, and Murdoch used to watch his father marking up the papers every morning. He would mark up almost every paragraph with advice or criticism. Then he would compare his paper with the *Argus* and often say the *Argus* was better that morning. He would tell his son his staff sometimes did not realize how good the opposition was.

'I can't remember any actual business discussions with him until much later when he was buying the *Adelaide News*. Then he talked to me a bit but not too deeply. But I was always brought up in the intense atmosphere of newspapers.'

A contemporary remembers, a little later on, coming back with Murdoch from the beach when Sir Keith was at Cruden, the family home. 'I don't know what we had been doing exactly,' he said, 'but we had been larking around. Anyway, we got back home full of the joys of spring, and Sir Keith was there, and he asked Rupert, very seriously, "Well, Rupert, what has been your most important thought today?" Poor Rupert had to start thinking very quickly. I mean, he couldn't really say he'd been thinking about sailing or swimming or girls. I can't remember what he said, but he thought of something very important rather quickly and spouted a bit of Latin. Sir Keith seemed to be satisfied. I got the feeling Rupert might have saved up good thoughts for such occasions.'

At Cruden, Murdoch's only real companion was his older sister Helen, now Mrs Hanbury, and to whom he was closer than either of his other sisters. She had a very big influence on him and probably still has. However far he goes in the world, both Dame Elisabeth and Helen are still quite capable of bringing him down with a bump. Helen is an extremely down-to-earth person. She is sensible, intelligent and totally unpretentious. She seems unawed by anything and lives a simple hard-working life in Melbourne where Rupert has placed her on the board of Southdown Press (a subsidiary of News International). It has been said several times that one particular Australian politician owes the wrath of Murdoch editorial columns which continually attacked him to the fact that he once sat next to Helen at an official dinner, and was rude to her.

According to Helen the Murdoch children were fairly lonely and consequently got thrown together a lot more than normal. It may have been because their parents had married at such different ages. Their friends—especially Sir Keith's—did not have many children of their own age.

Rupert was always a rather shy child and did not make friends easily. His sister was much more strong-willed than he, and some times a bit unruly. 'I think all this left-wing stuff at school had a lot to do with me,' she said. 'I was always spouting about the poor and the underprivileged.'

Family life at home in those early days must have been full of fun, happiness and security. It was a period that had a very fundamental influence on the life of Rupert Murdoch and I am convinced that Cruden is where his deep sense of family dynasty was born and bred.

Dame Elisabeth is a remarkable woman. She is deeply respected, not only in her own community but throughout

Australia and doesn't seem to have an enemy in the world. She is a good, old-fashioned woman packed with formidable energy, old-world wisdom and honest-to-goodness charm. She is full of minor eccentricities and a homeliness which she manages to combine with a quick and sharp wit. She, like her daughter, is totally unpretentious and despises all pomposity. She works fearfully hard with an energy which makes you weary to be in its presence.

She is perhaps Rupert's sternest critic, reminding him always that, however far he goes, he must not lose his principles or ever succumb to overindulgence. She puts every ounce of her being into living life to the full. She never stops still, always jumping up and down and running around doing things. It is as if eating is a waste of time to her and food disappears with such speed you are never sure it was there at all. She was made a Dame by the Queen in 1963 for her services to hospitals and charities in Australia. She attacks her charitable work with such a fury of activity that few obstacles remain in her path for very long.

She drives a magnificent old car with that inimitable smell of leather to it, never travels first class because she thinks it snobbish, is embarrassed about the sheer amount of money her son is amassing and, in passing, is one of the few women in the world who allows her date of birth to be printed in *Who's Who*. Her tenacious sense of purpose and her great perspicacity coupled with her energy and strength of character make her very obviously the mother of Rupert Murdoch.

Sir Keith was slower and surer than his wife. She was very much the backbone of the family, for while he was in many ways an excellent and loving father, his lifestyle often kept him away from his family. However as he grew older and more conscious of his age, he tended to value his time with the children very greatly and consequently he often indulged them. Dame Elisabeth felt she had to offset this by being the strict one in the family. This resulted in the children always thinking of themselves as closer to their father. 'We thought of our mother as being rather the spoilsport. Since then, of course, we have grown very fond of her and extremely close, but that was the picture we had as children,' Murdoch recalled.

Despite this, most people who knew the young Rupert contend that in those early days his real strength and influence came from his mother. At a recent interview she said, 'Many of the things which Keith was able only to toy with have come to fruition under Rupert. One of his great ambitions, for instance, was to start a national newspaper. He always loved the idea of getting involved with politicians and he was a great one for Australianism. A lot of people have probably told Rupert, "Your father wanted you to do so and so". This is a great mistake. My husband would have wanted Rupert to do what he had to do. I have always been very careful never to quote the dead. Too many people like the idea of saying someone said something when they are no longer around to confirm it.'

Murdoch told his mother recently when she was giving him some verbal chastisement, 'Come now, it's only natural I have *some* pride. If I was as humble as you wanted me to be we'd all still be in Adelaide.' As her son pursues his frantic career across the world, Dame Elisabeth occasionally allows herself to wish he had been just as humble as that.

IV

Throughout the period of Murdoch's childhood, Sir Keith was planning to build up his own journalistic empire and as the teenage Rupert was going through Geelong Grammar School to Oxford University, his father's plans were gradually coming to fruition.

At Geelong Murdoch appeared to be an unhappy child who was not obviously bright and who kept to himself. It is during this period that the paradox in Murdoch's life pattern becomes noticeable, a paradox which has been followed right through to the present day. On the one hand the schoolboy Murdoch was shy and reserved, not making many friends; on the other there was Murdoch the rebel expounding deep socialist principles quite noisily to anyone who would listen. His nickname at school was 'Red Rupert' and since then people have made great play of his early left-wing leanings. In fact, his reputed 'deep-rooted socialism', although sincere at the time, was merely childhood whimsy influenced by intellectual housemasters who bothered to spend long periods with him talking about the evils of being born into a privileged family.

There is no doubt that these men had a very profound effect on Murdoch the schoolboy. But this idealism was tempered at Oxford and, although streaks of radical thinking emerge in the Murdoch psyche every now and then, he is now very far removed from that original 'red rebel'.

He did not excel at sports, was always in the bottom half of the class (except in English language) and was regarded by the rest of the school in a rather negative fashion. Until a later brush with him sharply restored his memory, Sir James Darling, Murdoch's headmaster, said he hardly remembered the boy. Friends of the Murdoch family remember when, in later life, Darling was asked about Murdoch he thought about it for a long time and eventually said, 'Oh, that little nuisance.'

Murdoch admits he was never a member of Darling's fan club. He knew his father had little time for the headmaster and that may well have influenced him. His father had wanted him to go to Scots College. He thought Geelong was then academically weak. He felt the school spent all its money tarting itself up. 'For someone like me who didn't want to put my head down to work,' said Murdoch, 'Geelong was fatal. It would have been far better if I'd gone to a much tougher school.'

Murdoch rarely came up against Darling at Geelong. He feels the headmaster was tired of the school and was 'irrelevant' to the running of the place. Murdoch remembers he missed most of the classes he should have taken and the boys only saw him in chapel on Sunday morning. 'He seemed a very remote person, not particularly interested in his job at the time.'

Despite the suggestion of several schoolfriends Murdoch remembers that only the English master had any real influence over him at school. 'We would discuss anything. I suppose I must have discussed politics too.

'Both Helen and I had somewhere in us, either from school or ourselves, or perhaps from our parents, a sense of social obligation. And we were both by nature rather rebellious. I was much more so than Helen in some ways. She used to work out her rebellion on her mother, whereas my rebellion was against any form of conformity or authority at school. I hated organized sport, mainly because I hated being organized, and partly because I was bone lazy.

'But to say I had no friends would be quite wrong. I remember many of them by name to this day. In the cadet corps my mates and I used to give those in charge hell. All this lugging of rifles around and square-bashing so offended us, we convinced ourselves very quickly we were pacifists.

'We all, and I in particular, hated the old public school system of prefects who would cane you and so on. I found this offensive, particularly as I was always a victim. I remember one particular fascist type who caned me once or twice. I sometimes still see him standing at the bus stop. I must admit to a certain relish in not giving him a lift.'

Dame Elisabeth maintains he is being unfair to the school and that whether he liked it or not it did a great deal to help shape him into the type of person he is today. She admits that when he was there, both she and Sir Keith were worried about his lack of 'school spirit'. There was certainly little in Murdoch the schoolboy to indicate the powerful man he would become later. However, his parents seem to have been sensible enough to let their son work things out for himself. But there is evidence to suggest that Sir Keith was a little disappointed in his son's schooldays. If this is so, it may have contributed later to Murdoch's drive in order to prove himself to his father's memory.

'I was quite amazed when Murdoch became a newspaper tycoon,' a contemporary at Geelong commented. 'I would have said the odds against the quiet little boy I knew at school doing anything really positive with his life were very high.'

'I feel,' added Murdoch, 'that many people are unfair to me about this period. I showed a great independence of spirit, even if other people called this being a bloody nuisance.'

Murdoch was always a fidget as a child—even a portrait of Helen and himself painted at Richmond, and now hanging at Cruden, when they were children, shows he was quite unable to sit still. Helen is sitting serene and composed but the five-year-old Rupert seems—even within the composure of the picture—to be all over the sofa. His leg is cocked up characteristically on the couch and his fingers look as if they are fiddling with something. At Geelong his mother reports that during cricket matches Murdoch annoyed the whole school by doing cart-wheels all over the pitch when he got bored. It was obviously impossible for him to keep his mind interested in a game as slow as cricket.

It was also at Geelong that Murdoch discovered his passion for racing. He would sometimes play truant on Saturday after-noons in order to go to the Melbourne races. He was seen once by a master there and was sure he would be reported. However the master, a man called Pinner, turned out to be a fanatical punter too. He pretended he had not seen Rupert and his chum, as a gesture of honour among thieves. But it was enough to ensure that Murdoch behaved himself for the rest of the term, and when Murdoch passed his exams to Oxford, the punting master commented rudely, 'Wonders will never cease.'

Richard Searby, a prominent Melbourne lawyer, went to both Geelong and Oxford with Murdoch. He remembers Murdoch at school as being rather quiet and shy. No one could really make him out. He kept to himself, had no deep friendships and was not prominent in any school activity. Searby thinks of Murdoch's political views at the school as a bit of a joke. 'No one took him seriously,' he said. 'It seemed so incongruous that Sir Keith's son could be a rampant socialist.'

Searby believes there is no mystery to Murdoch's personality. 'The key to Murdoch, if you really feel you have to find one, is that he is a fidget.' He maintains that Murdoch has a clever, fast mind and a big overdose of energy. 'On top of this he likes everything to be nice and orderly. Inefficiency on any level annoys him. He has to straighten it out and leave it neat and tidy. He gets bored with things very quickly. He was a hopeless student. He simply could not settle down with a book for more than an hour at a time. His dealings in politics these days are a typical example of his lifestyle. He loves the game of it all and the feeling that he is getting the story behind the story. He loves the involvement. But he has absolutely no conception of political theory.'

It is difficult to assess the validity of this but it is an attractive theory because the fundamental thing about Murdoch is that, underneath the more obvious facets which everyone can see, there is very little else. Outside the dramas of big business Murdoch is really very ordinary. With the exception of work and gambling he does everything with dedicated moderation. His pleasures are simple, and I do not think he feels deeply about anything except his family. The depth of his love of art, his Australianism, and his inborn feelings for newspapers, is an unknown quantity. He certainly has a superb collection of modern Australian paintings but it is difficult to pinpoint how he feels about them as somehow it seems incongruous to talk to him about the meaning of art or the application of painting techniques.

V

While Murdoch was at Geelong, Sir Keith made it plain he was not content merely building up someone else's profit accounts. He wanted something for himself. He had a very strong desire, according to Jack Williams, to pass on something to his family—something more tangible than a formidable reputation. However much money he made he could never raise the millions needed to buy the *Herald*, but he had to have something where he ruled the roost. He eventually found what he wanted in the ten-year-old *Adelaide News* when he joined its board in 1931.

This small and rather humble beginning—an afternoon newspaper in one of Australia's smaller cities with a circulation of only thirty-five thousand—was the start of the Murdoch empire. But it was not humble for long. He also became principle proprietor, with a forty-five per cent holding, of two Queensland papers, the *Courier* and the *Mail*. He merged these with great success. They also had the *Adelaide Sunday Mail* in the stable.

Sir Keith also wanted to buy the *Argus* to supplement his other papers. Murdoch thinks that had his father been five years younger and fitter he would have gone through with his plans. But he did not because he felt in the end his name was so indelibly linked with the *Herald* it was far too late to live that down and start afresh with the opposition. He certainly flirted with the idea to the extent of cabling Cecil King, then chairman of IPC, who owned the *Argus*.

The *Adelaide Advertiser*, owned by the Herald Group, had previously controlled the *Adelaide News*. After World War 2 Sir Keith had persuaded the *Melbourne Herald* board into getting the *Advertiser* to sell him the shares. In return he gave them the clear legal first option to buy the *Courier Mail*, and, as the circulation rose steadily on the *Adelaide News*, so did Sir Keith's shares until, in 1949, he had a majority holding with a sum of about one hundred and fifty thousand pounds invested.

Sir Keith's pact with the *Melbourne Herald* turned into an expectation that they would acquire the *Courier Mail* on his death. Murdoch firmly believes that had he been just a few years older he would have been able to fight them off and keep this paper.

The Murdoch family fortunes had started life on the acquisition of the *Adelaide News*, but the newspaper itself had been born years before as the *Barrier Miner*, launched in the rather peculiar mining town of Broken Hill towards the end of the last century. It was bought by a man called Davidson in 1918. He had been fired from the *Melbourne Herald* under what Murdoch described as 'rather mysterious circumstances'. Davidson went on to buy a paper called the *Port Pirie Recorder*—at the port just north of Adelaide where all the metals from Broken Hill were exported.

In July 1923 he used the two tiny papers 'making peanuts' as the basis on which to float a public company called News Limited to start the *Adelaide News*. He put in the *Barrier Miner* in exchange for preference shares. Davidson went on to start an evening paper in Hobart called the *Hobart News*, which quickly failed, and the *Daily News* in Perth. Always thought to be a complete teetotaller, he was found dead in 1928 in the middle of a mass of empty bottles. For years he had been a secret drinker.

In 1923 Sir Keith had also taken the *Melbourne Herald* into Adelaide and they had bought a little morning paper called *The Recorder*. The new paper kicked up such a stink that the principal owners of the *Adelaide Advertiser* sold out to the Herald Group. On Davidson's death there was an exchange of shares between News Limited and the Herald Group so that, in effect, the Herald Group took over News Limited. It is true to say, then, that the Murdoch empire was started on a shoestring by a secret alcoholic in one of Australia's most unique outback townships.

VI

As the circulation of the Murdoch family papers went up and up, Murdoch prepared himself for life at Oxford, where he immediately blossomed out. He was outstanding neither academically nor socially, but for the first time he made solid friendships, took part in the activities of his surroundings and was noticed by his contemporaries. He mixed with a young, smart and intelligent set of Labourites led by Shirley Summerskill and Gerald Kaufman, who was to become principal private Secretary to Harold Wilson when he was prime minister of the 1964 Labour government and MP for a Manchester constituency in 1970. Murdoch also counted among his friends at the time, his tutor, Asa Briggs, now professor of sociology at Sussex University, whose prolific energy can be rivalled only by Murdoch himself.

Richard Searby remembers that Murdoch found it very difficult to sit down with a book. 'He would go to his room for a few hours dedicated to study. But then he'd throw the book down. He just got so bored. He'd have to be up and about. He just couldn't get down to it.'

Murdoch himself still relates with some glee how, when he set himself up for president of the Labour Club, he canvassed for votes. This was theoretically against the rules of university politics and Murdoch only narrowly escaped a minor scandal. He lost the fight, which is interesting as it was probably his first defeat of any significance. Murdoch played to win and the

fact that canvassing was a little unethical seemed rather
ridiculous to him.

'It was not exactly unheard of to canvass for votes,' said
Murdoch. 'Gerald Kaufman, for instance, canvassed better than
I did. The trick was not to get caught at it. I made the mistake
of having a list on my desk and Kaufman came in and pinched
it.'

Asa Briggs would often ask Murdoch to drive him down to
London for an appointment and Murdoch, bored with Oxford,
was always happy to comply. Down in London, Murdoch would
stay with an aunt in Oakley Street, Chelsea. A tenant of the
house at the time recalled that he was always popping in and
borrowing a fiver.

During his second year at Oxford his parents came to see him.
They stayed for several days and Sir Keith came to the conclusion his son was probably wasting his time. They talked
about taking him away but Dame Elisabeth persuaded her
husband it would be better to leave him there. They both
thought, on reflection, that to take him away as a failure would
hurt his pride too much. She maintains that, as it turned out,
they made the correct decision, and Murdoch's subsequent
career tends to back her up.

In fact, as the time to take his finals approached, Murdoch
himself realized he had little chance of graduating. He had
simply not done enough work. But before the exams Asa Briggs
took him off on holiday for six weeks and crammed enough
knowledge into him to enable him to get a second-class degree
in economics.

Murdoch remembers that he worked hard in the subjects
which interested him, but admits they were not many. He got
very involved with university politics and would rush off to
club meetings rather than get down to his course. Sometimes
he enrolled for a course of lectures which had nothing to do
with his subject.

He found Oxford a fascinating place. He loved sitting up all
night arguing with people and picking their brains. 'There
was always something more interesting to do than study,' he
said. 'But I think it was all immensely valuable.'

The brains around Murdoch were bright, intelligent and much to the radical side of politics in the fifties. Murdoch was certainly seen to be influenced by them. He loved the cut and thrust of small-meeting debate and spent endless evenings putting his point of view fairly aggressively to anyone who would listen. His early years in Adelaide reflect much of the social radicalism he was exposed to at Oxford.

In the main, however, Oxford was a stimulating and interesting interlude between his rather mundane schooldays and the aggressive tycoonery which would quickly show itself on his return home. Academically, university meant little to him but the exercise of an already agile mind. Perhaps, too, the place was a confidence builder. There was a freedom and away-from-home atmosphere which must have been very refreshing after the rigours of Geelong.

Rupert enjoyed an allowance of six hundred pounds a year from his father, from which he had to find his fees. Friends report he was fairly free with his money, sometimes splashing it around in quite an abandoned manner. He claims this is rubbish. He found he could live fairly well on the money in those days, but never had enough to throw around. He ate well but could never eat out unless he went down to the station canteen for some egg and chips for ninepence. 'I never had any high life. Not like some of those fellows with two or three thousand pounds private income, taking girls to expensive balls in London. That wasn't my life at all.'

In the last two years he had a little Austin A40. He frightened it out of his father after he had bought a small motor-bike.

In the summer of 1950 Murdoch spent the last two weeks he would have with his father, when he and a friend drove off on holiday to meet Sir Keith in Zurich. They planned to leave the friend there for a while and go off to Turkey for two weeks together. They found Europe bomb-shattered and ugly. Most of the time they had to camp rough in a large tent. Sir Keith paid all the expenses but they found little they could spend their money on. The roads hardly existed and the only comfort the two had on the trip was when they called in at the British embassies in Belgrade and Athens.

The plan was to drive to Istanbul where Asa Briggs would join them. Sir Keith would then fly back to Australia and the other two would drive as far as the Euphrates. But in the end they left the car in Beirut to be shipped to Australia. Unfortunately the car got shipped to Suez and was left on the wharf there for several months. When it finally arrived in Australia it was in a totally unusable condition. Searby remembers that until Sir Keith heard the full story he was quite livid. 'Sir Keith was not the type of man to bless someone who took no regard for expense or property,' he said.

Any journalistic comparison between Sir Keith and his son is difficult. Sir Keith was always essentially a working journalist first and a newspaper owner second. Probably the reverse is true of Rupert. It was said by a close friend of the family that Sir Keith was twice the journalist Rupert is—but Rupert is twice the businessman.

Reading back over the files of Sir Keith's journalism it is obvious that much of it was quite brilliant for its time. On the other hand there is very little signed copy from his son, although there is much testimony from every section of Murdoch's organization that he knows all the facets of publishing a newspaper. Whether the son excels in one field where his father excelled in another is a matter for conjecture. From a purely practical viewpoint, though, if the rare writings of Rupert are compared with the colossal mileage of words from his father, Sir Keith very obviously comes out on top on the writing side. To take an example, on September 14th, 1960, the *Sydney Daily Mirror* carried a well displayed double-page spread headlined 'Special Dispatch from Havana'. Underneath was a huge by-line and a picture of Murdoch, with massive sub-headings like 'Cuba holds the key to Red Control over Latin America', and '200 million people could be lost to the free world'. It is open to argument, of course, but the piece quite clearly lacked the depth and insight at which Sir Keith excelled.

Murdoch over the years has also written front-page editorials signed by him, dictating his attitude to the politicians. On February 10th, 1961, for instance, he blasted off on the front page demanding that the governor general to succeed Lord

Dunrossil should be Australian. He urged, with a good deal of style, that the then prime minister, Sir Robert Menzies, should take the job. Echoes of his father, certainly. But at a different time, in a different generation, when he was writing, not as an observer like his father, but as the outright owner of the vehicle publishing his views.

Commenting later on this piece Murdoch said, 'I wrote that piece about Menzies because I thought it was a very good way of getting rid of him. I agree with your assessment of the journalistic difference between my father and myself. The only time recently when I have really got down to hard day-to-day journalism was before the 1973 Australian election. I wrote most of the editorials for our papers and I really got stuck into it. I stand by them, I think they were all good campaigning stuff.'

VII

When Sir Keith died Murdoch flew home for the funeral and wanted to stay there. He felt he should get stuck in immediately and only a lot of urging from Dame Elisabeth persuaded him to go back to Oxford to take his degree before returning to his father's business.

Murdoch finally left Oxford in the early summer of 1952 and decided that, before going home to launch himself into the family firm, it would be very useful for him to have actually had some hard news experience. Fleet Street was the obvious place to get it and, although Murdoch was itching to return home, he went to see Lord Beaverbrook who had been a friend of his father.

Murdoch quite blandly used this friendship to get a job on the *Daily Express*. He asked Beaverbrook if he could spend a week on the back bench (the nerve centre of editorial operations). He felt he had managed to pick up so much after eight days that he decided to stay on. Beaverbrook benevolently put him at the bottom of the sub-editor's table (subs manipulate the words into the spaces provided and then headline them). And he spent several months at ten pounds a week subbing one paragraph 'shorts' and 'fillers'. An up-table sub of the time recalls, 'He was the cheekiest but busiest little whipper-snapper to ever sit at the end of the table.'

Murdoch played newspaperman furiously. He was unmercifully bullied by the up-table cynics but brashly ignored them and learnt enough about sub-editing and page presentation in two months to teach all his Australian staff a thing or two when he went back to rule the roost. It was this brashness which was to take him from the bottom of that particular table to the very top of Fleet Street within a mere twenty years. One night the *Daily Express* editorial staff were arguing about what a slow news day it had been. Apparently they had no idea what to lead the paper with and edition time was creeping up. Murdoch had noticed an Australian-orientated story in his own family-owned *Courier Mail* which had huge significance for Britain. He cannot remember the story itself, but realized it had somehow got brushed aside among the miles of words which daily come into a newspaper office. He broke into Reuter's and went back through their files until he found the newsflash and brought it back to the office. It was the next day's main lead.

He also attempted to accomplish what his father had abandoned—to buy the *Melbourne Argus* from Cecil King's IPC. He recalls he was extremely nervous as he went to see King at the then IPC headquarters in Geraldine House. He asked outright if he could buy the paper but King wanted to know who would run it. At twenty-one Murdoch did not yet feel quite bold enough to retort that he would himself. Murdoch tried to persuade King that IPC would get their money back over a long period. 'I hoped we'd have enough time to pay off all the debts before we paid him back, including the death duties.'

In fact this little trip to Geraldine House must be regarded as classic Murdochism. There he was, without a drop of hard newspaper experience; facing a hostile board in Adelaide and trustees who were already planning to carve up the company, small as it was, to pay death duties; and he calmly walked in and tried to buy one of Australia's most influential newspapers. Had they known, the board would have been horrified. But Murdoch's plan was sound, and with hindsight he could have probably got away with it. He felt that with the *Courier Mail* in Brisbane, the *News* in Adelaide and the *Argus* in Melbourne he would be stepping into something really worthwhile.

But Murdoch was not allowed to get away with it. The executors of his father's estate went berserk when they heard of the plan and King, in the end, decided he did not want to sell to Murdoch. King had been very interested in who Murdoch had in mind as editor of the paper. Murdoch, for political reasons, could not say he had Walton Cole, then editor at Reuter's lined up, so he told him he wanted Colin Bednal of the *Courier Mail* as editor. King said they had rejected him only a few months before. But, in fact, King hired him himself soon after.

When Murdoch finally returned home in 1952 he found himself embroiled in several battles to keep the empire, small as it was, at full strength. On Sir Keith's death, the trustees had sold the Brisbane interests to the *Melbourne Herald* to raise the money for death duties and Rupert himself had to start with the *Adelaide News* and the *Sunday Mail* alone. He believes it was the worst thing the trustees could have done. 'I would have borrowed on our assets, paid off the duties and repaid the debt from profits,' he said. With hindsight again, he probably would have been successful.

The main executor was also the chairman of both Murdoch's bank and of the Herald Group and was faced with listening to what he considered to be a very young boy. He wanted to clear everything up as quickly as possible. He thought very much in terms of looking after a widow and her three daughters. His attitude was that a son could look after himself. He could not tolerate the thought of the family going into a whole new phase deeply in debt. He thought the idea quite mad. 'When my father died he was hocked up to his ears and the death duties were half of the total estate,' said Murdoch. 'The *Courier Mail* more than met all that and still left some money over which was put into the *Adelaide News*.'

Murdoch while understanding the consternation of the executor (and why his mother sided with him) still deeply regrets losing the paper. 'I lost the battle, but not without a lot of protest,' he ruefully remembers.

VIII

Adelaide is a small, sunny, sleepy city with large sprawling suburbs flanked by beautiful hills and forests. Everything moves a lot slower than in most of the rest of urban Australia and the whole place is landscaped with well-planned gardens. It is the exact opposite of the brazen hubbub of Sydney, yet it keeps that indefinable spirit of Australia peculiarly intact.

When Murdoch returned to Australia he was met in Adelaide by a board of respectable men and a staff of talented journalists who had all been hand-picked by his father. 'My first attitude when I got back,' he said, 'was that I would take over. But they thought I was a young whipper-snapper who should learn the ropes first. I felt if I was going to do that I would do it elsewhere. But there was no time. The thing that urged me on all the time was the impending battle with *The Advertiser*. I was very confident of myself, although I was rather shy in many ways. I knew I was in for a fight as soon as I got back. So my mother and I wrote the board a letter from Cruden Investments [the family holding company] saying I should be given some executive power and the directors accepted that.'

He was immediately faced with a fierce newspaper war which he went into furiously. Sir Alexander Dumas, a former close friend of Sir Keith's, had gone to Dame Elisabeth on behalf of *The Advertiser* board to try and get her to sell the *Adelaide News* and *Sunday Mail* to them. The proposition was really in the form of a polite but firm threat. It was put to Dame Elisabeth that they would be starting their own rival Sunday, and that the *Sunday Mail* was a threat to them. They were sure they could run the *Sunday Mail* out of business and consequently lose a lot of money for News Limited. They had felt it polite, they added, to come along and give Dame Elisabeth a chance to sell to them at the market price before the fight started.

Murdoch was incensed and to this day has never forgiven Dumas. 'I told my mother we must fight them. She eventually let me have my own way.' His first action was to print the whole story of the threat in the *Adelaide News*. He front-paged a letter making the 'proposition' to his mother. 'I'm not sure I would do that today. I might have been a bit headstrong,' he said, 'but I have no regrets. They knew from then on we meant business. We made an emotional appeal about press monopoly. It was great stuff. They didn't speak to me for five years.'

Murdoch wasted no time. Representing his family's majority interest in the firm he asked to be made senior executive as a working member of the board. He put this proposal to the second board meeting he attended. According to R. B. Wiltshire, an Adelaide accountant who was on the board at the time, the board was split right down the middle. Wiltshire was asked to give the deciding vote. Wiltshire did not think about it for very long and turned him down. He felt Murdoch had not yet proved himself and they had other shareholders to think of. The board felt it was too early for Murdoch to be put in a position of such power. Although Murdoch was straining at the leash and was disappointed, he took it in good grace. He came back a few months later and said he wanted a title. He asked if they would mind if he called himself 'The Publisher' and no one objected.

It was not long before the Australian love of nicknames got to work. Throughout his days in Adelaide he was known by everyone as 'The Boy Publisher'. Murdoch counters that Wiltshire is romanticizing and that the three members of the board all voted against him. There was no split in the board and if there had been a vote it would have been three to one against him. 'They were horrified I should try to take over as chief executive at only twenty-two.'

Murdoch had accepted that he could not yet run the board meetings, but this did not stop him from plunging right into the middle of the organization and, with fists flying in every direction, he made himself thoroughly felt.

The new rival Sunday paper came out with a flourish and throughout the early fifties the fight between the two papers was intense. Eventually both sides decided to quit and they joined forces under one banner. Both owned fifty per cent, but

News Limited had all the executive control and the permanent print contract.

'In fact,' said Murdoch, 'we were beating them. They came out with a huge circulation on the first edition, but eventually went down to about thirty thousand. But my board of rather old men were seeing our competition costs and were having kittens. They kept asking me to be reasonable, but I absolutely refused. If we had been a private company I would have seen them off and they would have had to close. We should have done that. But in the end, under great pressure, I capitulated. We got a lot of money, the printing, and a half share.'

From that moment Murdoch flung himself deep into the bowels of the business and never looked back. He busied himself going to editorial conferences, digging up stories, learning the page make-up and nearly always putting the paper to bed. He supervised some remarkable exclusives, brightened the paper up, built the circulation, cut out a lot of deadwood, lopped off costs in every direction and proved himself to be a tough, hard, board-room in-fighter.

He spent nearly all the fifties in this sunny southern city and his time was crammed with activity right from the start. He geared up for battle with *The Advertiser*, fought his own editorial battles, leapt into television and, as a backdrop to all the other dramas, threw himself into the business of learning what he could about newspapers. He was quick to learn, although he depended, as he always has, on his energy, flair and intuitive inspiration rather than on any solid newspaper training. By the mid-fifties Murdoch had emerged as a clear force in News Limited, cutting and thrusting his way to the top of the board, expanding wherever the Commonwealth Bank would let him and eventually gearing himself for a forceful swoop on Sydney.

Frank Waters was company secretary both before and after Rupert's appearance. He recalled that Rupert quickly started lighting fireworks under the business. The old board had been taught by Sir Keith to look at every penny. They would never risk anything. But, although Murdoch showed he cared for the figures, he was prepared to take a gamble. The first thing he wanted to do was expand. These ambitions were motivated by the fact that a single evening newspaper in one of Australia's smaller towns gave him no power of initiative. He emphatically denies he was trying to beat the memory of his father, even though at this time he was treated very much as his father's son.

His expansion motive developed because he could not afford to buy Australian rights to articles or information. He had no connections outside the state. The paper could not afford its own correspondents, especially abroad. He realized early on that more newspapers meant better newspapers because they could complement and back each other up. 'That's why we bought the Perth paper,' Murdoch said. 'We just went ahead and got the first thing that came along.'

They bought the *Perth Sunday Times*, in Western Australia, and Murdoch started flying out to Perth every weekend, a journey of eight hours in an old DC4. Murdoch had an uncle of his father's living there, a Professor Walter Murdoch, who was a famous essayist. He stayed at his home and the professor had a considerable influence on him. They often talked right into the night. It seemed sometimes as if he was back at Oxford, and they grew very fond of each other.

Ron Boland, present editor of the *Adelaide News* and one of Murdoch's most trusted aides, remembers the paper was in an awful mess. The picture desk had been supported by old picture blocks. If the previous editor had a space in the paper he would dig under the table until he found a picture block of the right size. It didn't matter what the picture was of. When they first got the paper, Murdoch himself went over every week to put it together. He whipped the paper into shape in a very short while and before long it was making money.

On Saturday night when the last edition had come off the presses Murdoch and a bunch of his employees would charge off into the night. Murdoch was nearly always at the wheel. He was a mad driver. He would get the car up to seventy or eighty miles an hour and they would drive non-stop all night and half the following morning until they got to a place called Shark Bay, seven hundred miles north of Perth. They would arrive mid-morning at an old pearl-fisher's paradise. The pearls had run out and now just a bunch of fishermen and odd-bods lived there. They went there for the snapper fishing. You could apparently get good fifteen- to twenty-pound snappers. They would net some whiting for bait and sail off for an island in the bay which was used as a sheep station.

Maintaining a custom that has amused his friends all his life Murdoch always designated himself as chief cook, and would attack the food by slapping it down, bashing it, basting it, and sploshing it into the pan. He would experiment with all sorts of things. Some of them near disasters, and everyone else would have to do the washing up. Boland ruefully recalls Murdoch had a funny way of using every single pot, pan, plate and piece of cutlery in the whole place to cook a simple meal.

Most of the board remained sceptical of Murdoch's achievements—though they began to recognize they would not be able to keep Murdoch in his place for long. The first time they really knew he had it in him was when he acquired Channel Nine Television in Adelaide. It was his first major coup. It was a logical step and he pulled it off almost single-handed, despite opposition from Sir Robert Menzies.

He started the STV Corporation with a tiny capital of a quarter of a million pounds, borrowed from sources of every kind. The station started making money immediately and he paid everything back very quickly from profits—a typical business manoeuvre which was to become standard Murdoch practice. The battle for the television station was a 'consuming thing' for some time. There were a lot of public hearings and cross-examinations especially concerning the number of stations in the state.

Murdoch also tried to get the second Perth television station. His argument was that the *Perth Sunday Times* was just a little paper and wanted a small interest in the station, although they would probably have bought a majority interest later on. The opposition had the daily papers and all the radio stations and Murdoch argued that they were creating a monopoly. There is little doubt Murdoch was recommended for the Perth TV licence. 'Menzies also stopped that,' he claims.

Apparently before the recommendation got into printed form

it got the thumbs down from Sir Robert Menzies and the issue became another of several between the ex-prime minister and the forceful up-and-coming tycoon which were eventually to end up with Murdoch campaigning vigorously for Menzies' removal.

It was the second time Murdoch and Menzies had brushed over TV licences. Murdoch now believes he was wrong about the Adelaide licence. He wanted one station, although Menzies had insisted there was room for two. Murdoch now admits there was. But he claims the Perth issue was a straight veto where News Limited did not get a look-in and Murdoch asserts that the decision to stop his bid was taken at cabinet level, on the eve of an election.

Murdoch has retained scant regard for the Australian Broadcasting Board ever since. His critics point out this is sour grapes because things did not always go his way. But Murdoch claims the ABC board, with all its public hearings was merely a front to make things look respectable. At the end of it all the prime minister of the day can veto the findings and the real power over such issues belongs very firmly to him.

IX

Old Adelaide aides remember Murdoch as being carefree and good fun in those days. He went everywhere with a huge great dane called Webster who would run away, stopping all the traffic, until he got to Myers Emporium where he would wait to be picked up by a Murdoch delivery van.

Murdoch lived a full life and managed to find time for indulging in his favourite pastimes. Boland remembers that Rupert loved swimming and surfing and it was difficult to keep him away from the sea. He had a small flat down by the beach and spent all his free time perched on a surf board. He apparently did not bother too much about the finer things in life, and would sometimes borrow a shirt and cufflinks from Boland to go out to dinner.

It was also in Adelaide that Murdoch learned his favourite trick of walking up to a news-stand and changing the formation of the newspapers so that his own publications were on top. (He still does this today and often embarrasses his wife, Anna by the tactic.)

Buying the Perth paper and the TV station constituted most of the drama during Murdoch's early Adelaide days. But he had some fun and games with the *Adelaide News* too. He brightened the paper up considerably and immediately increased its circulation. He became a sort of glorified editor-in-chief without a real title and the board, which had started by keeping a restraining hand on his shoulder, began to let him have more and more authority.

At any given opportunity Murdoch would rush off by car into the countryside. When, in Canberra, politicians were shouting about the state of the aboriginals and how badly off they were, Rupert gathered together a bunch of colleagues and flew around Australia in a four-seater plane. They criss-crossed Australia a dozen times and stopped off right in the middle of the bush at sheep stations and slept where they could. They went everywhere the trail led them and followed up rumours, talked to hundreds of people like missionaries, and generally covered the story in every possible way. One of the people with him on the trip said, 'We found—and Rupert subsequently wrote—that although many aboriginals were suffering from malnutrition, the reports had been highly exaggerated. But it was a hell of a trip. I don't know to this day whether Rupert wanted to know about the state of aboriginals—or whether he just wanted a bloody good jaunt around Australia.'

Rohan Rivett was Murdoch's first editor of the *Adelaide News*. But later he was also the first editor to be sacked by the young tycoon. By all accounts he was a good editor, a radical man who believed firmly that the power of the press should be continually utilized for the exposure of that which was not to the public good—a good working manual for almost any editor.

At first the two hit it off. Murdoch was still influenced by his radical Oxford days. Rohan Rivett, a dedicated man, wanted to have a bash at the establishment in every edition. The two raised issues which were highly controversial. For example, they supported an aboriginal called Stuart against corrupt practices by the police, and although they won eventually it was a case which left a bad taste in everyone's mouth. The climate of opinion was that both sides were as bad as each other. 'There is now no doubt Stuart was guilty of murder,' said Murdoch, 'but there is also no doubt the police fabricated evidence.' When Stuart eventually got off, Murdoch and his colleagues were taken to court for sedition. They won the case but no one is convinced they won much popular support.

Murdoch remembers Rivett as 'a strange mercurial sort of Welshman'. He had known him when Rivett was in London working for the *Melbourne Herald* when Murdoch was a student. They were very close friends but Murdoch's theory was that Rivett became a little unhinged over the Stuart case. Not through the conducting of it in the newspaper—they were both in that together—but because of the court case itself.

The government quite clearly wanted to send Rivett to prison. Murdoch and Rivett heard from their own sources that the state premier would be delighted to send him inside but they were determined to keep Murdoch out. It would have been too much for them. Ken May, now chief executive of News Limited, went into the box to give evidence that Murdoch had in fact been deeply involved and had written the offending posters. 'Of course, they weren't even faintly seditious,' Murdoch said. 'Anyway they then went a bit quiet and we eventually got off on all eighteen charges.'

The case tore Adelaide in half. It was a violent time for everyone. Murdoch could never make out whether Rivett wanted to go to jail or not. One day he seemed frightened of it—the next he rather liked the idea of being a martyr. Murdoch claims Rivett was not a heavy intellectual although he liked to appear that way.

X

In 1958 Murdoch conceived the idea of a national TV paper which would give all the TV and broadcasting programmes in a single periodical. He decided that as he knew nothing of such papers he would fly to America and give himself a crammer course. Ron Boland and he took a thirty-three day trip jauntily criss-crossing the continent looking at all the TV papers. Murdoch made sure they passed through Las Vegas, where, it was said by a highly reputable source, Murdoch once had to hitch-hike back to his hotel after spending his last cent at the roulette table. 'Just coming through the outskirts of town Rupert got quite excited,' Boland remembers. 'Las Vegas simply fascinated him.' Murdoch won and lost small fortunes during the few days they spent in the gambling city. 'He had a go at everything. One-armed bandits, roulette, blackjack—the lot. You couldn't keep him off them,' Boland added.

On the same trip the roving couple bet on the big interstate Kentucky Derby. The night before they had been on something of a session with the UPI man and asked him to stake them one hundred dollars at five to one on an Australian horse called Sailor's Guide. Boland recalls that they got really excited during the race. After a mix-up and a subsequent investigation into the race, Sailor's Guide was declared the winner. Murdoch and Boland collected the five hundred dollars, flew to Bermuda and blew the lot celebrating.

Despite the fun and games of this trip, Murdoch was also managing to think very deeply about his business back home. While he snoozed on aeroplanes between the major cities, he was hatching a sensational plot for his homecoming. This resulted in the opposition paper *The Advertiser* (whose board was watching Murdoch's activities with keen interest) waking up one day to find Murdoch had been audacious enough to attempt its takeover.

Murdoch had made himself felt in Adelaide. First of all with his own board. Then, as he rather brashly started spread-his wings, his acquisition of the TV station. The opposition thought that would keep him happy. No one on *The Advertiser* could possibly dream that he would suddenly turn round and try to buy them out too. They had thought they were all sitting pretty when suddenly, with one cheeky bid, they saw how vulnerable they were.

Ron Boland remembers it had all started when he and Murdoch were returning from the USA via London. Apparently Murdoch sat in the bath at the Savoy Hotel and pontificated about the possibilities of a takeover bid for *The Advertiser*. He leant back in the bath pouring in hot water every now and again, and spent hours musing to himself on how it could be done. He had a plot and he spent about two hours spelling it out to Boland. He gave him a running commentary about how it might be pulled off—and what his opposition might be and so on. 'I suppose he was just thinking aloud and needed someone as a sounding board,' said Boland, 'but at the time I thought he was loony.'

That evening Murdoch continued his planning and doodled on the back of a menu in a Soho restaurant where he and Boland were dining. On his return to Adelaide he quite remarkably put his doodles into operation. Even Murdoch's own board was startled at his affrontery. *The Advertiser was* Adelaide. It was so establishment, Adelaidians treated it like a maiden aunt.

It was the biggest takeover bid of this period of his life. He found fourteen million pounds from various sources which really surprised *The Advertiser*'s board. They just did not believe he could raise cash like that. The bid was a viable proposition and the paper could have gone for less than that. However, the old guard at *The Advertiser* would have none of it, and the bid was foiled. This left *The Advertiser* in a very weak position because the bid exposed to the shareholders the real worth of the paper and for years their shares remained much lower than Murdoch's offer. This was constantly hanging over the directors and a lot of shareholders kept needling them about the bid. They were put in a position of straining at all times to pay much higher dividends than they could afford.

Jack Williams later told Murdoch that if he had come to him quietly they might have been able to do a deal. But, as it was, the *Melbourne Herald* owned forty per cent and they immediately got some of the big family shareholders to pledge support. Before the bid got off the ground they had more than fifty per cent. 'I think the Williams deal would have meant them taking us over—with maybe me running the whole

Adelaide set-up. I would have lost forever any chance to make my own way,' was Murdoch's comment.

The Advertiser takeover attempt was a classic in everything but its failure. It is wrong to assume, as many did, that this was Murdoch merely being cheeky. He meant it, although he must have known that the odds were stacked against him.

It was also during the closing stages of this period that Murdoch's first marriage began to break up. Most observers of the situation at the time say Murdoch was an impossible husband. He would bring fifteen people home to dinner at ten minutes' notice. Then his wife would arrange a nice little dinner party to find that her husband had flown halfway round Australia to fix a deal and had forgotten to tell her. It is firmly believed by many people who were close to Murdoch that he was greatly upset by the breakdown and flung himself into his work with a formidable energetic hangover.

By the time Murdoch was ready for Sydney he had built News Limited into a flourishing business. He had acquired the Sunday in Perth, a paper in Alice Springs, Channel Nine Television, started *TV Week*, and kept the *Adelaide Sunday Mail* as a thriving concern. He had cheekily bid for the opposition, got himself into a position of confidence with the bank, and learned enough about newspapers and publishing to feel confident about moving into the guerilla warfare of Sydney publishing.

His chance came when he was offered a string of provincial newspapers based at Parramatta, a little to the north of Sydney. He had to find a million pounds and needed his chairman's signature on the deal. The chairman was fishing off Kangaroo Island off the Adelaide coast. Murdoch and Frank Shaw (now company secretary in Sydney; then, among other things, aviation correspondent of the *Adelaide News*) flew over and rowed out to a smaller island where the chairman was. It was almost dusk before the two rowed back to the main island where they found an irate pilot who said it was too late to fly back because they did not have landing lights which were required by Adelaide airport. The pilot was livid because he had got married that morning and his new wife was waiting for him. The sorrowful trio repaired to the only pub on the island and found that none of them had a bean between them. Murdoch, with a deal worth a million pounds in his pocket, had to throw himself on the mercy of a highly suspicious landlord and request they be given food and board—on tick.

Chapter 3

Barons and bandits

I

In the twenty-two years from Murdoch's homecoming in 1952 to 1974, there was a dramatic growth pattern in the Murdoch saga. From the small sunny city of Adelaide to an empire spanning the globe, Murdoch has moved fast. In Adelaide he learnt how to produce a newspaper and how to expand his business. In Sydney, Murdoch began to learn the cut and thrust of newspaper politics. He was an ardent student, quickly assimilating more than his rivals and eventually leaving them all behind. Sometimes he lost, but he never failed to learn.

When he had acquired the Parramatta papers he moved out of Adelaide and started concentrating on big-city journalism. The Parramatta deal was a foot-in-the-door operation which became typical Murdoch strategy in later years. He certainly had no intention of sitting around in the suburbs.

In the 1950s, Australian newspapers were roughly divided into two camps—Sydney and the rest. Outside Sydney there were the big prestige papers like the *Melbourne Age* and the *Melbourne Herald* which stood unchallenged. But in Sydney there was guerilla warfare. Before Murdoch began, three big rough and tough characters dominated the scene: Frank Packer, John Fairfax and Ezra Norton. Frank Packer was a big, sometimes oafish man, who had once been a top professional boxer and liked to throw his weight around. Fairfax was shrewd, but not so robust. Ezra Norton was a peculiar little man who possessed an inherent evil streak which seemed to ooze out of every pore. The three spent a great deal of their journalistic lives hurling abuse at each other. Norton was said to tote a gun around in case he met Frank Packer who he was convinced would hit him. Surrounded by henchmen, they would fling

angry insults at each other at the races. They eventually did
come to blows and Packer was said to still have Norton's teeth
marks in his ear when he died in 1974.

Their newspapers were hardly better than their behaviour.
Each would not hesitate to insult either of the other two.
Delivery lorries were sabotaged, reporters were bought off. Posters
were ripped down and fights were always breaking out among
reporters from opposing sides.

The three main papers of these rumbustious tearaways were
Packer's *Telegraph*, Fairfax's *Sun* and Norton's *Mirror*. Each
of them also had a sister Sunday in the stable. The wars between
Northcliffe and Beaverbrook were but child's play to the angry
gangsterism of Sydney in the thirties and forties. The situation is
summed up by a remarkable newspaper cutting in Sydney,
dating back to the pre-Murdoch era.

The public has been intrigued more than somewhat over
the war of words that broke out this week between certain
big guns of Sydney's newspaper world.

In one corner is Granny *Herald* [Fairfax's *Sydney Morning
Herald*] the wasp-waisted widow of Wattle St; in the other
is The Terrible *Telegraph*, the undisputed champ of that
area of Castlereagh St between Park and Market St.

Granny's seconds are Rupert Albert Geary Henderson
[managing director of John Fairfax Ltd] and Warwick Oswald
Fairfax [chairman of directors]. In the *Telegraph* corner,
seethingly indignant and scowling darkly, are Douglas Frank
Hewson Packer [managing director of Consolidated Press
Ltd] and David McNicoll [editor-in-chief].

At the ringside no doubt wincing at every contact, is
Telegraph columnist Jim Macdougall, who once used to write
for the *Sun*.

Nobody seems to be too sure of what the trouble is all
about, but the contestants look like reaching the hair-pulling
stage at any time now.

Already words like cowards, liars, blackmailers, libellers,
dishonesty, etc. are being tossed about with reckless abandon.

Tch! Tch! Isn't it disgraceful!

Packer and Henderson quickly realized that Murdoch could become a real threat to them. He was already losing them circulation in the northern suburbs and his next move was to buy up a TV station at Wollongong, south of Sydney. They soon spotted Murdoch's plan to ring them in and carve up their circulation areas outside the city itself.

Packer and Henderson got together and formed an unlikely alliance to beat Murdoch. They decided to pour all their time, effort and money into a suburban circulation war with him and go on losing money until he was beaten.

Murdoch was always wary of Packer and was not surprised when he was invited to a 'welcoming party' and told of their plans. They informed him loudly and brazenly that they were both prepared to lose five thousand pounds a week each until they had ruined him.

Murdoch's first reaction was resentment. His second was a resolution that, no matter what, he would survive. Murdoch's energy and will have always been quite formidable. Without realizing it Packer and Henderson managed to strengthen Murdoch's spirit to its ultimate limit.

Most people who knew Packer either loved him or hated him, but few ever tried to maintain he was not one of the most interesting characters in Sydney. When he died he was a mere shadow of the man he had been, but in those days he was fighting fit and clever with it. He was a crafty businessman, a tough negotiator, a loud-mouthed political agitator, and quite open about his pursuit of power. He lambasted politicians who did not kow-tow to him and abused those who did. *The Australian* newspaper said of him the day after McMahon had beaten Gorton to become the new prime minister (with Packer's backing), 'Sir Frank ... the big shambling man who has now hacked his way up from the slaughterhouse of old Sydney journalism into today's penthouse power game.'

He was a ruthless boss, hiring or firing on a whim. He drove his staff hard and expected utter loyalty at all times. He was capable of almost any kind of deviousness to get his way in politics or business. And every time he won he lorded it with swaggering pride.

The Australian article, which was a general summing up of his life and times, went on, 'Packer sat like a mighty feudal baron yesterday while his little champion, Billy McMahon, cantered back after toppling Gorton.'

Like all Australian newspaper proprietors Packer was devoted to sailing and owning racehorses. Unlike Murdoch, who got bored quickly with both, Packer loved the image of himself as the healthy, captain-hatted, pipe-smoking, sailor with the chunky chin and the sea breeze rustling the tufts of distinguished grey hair which popped out beneath his starched white cap. He loved to be in the members' enclosure at a big race. He loved power, but more than that, he loved to be seen to be powerful.

Packer, the ultra-conservative, always backed his own man with a bluntness which would have appalled many serious political observers outside Australia. He bullied or cajoled his way through every parliament. Not the slightest bit of scandal about the opposition escaped his daily tirades. There was nothing any of 'his boys' could do wrong. And in the end he got so powerful to the Liberal and Country Party coalition that he was able to almost inaugurate his own bills—or quash ones he did not agree with.

This then was Murdoch's principal opponent when the young tycoon found himself battling like fury in every direction. But Murdoch, after putting his foot in the door, was looking around for something bigger. He found what he wanted in the ailing Sydney *Daily Mirror* and, as Cudlipp was to with the *Sun* in London many years later, Packer and Henderson decided that if they gave him the paper it would be the final stone around his neck.

Years before, when Norton had owned the *Mirror*, Murdoch had tried to buy him out several times. Norton evidently never took him very seriously although he kept talking about a deal. He once intended giving Murdoch the papers, afterwards taking fifty per cent of profits. 'He wanted to run off to France and play racehorses or something,' said Murdoch.

Suddenly, out of the blue, Norton sold to a company which

was controlled by the *Sydney Morning Herald*. The *Herald* could have put the two papers together into a profitable monopoly position. Packer would never have caught up. But they kept it going as a separate paper.

When Murdoch emerged they had run the paper down very badly and had drained the company dry of talent. They sold it for what it had cost them and gave Murdoch five years to pay for it. He had bought the old Norton empire. The very sick *Daily Mirror* and *Sunday Mirror* in Sydney, the *Sunday Truth* in Brisbane and *The Truth* in Melbourne. This deal meant that overnight, from merely having printing plants in Adelaide and Perth, he now had a printing plant of sorts in every capital city in Australia, and a distribution organization thrown in. This eventually gave him the ability to start *The Australian*. It can be fairly stated that Murdoch is the weakest publisher in every state—but he is also the only one to have a toehold in every state.

The *Mirror* was losing so much money that everyone outside Murdoch's organization was convinced that this would be the end of his activities. The only people in Sydney who desperately wanted to believe in Murdoch were the poor souls left on the paper. They clung on to a vague hope that everyone else was wrong. It was characteristic of Murdoch that he should play his favourite game and win. He took from the *Herald* a damp squib and turned it into a whip with which he savagely beat them back.

Murdoch cracked that whip with an energy which immediately made the opposition sit up and blink. He attacked them on all sides. He chastised his editorial team into shape, stole a great deal of talent from the *Telegraph* and *Sun*, and immediately started putting on circulation.

The first two years of the new Murdoch ownership were fraught with difficulties. 'We didn't know whether we were coming or going,' Murdoch admits. 'I had told them they had made a mess of it. Now I began to wonder whether I could do any better.'

Murdoch learnt very quickly how vulnerable he could be to Sydney-style union activity. Within a few weeks the militant unions had forced more money and extra holidays out of him. He had made the critical mistake of telling the other newspapers he would deal with his unions on his own. The unions quickly realized he would not get the support of the other papers and they acted very quickly. 'It was the greatest lesson I ever learned. Nowadays if one paper closes down, we all do. It was heartbreaking at first. It took us years to recover,' he added.

At the same time Murdoch was having difficulty back in Adelaide. He wanted to leave everything there in a stable position so that, from then on, although he would keep in daily contact, he would only have to make the executive decisions.

Murdoch felt the *Adelaide News* should have a period of peace for a few months. They had initiated dozens of controversial campaigns, including the Stuart case and had endlessly needled the authorities. Murdoch's attitude was that now they were established as a radical paper, they should begin to get more authoritative.

He had discussed this at length with Rohan Rivett and the editor had agreed with Murdoch wholeheartedly. But Murdoch was horrified to see, the Monday after this discussion, that the paper had launched a huge campaign against the state premier. Murdoch felt the story was libellous and unfair. It was certain to rock the boat in Adelaide and Murdoch flew back to sack Rivett. Murdoch felt the situation in Adelaide was tricky enough anyway. While he and Rivett had had a partnership going which he could control, the formula worked. He decided Rivett could not handle the job alone and felt he did not have the right mentality for Sydney. 'I had no real alternative but to pay him off,' Murdoch said later.

There was a huge leaving party which Murdoch attended and he has always felt he and Rivett should become friends again. Rivett, however, the first sacked executive in a long line, was later to join with most of that line in condemning Murdoch in no uncertain terms.

II

The ensuing war between Packer and Murdoch (with Henderson sparring with each of them now and then) did not end until Murdoch was firmly entrenched in London. In 1972 Packer finally gave up the fight and sold Murdoch his *Daily Telegraph* and *Sunday Telegraph*, but the early Sydney period came to a head in the famous Anglican Building brawl. The tough, old-style Sydney journalists still relate the story with tremendous relish and sigh with nostalgia for the old days. Packer and Murdoch were then fighting on two fronts—the city and the suburbs.

The brawl occurred during the closing rounds of the suburban battle between Cumberland Newspapers at Parramatta and the alliance between Packer and Henderson. At that stage Murdoch was not only holding his own outside Sydney but actually stealing valuable advertising revenue from them. One day 'out of the blue', as Murdoch recalls, a columnist called Francis James, who was to become one of Sydney's most colourful newspaper characters, turned up on Murdoch's doorstep with two bishops. James told Murdoch that the two churchmen ran an Anglican printing press but were on the point of bankruptcy. The bishops explained that the official receiver was going to sell the business to Packer at five o'clock that afternoon. It was then a little before three.

Murdoch acted fast. The Anglican building was right in the middle of his circulation area. If Packer got in he would have not only printing machines—but bricks and mortar in the centre of Murdoch's suburban operations. James had persuaded the bishops to come to Murdoch and try and make a deal. They asked for, and immediately got, thirty thousand pounds for the lot and they returned to their building to start packing.

When they got there they found Packer had jumped the gun and his eldest son Clyde had already taken possession of the building. James rang Murdoch and asked him if he minded if he got hold of a gang of toughies to oust Packer. Murdoch did not give permission but managed to turn a blind eye. Soon after, James assaulted the building with his gang and a huge hand-to-hand fight ensued. Eye witnesses remember people were climbing all over the roof, smashing windows and battling with each other. James's mob eventually operated a huge battering ram and beat the front door down. Clyde Packer had most of his ribs broken and many say he was lucky not to be killed. For months he sported a limp he had obtained during the fight.

Murdoch surrounded the building with his staff-photographers and one of them operated a two-way radio so that Murdoch could listen in to a running commentary of the battle at home. One of his editors, Ian Smith, was jumping up and down, wild with delight. He kept saying they would have a lovely scoop for the morning edition. The next day the *Daily Mirror* had right across the front pages, 'Knight's Son in City brawl', and a picture of Clyde Packer, who was about twenty stone, dropping out of the front door holding, by the scruff of the neck, a one-legged Anglican clergyman. 'You couldn't have had a more damaging picture and they pasted it right across page one,' said Murdoch. 'Clyde hasn't forgiven me to this day. It was my retaliation for him being so bloody rude and telling us he was going to run us out of town and things. He still thinks I personally hired the thugs, which is not true. However I was sufficiently compromised not to be able to cross my heart and say I knew nothing about it all.'

An account of the battle was also printed in the *Sun*.

Monkey wrenches and mallets were wielded, a door was bashed in and windows smashed.

In the disturbance the printing house of the Anglican Press changed hands three times within two hours.

Punches were thrown, blood was spilt, and police were called in—after the son of a newspaper executive was knocked down with one eye 'closed'.

The extraordinary drama opened soon after 9 p.m. when eight men drove to the three-storeyed premises of the Anglican Press, in Queen Street, Chippendale.

An hour later a well-known newspaper columnist arrived with some companions. In response to a knock on the door, a young man came out. Almost immediately there was a fracas. One man finished sprawled out on the footpath. Soon afterwards a monkey wrench was thrown through a front window.

Simultaneously two men climbed through a rear window to be followed by a third. Sounds of a brawl could be heard and eventually the members of the 'visiting party' left the building.

A conversation between a *Sun* reporter and the columnist was conducted at the front door of the building.

The door was opened an inch. Behind the columnist stood two men, one with a monkey wrench, the other with a mallet. The columnist added, 'I'm sorry I can't open the door—I'm only a visitor. The thing worrying me most is that our visitors have taken my coat with my spectacles. I'm as blind as a bat without them.'

The Anglican Press turned out to be a complete wash-out and Murdoch lost about fifteen thousand pounds before he tossed it out and wrote it down to experience. But it had served its purpose in keeping Packer well out of his suburban camp.

III

After the heat of the Anglican brawl, the battle between Packer and Murdoch became more or less a cold war. The *Daily Mirror* gradually crept up the circulation scale and finally beat its rival *Sun*. It has kept a small majority ever since. The paper soon became the mainstay of the now flourishing Murdoch organization and was to remain the flagship until *The Australian* was started a few years later.

Unlike in London, where most evening papers sell in the evening rush hour, in Sydney the *Daily Mirror* sells steadily all day. It is in the literal sense a daily paper more than a morning or evening. This means that some members of the staff have to start work at four in the morning—often not finishing until four in the afternoon. The rush—starting at six in the morning —to get the first edition on the streets by half-past ten is a daily miracle. Despite a glut of early-morning hangovers and a bevy of bleary eyes, the whole thing swings into action with proficient speed. There is a seven o'clock conference in which the main stories of the day are discussed. But little of the copy filters through until about eight. Between then and quarter to ten the back-bench hums like a top with a swarm of bees in it.

The *Daily Mirror* has had to fight a constant battle to get itself accepted as a decent newsy newspaper. Murdoch, for a time, waged a personal defence for his new acquisition. He remembers one day a Methodist Church leader rang up and complained about one of their posters. Murdoch checked it out and called him back to tell him he was complaining about a *Sun* poster. Because the minister had seen a 'bad' poster he had automatically assumed it came from the *Daily Mirror*. This relates to the history of the character fight between the two papers. The *Sun* was always seen as the middle-class, respectable paper. People thought of the *Daily Mirror* as a rag, although it was always the traditional pacemaker. But then the *Sun* suddenly went ahead and beat the *Daily Mirror*—eventually getting on top. When Murdoch bought it, it took him years to climb back. It did not matter what they did—the *Sun* always outdid them. 'Now it is very hard to judge the *Mirror* from London. I saw a copy only yesterday and thought the headlines were overdone and there wasn't enough news,' Murdoch said. 'But it's a better paper than the *Sun*, I don't think there's much doubt about that. Sydney's a hard cosmopolitan city, a very masculine sort of place and I think the *Mirror* is a definite reflection of that.'

The composing room at Holt Street is little short of fantastic. Three daily papers and two Sundays come out of the one room every week—that is something in the region of two and a half thousand pages a week—compared to, say, the Bouverie Street presses which churn out, on average, a mere two hundred and fifty or so. By putting his whole Sydney operation into one building, Murdoch has managed to split his overheads among them all. (It was because of this that the subsequent buying of the *Telegraph* was such a sound investment.)

From the composing room the pages are wheeled by trolley to the printing department. The papers are printed and vans distribute them all over town. Standing by in town are spies who immediately report back on the opposition posters and front pages. During the course of the day they will receive reports from key news-stands. From these reports they are able to tell in advance how the paper is selling, and they can also tabulate the opposition's figures.

The *Daily Mirror* went through various stages of evolution before it emerged as the bright and newsy pop tabloid it is today. The journalistic side of Murdoch's Sydney era was dominated editorially by Douglas Brass with whom Murdoch had a deep and long association. Brass was a sort of glorified editor-in-chief and general editorial director of the whole group. For a long time he was very close to Murdoch and had a sound influence over him.

Brass, a brilliant writer-journalist, was the first journalist in Australia to profoundly attack the government over its policy in Vietnam where Australia had committed troops. His editorials on the subject are reminiscent of the old Sir Keith days—hell-fire and damnation neatly tied in bundles of clever phrases and adjectives. He had a turn of phrase which for a time was the cornerstone of good journalism in Australia. He was also a very 'correct' man, fastidious about his appearance and almost aristocratic in his countenance. A New Zealander by birth, he had the reputation of being more British than the British. Brass was considered to be one of Murdoch's best influences and certainly did much to tame and build several of his newspapers, during this period, into sound winners.

He eventually crossed swords with Murdoch when his boss went to London and is perhaps one of Murdoch's most unfortunate casualties. In the early *Daily Mirror* days he made several attempts to tone down the paper. All of them were thwarted by Murdoch.

His views on Murdoch are neither generally pro nor anti but prolific and objective. He shows little of his own sentiment, rather going back in his own mind to what he really believes to be the truth. He says he recognizes Murdoch's brilliance but that he also has a few warts and scars. He disagrees more with some of his business ethics than he does with Murdoch the journalist.

Brass is one of those who feel Murdoch had a deep-rooted jealousy of his father. He thinks of him as being 'reckless, brave and cheeky'. Brass, in fact, replaced Rohan Rivett when the latter got fired in Adelaide. 'I was London correspondent and enjoyed it very much,' he recalled. 'Rupert came over and hired me as the chief editorial manager. When we moved into Sydney I moved with him. I disagreed with some of the things he immediately tried to do. I wanted to make the *Daily Mirror* into a rather more respectable newspaper. But the circulation fell and Rupert's idealism was gradually eroding. He quickly changed the *Mirror* back to the pop tabloid it always was. He was a great idealist once. It was wonderful working for him. I think we developed a sort of love-hate relationship, but in the end I feel he thought of me as a rather elderly annoyance. He certainly did not like me quietening his papers down. He felt survival in the industry was popularization—and in my opinion the *Daily Mirror* got more and more lurid.'

Years later Brass has not actually joined the anti-Murdoch lobby, and still speaks fairly of the man. He did not show bitterness at their parting—just a sort of overwhelming disappointment. 'I begged him to stay,' said Murdoch, 'but he felt we should part company.'

IV

By the summer of 1962 Murdoch's race for expansion was getting even hotter. In one furious year he started going international, began *The Australian* and tried to start a Sydney TV station.

This period began with a controversial bid in New Zealand which to some extent was thwarted by the New Zealand government. He bought the *Asia* magazine in Hong Kong, which is now a nice little money spinner, and he cast his eye over Singapore and other areas of south-east Asia.

The New Zealand bid was interesting because it was a free-for-all fight between Murdoch and Lord Thomson for the prestigious Wellington daily, *The Dominion*. Thomson made a bid which caused an outcry and a large deputation of angry journalists rushed off to see the then prime minister, Mr Holyoake.

Murdoch was in fact sailing in his yacht *Iliana* just a little way off South Island when he got the message about the Thomson takeover. It was not long before he was buying up shares in the New Zealand company for all he was worth. 'You might say he was being a little unethical,' Douglas Brass said later. 'After all, no one else was allowed to buy shares. Before Murdoch declared an interest he had a fair few under his belt. Mr Holyoake was said to be less than pleased.'

Murdoch countered, 'That's complete rubbish—everyone was buying for all they were worth.'

At one stage Cecil King added to the speculation by saying that he too was on his way to New Zealand for a 'holiday'. In fact King never did join the fray. The *Auckland Herald*, however, did. It joined in with a great deal of local backing against all the outside bidders.

At the end of the day all sides had to withdraw their bids and the takeover, as such, did not happen. News Limited still has a large and influential interest in New Zealand, but *The Dominion* cannot be regarded as belonging to the Murdoch stable.

While this wheeling and dealing was going on it was announced that Sydney was going to be granted a third TV channel, Channel Ten. It was very natural that Murdoch should prepare to pull out every stop to get it. The odds at first seemed stacked against him and eventually he lost the joust. But it was not for want of trying. It was one of Murdoch's rare losses and it was a battle in which he came under direct personal attack in the witness box.

Until then the two existing TV channels had been dominated by Packer and Fairfax—giving them an unfair advantage over Murdoch's *Mirror* group. In Australia, unlike Britain, television and newspapers owned by the same company do all they can to boost each other. The paper plugs programmes on the TV and gives nice reviews while the TV programmes, especially the news programmes, butter the papers up. It is an accepted part of Australian media practice.

Murdoch claims the Sydney TV hearings were a political farce. They were staged only to make the whole thing look respectable. It was a huge issue and would have involved many millions of pounds. Murdoch and his colleagues fought it hard for eight weeks. He claims that at the end counsel who summed up for the board clearly gave the whole thing to them. They had gone in there as one of the three main contenders. They came out of it as the clear winner. Murdoch was resentful because the people who did win it already had a TV station and had sold out for big profits and were going in for a second dip. 'And in my opinion they made a bloody awful mess of it,' he said.

They sat about waiting for the final decision on tenterhooks. Then Brass went to see Menzies. Brass and the prime minister had always had a rather sneaking regard for each other. The message came back that Murdoch was quite clearly not going to get it. He intimated that it was not a matter of him not liking Murdoch, he just thought Murdoch was in too much of a hurry. He also let drop that Reg Ansett, the airline king, was going to get the new Melbourne licence. According to Murdoch he kept telling Brass things like, 'Australia is made of people like Ansett'. 'When Menzies put it to cabinet our friends there raised their eyebrows,' said Murdoch. 'Other people obviously had more influence there than us. I have always had a suspicion one cabinet member had shares in our rival.

'Menzies expressed great shock at the decision and said it was terrible "but if there is this independent body—what can you do?" etc. He was a wonderful old actor and great the way he controlled things. He even asked if they could throw it out (knowing of course, full well, that they couldn't).'

Murdoch still feels that Menzies was always able to succeed in kidding his cabinet that they were really working as a cabinet yet remain completely dictatorial. It is true to say that Murdoch retains a deep resentment for Menzies which some people call sour grapes, but Murdoch sycophants like to say he was not serious in his bid for the TV station. 'He did it to needle Packer,' one said. 'We all knew he hadn't a chance.' This is, however, highly doubtful. Murdoch fought as hard to get

Channel Ten as he ever fought for anything before or since. He accepted that the confrontation would be hard, and probably knew his chances were slim, but there is little doubt he went into action with every banner flying.

By looking back over methods Australian newspapers enjoy to buy up television stations a general pattern tends to emerge. A publishing house floats a TV company in which it has probably up to one third of the shares. Another forty per cent of the company is generally offered to organizations and prestige individuals and the rest are put on the open market where, very shortly after the deal is done, the newspaper buys up the balance, thereby giving it a clear shareholding majority.

This was certainly the Murdoch plan. The share ratio offered did fall into a similar pattern. Murdoch managed to get together a formidable collection of 'worthy organizations'. Apart from his own group he had several churches and trade unions along with him in the stable. He formed a company called Channel Ten (Sydney) Limited, under the chairmanship of Sir William Gunn. The share ratio was divided up into $17\frac{1}{2}\%$ for Mirror Newspapers, 10% for Murdoch's Cumberland Newspapers Ltd, $7\frac{1}{2}\%$ for Elder, Smith & Co., and 5% for American Broadcasting-Paramount Theatres Inc. Two churches and two unions, plus Channel Ten staff, would share a further $22\frac{1}{2}\%$. Aided by these prestige names the new company offered more programmes, especially of a 'serious' nature and of Australian origin, than their rivals.

With this manifesto they moved into battle. The Broadcasting Control Board began hearing applications for the licence in August 1962. Altogether nine applications were to be heard. It very quickly became obvious that it was Murdoch versus the rest. Two top QCs battled it out before Murdoch eventually took the witness stand. He clearly outlined his company's proposals and put up a very strong case. Then Mr J. W. Smyth, the senior QC for the opposition Sydney TV Broadcasting Corp. Ltd, got up and began trying to roast him.

Murdoch batted very well and managed to score several sixes against some pretty tough bowling. Nonetheless he lost the bid and it fostered his already large resentment for Menzies.

V

Smarting but undaunted, Murdoch's defeat in the Channel Ten fiasco did not stop him from continuing his ambition for a Sydney TV station. Before the new station got on to the air he had already plotted a brilliantly devious plan to outwit his new-found rivals.

The background to the forthcoming deal was that Packer and Henderson had wanted to carve up all the country TV licences so they could use them as boosting stations for their main Sydney stations. This had clearly been politically un-acceptable and the country stations had been made up into separate, small companies and sold mainly to local shareholders.

Before Murdoch had arrived on the scene Packer and Hender-son had both realized that stations in Newcastle to the north and Wollongong to the south could beam over parts of Sydney. To ensure they did not encroach upon their own territory, they more or less blackmailed the big American film companies into not selling the small stations any programmes. They did this, according to Murdoch, by threatening not to buy a single pro-gramme from a particular film company if they sold anything to Newcastle or Wollongong. 'You can imagine the rubbish the stations ended up with,' said Murdoch. 'No audience either. They were right out of bounds. Wollongong eventually went bankrupt. That was how I was able to buy it.'

Before acquiring Wollongong WIN-4 the Murdoch camp had toyed with the idea of starting a new TV company up in the Blue Mountains and beaming down over Sydney. He planned to buy some studios right in the middle of Sydney for making programmes which could be beamed back to Wollongong and out of there right back across Sydney. He would have to make it so good a lot of people would buy second TV aerials to get it. In this way he could invade Sydney before the third licencee got on the air.

But the crucial part of the Murdoch plan was yet to come. If it was to be successful he needed an ally and he eventually found one in Reg Ansett with whom he started top-secret negotiations. With Ansett, who by now had his TV licence in Melbourne, and Murdoch in Adelaide and hopefully Sydney, he felt he had enough behind him to sabotage his big-city rivals.

Murdoch raised two million pounds and Ansett offered to match him pound for pound. Murdoch then coolly flew off to the USA and started buying up every single film that every single film company was making that year. He completely scooped the board.

Stories quickly filtered back to Packer and Henderson in Sydney; rumours flourished, and it was said Murdoch had spent a fortune. 'In fact, surprisingly, I did not spend that much,' Murdoch said.

It was on this trip Murdoch got his reputation as the 'tarmac negotiator'. Indeed, since then, countless other deals of significance have been conducted by Murdoch in airport lounges. In America everywhere he stopped, often between flights, Murdoch bought, bought, bought. It was a huge spending spree, and companions at the time remember he loved every minute of it. Murdoch has always been a compulsive buyer and one executive remembers an occasion when he went shopping with him. They were in a greengrocer's shop and he was most embarrassed when Murdoch looked at some avocado pears and asked, if he bought six, could he have a reduction. He managed to knock a few pennies off. Then he just started buying everything in sight. He bought vegetables, fruit, salads. They both came out laden to the hilt. He eventually spent a fiver—and saved about five shillings.

The American ruse worked. A panicking Packer jetted over to the States to find Murdoch and try to get him to sell him the programmes. Packer admitted quickly he was completely outflanked. The two met eventually in an airport lounge. The deal they worked out was that, with a little bit of arithmetic jostled about, Packer would let Murdoch have twenty-five per cent of his television company in Sydney, in exchange for the programmes. Murdoch accepted.

Although the two continued to spar like gladiators they shared for a short while at least, a strange liaison. The two men made odd bedfellows and eventually, through sheer chicanery, Packer got his own back in a brilliant move. The gist of the matter was that, while Murdoch was on a business trip to America, Packer merged his TV company with his Consolidated Press. Whereas before the newspaper company had owned the TV company, he now reversed the process. It was a brilliant piece of knavery. Consequently, after the share shake-up, Murdoch suddenly found he had less than ten per cent of the shares. In one fell swoop Murdoch had lost more than half his share in the TV company. The ruse cost him a million pounds. 'That was why,' Murdoch ruefully recalls, 'years later when the Packer boys started courting me again, I at first told them to get lost.'

Apart from the few remaining shares in Packer's station, Murdoch never did realize his ambitions to have his own Sydney TV interest.

VI

It was only a little while after he had returned from his TV trip to America that Murdoch started planning his most important project of the sixties—the launching of *The Australian* newspaper. By now his divorce was over and he flung himself into the making of the new national newspaper with a fury unknown even to the close aides who were used to seeing their boss at work. Dame Elisabeth recalled that he desperately needed something to occupy his mind. He dedicated himself to his business which helped him forget the mess his private life was then in.

If nowadays *The Australian* is no longer the most important single aspect of Murdoch's publishing interests, it has certainly always been the most interesting and controversial. It was a Murdoch family dream, emanating from his father, that they should give Australia a national newspaper. It is a paper which has lost a lot of money and still fought back. It is a conception closely in keeping with Murdoch's nationalism. It has had a very up-and-down existence, using up a great deal of talent, effort, money, heartbreak and occasional high drama. It is the flagship of his Australian newspaper group and certainly very close to Murdoch's heart. A policy change on *The Australian* causes huge general controversy and a great deal of strong feeling on all sides. The paper is both a miracle and a graveyard. It is regarded as being Australia's second most influential paper and if it does fail, most people feel Australia will be a great deal poorer.

The debate that has raged over the course of *The Australian*'s ragged history becomes highly frustrating because both sides have such valuable arguments. It is more than just a storm about a newspaper—however important that newspaper is—it is more an argument about the state of the Australian press as a whole. It is a valuable debate because it concerns all the major issues of the media and could be transplanted to any newspaper community in the world.

On the one side is a newspaper tycoon who had the idea, put up the money to initiate the possibility, fed the nucleus with energy and fire, refused to fail whatever the odds, and finally had to struggle hard to keep the fire alight. On his side also is the fact that without him the newspaper would never have been born.

On the other side are a bunch of very clever men who believed in the product (for a short time putting their whole lives in it) and who thought at last there was a newspaper of foresight, vision, argument, intelligence, controversy, guts and emancipation in a country which desperately needed all of those things. Murdoch himself insists it is all these things. His critics chide him constantly that it is not.

From the beginning, *The Australian* faced every conceivable difficulty. The first was simply getting the concept of itself accepted. Australians are not over-interested in the issues of states outside their own. The printing and distribution difficulties are formidable and always have been. The competition of every other newspaper on its own ground is frightening.

Many harsh things have been said about *The Australian* but few people have tried to take the credit away from Murdoch for starting the paper in the first place. Even his sternest critics grudgingly admit they admire him for keeping the newspaper going through one potential disaster after another. Even former editor, Adrian Deamer, who later became one of Murdoch's most bitter enemies, had little but praise for his former boss during the opening stages of the paper's life. He admitted, 'It was a hare-brained scheme and would have not had a chance of success for anybody except Rupert Murdoch.'

The newspaper started life in Canberra in June 1965. It spent its first thirty-two months there before editorial operations were moved to Sydney. Against all contrary opinion the newspaper did not miss one edition from Canberra, though it was sometimes very late in reaching Sydney and Melbourne.

Winter fog settles on Canberra's runways just before midnight most nights. By midnight the airport is almost completely closed in. But, Deamer recalls, by flattery, cajolery or some other such means, the planes always took off for their two-and-a-half-hour flight to Sydney except on those few occasions when the fog was too thick and even the exceedingly tolerant officials in Canberra said no.

Then half the matrices (*papier mâché* impressions of type from which printing plates are made) were driven to a place called Cooma to pick up a waiting plane for the flight to Melbourne while another truck dashed off with the rest of the matrices to Sydney. If Melbourne was closed in—not an unlikely event in the middle of winter—the plane would land at Mangalore and a truck would rush the matrices into the Latrobe Street presses.

Deamer goes on, 'It was exciting and entertaining; real frontier newspaper stuff right out of an old 'B' class movie—with Murdoch in the early days, standing on the tarmac in his pyjamas, egging the pilots on, convincing them and the DCA officials that the fog was really only a light mist. But it was not the most reliable way to produce a newspaper and reliability, however dull it sounds, is the first requirement of a newspaper.'

Deamer spelt out his full views in a 1972 lecture to Melbourne University which was answered the following year by Murdoch. He said he felt *The Australian* had begun to build up a unique quality over its first seven years. Pointing out that the paper could not compete in local news with local papers, he said it had to look to the small segment of the adult population which cares about national and international events and issues. He maintained this segment comes from the better educated, more mobile, professional and semi-professional groups in the community, who are more likely to think for themselves, to be more politically aware and politically independent than the average Australian. They are prepared to read and discuss views with which they may often disagree.

He argued that a great many left-thinking and radical students were buying the paper and they were buying it for the views rather than for the news. Of the eventual one hundred and forty thousand circulation at least one hundred and twenty thousand were loyal, hard-core readers. They did not buy the paper every day, but they were intensely devoted to it in a way he had not come across before. The readers felt somehow that the paper belonged to them and they cared about it, argued about it, disagreed with it, but kept on buying it. The problem was that there was not enough of them to satisfy the management and the advertising people and basic changes in style and content of the paper were demanded, and made.

'Petitions going around certain universities in Sydney call these changes the trivialization of *The Australian*. But the managing director, Mr Murdoch, called them editorial "improvements" in his recent annual report,' Deamer added.

When he was sacked from the paper a few months before the lecture Deamer claimed that Murdoch had returned to Australia for one of his 'quick periodical visitations' and received a number of complaints about *The Australian*. Deamer did not know where the complaints originated, how many of them were Murdoch's or how many had been fed to him by his local management subordinates, who he said had always regarded *The Australian* with 'suspicion and something close to terror'.

He added, 'But the gist of his [Murdoch's] complaint, wherever it came from, was that *The Australian* had become too intellectual and too political. It was anti-Australian, it preferred black people to white people, it wanted to flood the country with Asians. He complained it took up every "bleeding-heart" cause that was fashionable among the long-haired left; it was not interested in the development and progress of Australia; it criticized the political leaders he supported. It was dull, it was a knocking paper, and it stood for everything he opposed and opposed everything he stood for. There were a number of other complaints, but that was the main line.' He went on that orders went out to make *The Australian* a middle-brow paper for middle-class readers. The old readers were not wanted, and a new type of reader would have to be found.

This strongly-put assessment does seem to reflect some of Murdoch's thinking fairly accurately. Murdoch counters that he is not anti-bleeding-heart causes but that *The Australian* was turning into a paper which contained very little else. 'Deamer would listen to every little gripe, however insignificant. It just wasn't my idea of what Australia's only national paper should be,' he said.

Deamer went on to describe the changes made to the paper, all of which he claimed were detrimental. He agreed it was pointless to oppose change, but disliked changes that radically altered the style of a paper. He did not like to see the aspirations and hopes of so many people dashed for such doubtful gains. Deamer rounded off his official speech with a strong assertion that Murdoch was no longer interested in Australia.

He felt the important thing to realize when attempting to assess Murdoch today was that he was now only one part Australian. His interests were more in London with the *Sun*, the *News of the World* and London Weekend Television than they were in Australia. 'He is an absentee landlord visiting Australia for short periods three or four times a year and making snap decisions while he is here, often based on incorrect, incomplete or misleading data.'

Deamer admitted Murdoch was unlikely to lose all his enthusiasm for the paper he founded and which gave him so much prestige at a time when he wanted it badly. But Murdoch's need for status in Australia had dropped and would become less necessary to him as his international reputation grew.

Several people who attended the lecture said they were impressed with Deamer's argument. However, it was later reported to Murdoch that, when the published speech had been delivered, Deamer launched into a personal and vitriolic attack on Murdoch which had not been prepared in note form and which was never published. It came right off the cuff and represented, presumably, the years of pent-up anger Deamer had found difficult to express when he was directly in the employ of Murdoch.

Murdoch described the speech initially as being a lot of hurtful rubbish, but then agreed that Deamer, in the main, was certainly entitled to his published views. It was his unpublished views, delivered completely unprepared, which had annoyed Murdoch. The following year, at the 1973 lecture, Murdoch made no reference to Deamer by name and mentioned *The Australian* only in passing. But both Deamer and Murdoch were aware of the importance of that particular audience.

Murdoch's actual reaction to Deamer's unofficial lecture was the same as he showed to several other deep criticisms of himself. He was not so much angry as completely perplexed that someone could dislike him to such a degree.

There are parts of Deamer's speech which seem unfair. Until very recently, although Murdoch must be considered an 'absentee landlord', he has managed to stay remarkably close to every aspect of his business. It might now be strongly argued that with the American acquisitions his affiliations are stretched too far for the kind of relationship he had. But, when Deamer spoke, America was still across the horizon. And even now it is too early to say how much actual difference the States move will make to the Murdoch method of operation.

Murdoch aides maintain it is of little consequence that he speaks to Australia by telephone from London or New York because he would probably have done so from two floors above in Holt Street anyway. His finger is on the pulse at all times. He may well be under the influence of his Sydney management but Murdoch points out he does not listen to them alone— apart from anything else he reads all his own papers every day. He feels he should be allowed to make up his own mind on whether or not he likes what he is reading.

VII

It was only a matter of time before Murdoch and his colleagues started thinking of bringing out a *Sunday Australian*. It was a logical step. When the event occurred it was with a great deal of excitement. The paper was Sydney-based and competed strongly with the *Sunday Telegraph*. It lost money and when Murdoch acquired the *Sunday Telegraph* from Packer, he merged the two papers.

This alone caused as much ferment as the policy change on the daily. In fact while looking at the paper before and after the merger I feel there is some justification for lament. It is not the paper it was. Somehow the two styles did not gell. These days you have a paper which is half serious and half pop. It does not seem to be quite sure exactly what its identity is.

Murdoch claims there were two or three things against the paper's success. There was no Sunday paper in Victoria. The *Melbourne Herald* has a virtual monopoly there with the *Age* which was a six-day paper. They had the unions and the news-agents sewn up. The *Sunday Australian* sold quite a few copies but only through sweet shops and delicatessens. They could not get a home delivery service for a national paper. The other barrier to the newspaper was money. 'If we had said, "Look we don't mind losing three or four million dollars a year" and investing it in a colour magazine we might have made it. We might also have had the courage to charge more for it,' he said. They started with a two hundred thousand circulation, and Murdoch thinks they could have held it. He admits they could have afforded to keep the quality up. But in the very end, they ran into a strike which began in Sydney and started all sorts of intricate problems. They were losing a lot of money on *The Australian* too at the time. And Murdoch admits frankly, they squeezed the Sunday down a bit too much. 'The thing began to get a bit too in, and sort of trendy. It even had a column on women's lib. It became a bit of a bore. We might have persevered but we were at a point when we were going to have to make a decision one way or the other. Then Packer's sons chased me round and said, "Why don't you buy the *Telegraph?*" '

Then, claims Murdoch, everything happened overnight, and they merged very suddenly. He says they took the best of the *Sunday Australian* and put it into the *Sunday Telegraph*, calling it the *Sunday Australian & Telegraph*. They got nothing but complaints from the old *Sunday Australian* readers calling it dreadful. But controversial or not, the new Sunday held the circulation of the combined newspapers and it is very obviously there to stay.

The buying of the *Daily Telegraph* and *Sunday Telegraph* in 1972 from the Packers formed the final triumph of Murdoch's Sydney operations. He bought the two banners for fifteen million dollars, without any assets, and immediately put them into operation in Holt Street, thereby splitting his own overheads up even further.

When the deal was first suggested Murdoch thought Clyde Packer was joking. He ruefully remembered Packer's last deal when Murdoch had been trounced on the television venture and at first treated the offer with amusement and cynicism. But the two Packer brothers came over to Holt Street and made it perfectly clear they were deadly serious. The two papers for fifteen million dollars, no holds barred and no conditions. A straight deal. Murdoch said he would call them later that evening. He raised the money in a matter of hours and, still wondering exactly what the game could be, held a hurried conference with his staff.

They all came to the conclusion that Frank Packer had finally given way to his sons who had always been more interested in the television side of the Packer fortunes. Murdoch felt that, with Whitlam winning the election, Packer had finally given up his political intrigues. As such the two newspapers were no longer of any real importance to him. The Packers were certainly not in desperate straits for cash.

On the face of it the fifteen million dollars seemed to some people a lot of money to pay for two titles. But in fact, because they both had such a large guaranteed circulation, and because Murdoch was able to house the two papers without real extra cost, they were a bargain. Neither side haggled for a penny and the deal was completed in Canberra two days later.

VIII

Australia is basically an open prairie with some thirteen million gamblers running across it. Gaming and betting are deeply inherent in the Australian nature, despite the fact that they are almost universally illegal outside the racetrack. Along with perhaps downing cold beer, gambling must be regarded as the obsessive down-under national pastime. An Australian will bet on anything and does so frequently with anyone he can find and, to be sure, if gambling had not existed, an Australian would certainly have invented it.

An Australian I knew in London regularly bet on the time—to the exact second—by 'phoning up the time signal. It is not very long in a Fleet Street pub these days before one Aussie or another spins a coin or bets on the numbers of a note. They are all impulsive, compulsive gamblers. But unlike their British counterparts who are mostly content with a quid on the football pools or a fifty pence each way tickle in the betting shop, the Australian is far more interested in a personal bet, almost as if it was an extension of his ego.

An Aussie has to prove his friendship or animosity to people by testing their gamesmanship. Although he will bet on the pools, by and large lottery betting is far too academic for him. He likes to swagger about with a fist full of notes challenging his friends and enemies as if it were a Western gun duel. Gambling then becomes an actual part of his personality and character. He proves himself by his abandonment to chance and his total unconcern when he loses.

Murdoch shares with his fellow countrymen a deep love for any game of chance. The fashion in which he gambles would spell disaster for most men. He bets on whims and fancies and gets an incredibly deep satisfaction out of winning. He is normally a lucky man. He once marched up to two one-armed bandits with a few coins and, playing them together, struck the jackpot within a handful of pulls. Gamblers are a strange breed and the psychology of gambling is more often than not based on the man's secret wish to lose, not to win. Murdoch is very different. His success as a gambler is said to be based on his sense of timing, his ability to make forthright and quick decisions, his peculiar brain which can sum up odds like a computer (he excels at backgammon which, when it is played seriously, goes into almost infinite mathematical complexities based on odds), and his uncanny method of plucking ideas out of the sky.

But Murdoch is more than a 'chance' man. Although he gets infinite fun out of a game of 'two-up'—a highly illegal game played everywhere in Australia which is based simply on two coins being tossed in the air and coming down heads or tails— he is also, in every sense of the word, a poker player as well.

His rise to power is inundated with moments when Murdoch has played poker with the actual situation. He calculates the chances and calls his own odds. He is able to bluff with supreme confidence and lull a man into being careless when he himself holds all the cards. He is a 'shoot from the hip' gambler with an impetuous habit of shooting without rhyme or reason, but of nearly always hitting the target.

His obsession with gambling made the rather incredible outback mining town of Broken Hill a very significant place in the legends of the Murdoch empire. Broken Hill was one of the places where Murdoch would take newcomers to Australia —or Australians who he felt had not seen enough of their own country. He would hire a car and take off into the bush at eighty miles an hour over rough bush tracks wildly pointing out various aspects of the outback which he loves.

Most hired cars in Australia have a speed-limiting device attached to them, but Murdoch would have none of it. As soon as he had got into the wilderness he would up the bonnet and wrench the device off. Then his passengers just had to hold tight and hope for the best. He would charge off across the bush at a hell-raising speed with kangaroos jumping out of his path in every direction.

The basic excuse for going to Broken Hill was his *Barrier Miner* newspaper. But executives and outback journalists both

Top left Rupert Murdoch discusses the aborigine problem with the superintendent of a mission (*right*) in his round Australia fact-finding tour.
Top right Playing "Two-up" with staff from *The News*, Adelaide, Christmas 1956.
Below The Adelaide *News* building – the beginnings of an empire.
All pictures by courtesy of News Limited

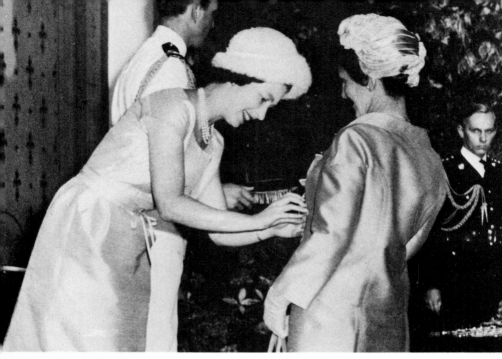

Murdoch's parents. *Above* His mother receiving an honour from the Queen. *Below* Sir Keith, founder of the family's newspaper empire.

Rivals for a newspaper. Robert Maxwell (*left*) and Rupert Murdoch (*right*) at a crucial meeting during their battle for *The News of the World*.

The tycoon as proud father. Rupert, Anna and daughter Elizabeth at home in Australia.

Left An informal meeting between President Kennedy and Rupert Murdoch.
Right Murdoch, watched by Larry Lamb (*left*) and Bernard Shrimsley addresses a press conference at the inauguration of *The Sun*.
Below Watched by the board of *The News of the World* (*facing camera*) Murdoch explains to shareholders the terms of his bid for their paper.

Frank Packer (*foreground*) who, as proprietor of the *Sydney Morning Telegraph*, was one of Murdochs' keenest rivals.

recall Murdoch was keen to get the official business done with so he could recess to the back rooms of the vast number of pubs for any game that was going on.

Murdoch attacked his gambling there with a vengeance and, as one journalist remembers, 'as if there was no tomorrow'. He would pass from two-up schools to the card tables and use up all his loose change in the one-armed bandits. From the occasionally effete board-room politics of his various concerns Murdoch loved the sweat and grit of outback Australia. In Broken Hill, because of the awesome and peculiar political structure of the town, all men are equal. And Murdoch, as he excitedly tossed coins or turned over his aces, was just another chance-crazed outback Aussie.

He has since grown out of Broken Hill but at the time he loved the hard toughness of the place. The crowded beer halls, the dusty streets, the loud swaggering men and the incessant gambling which went on all night, every night, before the eyes of an incredibly benevolent police force.

Broken Hill is run by the unions which have an eleven-man committee called 'Big Brother' which directs every last detail of the lives of its thirty thousand members. They operate from an imposing building called 'The Kremlin' and have such a tight hold on the city—imposing their own penalties and expounding their own laws—that no less than six full-blown police inquiries have done nothing to usurp their power.

Broken Hill could only happen in Australia and the very name mentioned in a Sydney bar conjures up anecdotes and memories—all told with a noted hilarity—which could be found elsewhere, perhaps, only in the pages of *Alice in Wonderland*.

This, as much as anywhere else in the world, was a confirmed Murdoch stamping-ground in the days before the young tycoon discovered the sophistication of international publishing.

While recalling his frequent visits to the two-up schools Murdoch fell immediately into the pattern of anecdote with the same kind of relish with which he remembers a major takeover. 'A great game. Most exciting. I love to play it. You bet on a run. You go in with a couple of quid and two, four, eight, you double it all the time. If you're betting on, say, heads, you can make hundreds if you get a run. Then it comes down tails and you're all through. The real game is the gamble on exactly when to stop. Then you can have side bets. I could play it for hours and frequently did.'

People would take it in turns to spin the coins and the others would all stand around him calling their bets. Ron Boland says he will never forget when Rupert was the man in the middle. Murdoch would do a little dance and every time he flicked the coin he would jump with it. He used every part of his body with the flick and loved every minute of it.

Murdoch enjoyed it most after the races when the book-makers would turn up with fat wads of winnings or on a Friday night—pay night—when there would be a great deal of money 'floating about'. Then, he said, 'You'd get a couple of hundred people shouting and screaming like mad and they would build up a terrific atmosphere. It got really exciting.'

The man who runs the two-up school takes ten per cent from the winners. This is not compulsory but Murdoch remembers it was always wise to make sure the boss was looked after or you would probably need protection on the way home. On the other hand he once landed a cool thousand pounds on a winning streak and the owner, who considered he ran a 'proper establishment', loaned Murdoch a couple of gangsters to ensure he got home unmolested.

Chapter 4

The political campaigner

I

From the very beginning Murdoch has always been involved with politics. He got the bug at Oxford, mucked about with state politics at Adelaide, and flung himself furiously into national politics when he got to Sydney. He has not got the prestige enjoyed by the heavy Melbourne press, but he does enjoy a far-flung readership. The launching of *The Australian* enhanced his reputation and brought him a certain amount of kudos, but so far it is not yet considered the most authoritative newspaper on the Australian continent.

In his Sydney decade he played politics hard and long. While he built the *Daily Mirror* into the hot-seller it is today; started the national newspaper; fiddled with television; strengthened his company throughout and flirted with Fleet Street; he kept a ferocious eye continually cocked on Canberra where, bit by bit, he became a man to be reckoned with.

Wherever he is in the world Murdoch somehow manages to keep up with Canberra movements. The idea behind Cavan, Murdoch's five-thousand-acre farm at Yass, fifty miles from Canberra, was first conceived by his father, Sir Keith, who once had another farm nearby. Sir Keith always maintained that a newspaperman who was involved with the destiny of his country should make himself felt in the capital of that country. Apart from that, Sir Keith, like his son, found an impish delight in interfering with politics. Rarely a Sunday lunch went by at the farm in the old days without Sir Keith having a politician or two in attendance. Rupert carries on the tradition.

Many of the personalities in Australian politics have at some time traipsed over to the farm where they have been treated to informal barbecues around the swimming-pool, a game of tennis or a wander or drive over the fields. But more than tennis is played at the rich sprawling cattle farm. Murdoch manages to survey the whole Australian political scene and then goes on to intrigue and persuasion.

The Australian political game is somewhat different to the political rigmarole played in London. Essentially, Australian politics resembles a game of cowboy and indians. It is probably a lot more fun than in London or Washington, and Canberra is rather like a village in which every villager is the mayor. They openly court the media and the media responds by very openly asking, and getting, political favours. Murdoch is quick to point out he has never asked for, nor got, one political favour in his life, although he has quite clearly demanded policy changes in exchange for his support.

There are few corridors of power in Australia. The game is played rough and ready across the open prairies. People insult each other very rudely inside and outside Parliament House. The civil service is quite happy to be seen arguing with the politicians. And the newspapers—in an almost American style— headline the whole lot with abundant glee.

There is also a purely practical side to Murdoch's political interests. He publishes some of Australia's most important newspapers and takes a purely journalistic interest in current affairs at Canberra. His lunches at Yass keep him a lot more abreast of cabinet thinking than most of the more able political roundsmen. This situation is helped by the fact that politicians might well say things to Murdoch they they would not say to others. Their motives for doing this are clear. Firstly, they are likely to tell Murdoch things they would like to see appear in his papers. Secondly, they inform on their enemies, hoping Murdoch will agree with them and support their attack. Thirdly, they want to curry favour themselves with Murdoch and are more than willing to give him inside information in exchange for the hope of a friendly nod and wink when the time is right.

In the world of chicanery and intrigue which is, almost by

definition, the world of politics, Murdoch is an important contribution to the whole. And generally speaking a lot of politicians
fall over themselves to keep in with him.

In turn Murdoch is no amateur when it comes to playing
this particular game. He has an almost uncanny knack of having
a one-sided conversation. It appears as if he is chattering away
quite happily but in fact he hardly says a word. At the end of
the day the politician finds he has been speaking non-stop and
has, in turn, learnt nothing from Murdoch. This is of special
interest because Murdoch is thought of by most people as being
a very bad listener. There are countless accusations of him
fiddling when people are talking to him. Or even just walking
off and leaving them in mid-sentence. But Murdoch *can* listen
very attentively when he is interested in what is being said.

His ability to have this kind of conversation was summed
up in his own words when he was talking about one rather
pompous individual who has graced his table from time to
time. 'The only thing you can do with that particular man,'
Murdoch said, 'is to butter him up because he likes the sound
of his own voice. Then sit and listen. You hear all sorts of
things. But you have to make sure you don't tell him anything
because you know that next week he'll be sitting at someone
else's dinner table doing the same thing about you.'

Murdoch eventually found some kind of harmony with
Australian prime ministers generally, including Gough Whitlam, but, as a rule, although he loves to play politics himself
he has a lot of contempt for politicians and political pressure.
During his 'Publishing in the Seventies' lecture to Melbourne
University he alleged that what politicians could not get by
stealth and charm—they would try by other means.

'Everyone who is involved in journalism knows that news
management exists everywhere,' he said. 'One only has to recall
the sacking of the former Australian external affairs minister,
Mr Bury. Axed on Thursday, leaked on Friday, and on Saturday the telephones of every Sunday paper newsroom were
running hot as several surprised journalists answered them to
find themselves talking to the prime minister and receiving
his personal background version of events. Needless to say, it

was a version that was hardly flattering to the victims. Yet Mr McMahon still refused to confirm, on the record, that Mr Bury had been fired.'

According to Murdoch, Australian editors have to put up with 'news management' from many outside sources. He accused advertisers and politicians of attempting to put pressure on his newspapers and said there are other pressures common to newspapers everywhere, particularly the growing skill of governments and other organizations at managing the news. 'Here I'm afraid, our politicians and our prime ministers, not to mention our local advertisers, tend to be great enthusiasts for the telephone.'

He maintains that hardly a week passes without a telephone call to the editor of one of his newspapers by an advertiser seeking some particular favour. There are, he says, grey areas where department stores and car makers seek free plugs. They may ask for pictures of their products to be given special treatment and, in such cases, will always be offended if the exigencies of the night conspire to frustrate their desires. Some of their requests are reasonable, some are not. Murdoch feels this is an area where editors have to feel their way.

Murdoch's idea is that if a newspaper, by brilliant staffwork, secures a picture of a new car, it is obviously news and should be printed. But if it is sent in to all the newspapers and embargoed and the editor breaks that embargo, he is securing a cheap beat and deserves all the fury he will stir up. In this grey area, the rules of the game are well known. Murdoch adds, 'There are the straightforward commercial pressures of advertisers which must be resisted. There are also the politically inspired pressures of advertisers which have been felt from time to time in most Australian cities, and which must be resisted even more fiercely. These can be serious, but the worst danger in them is that they can produce a counter-reaction which leads a paper into a more extreme position than is justified—or originally intended.'

II

Even after his major onslaught on Fleet Street in 1972, Murdoch was back in Sydney, with his sleeves rolled up, working a twelve-hour day and directing the front-page battle for a Labour government in the election of that year.

Murdoch met the future prime minister, Gough Whitlam, on a boat (no one has yet been able to find out who paid for it) for a joyride around Sydney harbour. Aides from both camps were present. The two discussed in wide detail the whole manifesto of the Labour party. But it was more of a row than a discussion. Murdoch wanted—and eventually got—changes in the election programme for his support. The most publicized change was for an economist of Murdoch's backing to be included in the new cabinet. But several concessions were made on that two-hour trip around the famous harbour. The housing policy was trimmed, for Murdoch let it be clearly known he was far more interested in the Whitlam economic policy than he was in the new prime minister's social changes. Murdoch was, for instance, highly suspicious of Whitlam's abortion law reforms. Indeed, over most social questions Murdoch is surprisingly conservative.

Murdoch felt Australia very definitely needed a new government. But more important, he and Whitlam both agreed Australia needed a new attitude towards itself. This was epitomized by the famous down-under phrase, 'It's time for a change', which Murdoch and Whitlam are credited with inventing.

There were few people around in Australian politics who had the charisma necessary to put that phrase into effect. Those who were around belonged to the Labour party. Whitlam was quite clearly their boss—and he had, either through a sense of inherent theatre or a policy of tactical finesse, the necessary charisma to hold the election stage.

It is generally felt Murdoch was keen to put a new government in and was certainly not averse to it being Labour. However, he was not necessarily regarded as Whitlam's greatest fan. For in fact he was capable of being quite critical, if not hostile, to the new regime.

But to get the party in, Murdoch was the first to realize it desperately needed Whitlam's general popularity and showmanship. And it was almost certainly the way in which Whitlam handled his campaign which took his party from a 'nearly' to a 'certainty'. This did not mean the Murdoch press would remain pro-Whitlam when the prime minister went offbeam in Murdoch's eyes. Murdoch was backing an ideal not a man or a political dogma.

He told an audience in London shortly after the election, 'I hope no one here will accuse me of making a party political speech, although it is true that the newspapers which my company publishes in Australia supported a change of government at the last election. This was not done out of any allegiance to Labour party dogmas. An important reason—perhaps the principal reason—for our policy was a belief that a change of government would help release the energies of the Australian people, and rekindle the spirit of national purpose that alone can make a country great.'

Whitlam and Murdoch may have widely differing views on how the country should be run, but they are both 'good Australians' and they recognize this in each other.

The background to Murdoch's involvement with Whitlam goes back several years. Over the past ten years Murdoch has switched parties freely whenever he felt the man was a good nationalist. He despised the ultra-conservatives who he felt were allowing Australia to be held back by the dubious glory of its past. And he distrusted the weird lefty who wanted a socialist paradise.

The 1972 Labour landslide in Australia was fascinating in this regard. There is no doubt Murdoch did give expression to a public mood which was important.

'I suppose I got far too involved in it. Frankly,' he said, 'when I get into a fight, I get too involved. I certainly got very close to the Labour boys. But some of the things we did then were fundamental to the throwing of the Liberal party right off balance. We built up a mood.'

Murdoch claims it got to the point where practically no cabinet minister would be seen on the platform with the retiring prime minister. At the end they were all looking after themselves. He feels his newspapers contributed very greatly to that. He does not think anyone went to a polling booth and voted Labour because of a leading article, but he believes that a leading article can give courage to the voter who has already decided.

It was in that Australian election where Murdoch first publically showed his mettle as a political agitator. He went into battle with fists flying and boots kicking. Even the trivial *Melbourne Truth* carried front-page political stories and agitating editorials.

Murdoch went back to Sydney for the election and sat in as virtual editorial director of his group of papers. He coordinated policy, dictated news stories, gave advice to the Whitlam camp and generally worked a twelve-hour day making sure that advice was used to the best advantage in his own editorials.

It can be said with utmost certainty that the Murdoch-Whitlam team won the election; the rest of the campaign, if not irrelevant, was grist to the mill.

A book by two politically experienced Australian journalists, *The Making of a Prime Minister*—a runaway best-seller in Australia and a comprehensive study of that general election—pinpoints in some detail the Murdoch involvement in the course of events. Murdoch said, 'As far as my own involvement is concerned, it only tells half the story. A lot more happened than even they have managed to find out about.'

Murdoch the politician is involved on three separate, but interlocking levels. Firstly, his pure sense of impishness where he sees a game and cannot resist playing it; secondly, as a newspaperman who sees his own corner of the media as being an important part of the whole political scene and likes to be kept informed of what is going on; and thirdly, probably by far the most significant and important, Rupert claims he wants to help push Australia and her future towards his own nationalistic ideals. He sees the destiny of the Murdochs closely aligned with the destiny of the nation. His attitude is that he, for one, is not going to sit around and let the future of Australia fall into the hands of the politicians alone.

The key to Murdoch's involvement in Australian politics is found in this intense nationalism. It is argued by many that he is seeking political power for the sake of political power. But others feel his prime motive is his desire to give the Murdoch dynasty a hand in Australia's future.

This part of the Murdoch Australian political philosophy is sometimes difficult to capture. He managed to quip away most of the interviews he once gave and nowadays simply does not give interviews. He is not a letter writer or even a sender of memos. He uses the telephone avariciously and there are few sources, save word of mouth, which exist to verify his feelings. In London in 1974, editorial director, Larry Lamb installed a tape recorder on his telephone so he could go back over conversations which had legal connotations. Murdoch decided he wanted one too. For a time there was an actual record of Murdochology which might have been useful to future historians. But, typically, Murdoch got impatient with the device and could hardly even be bothered to switch it on.

He has made two important speeches in his life and they are virtually the only official sources of information available to the biographer. The policies of his newspapers, from time to time, reflect his feelings, especially his political feelings. But determining direct Murdoch philosophy through this indirect channel, can be dangerous to pundits of his views.

His nationalism is well known and many quotes exist to show he feels there is an essential difference between Australia and the rest of the world. He feels Australia is a nation with virtually no real sense of its own history and with only a dawning sense of national pride. He feels they have little collective national identity.

Murdoch says there is presently a great mood of important and far-reaching change in his native country. He likes to feel he is very much part of this change. 'What we are witnessing,' he told an audience in London on Australia Day in 1972, 'is the rebirth of a vigorous Australian nationalism, something that has lain dormant for most of this century—to the heavy detriment of Australia's progress and enlightenment.'

Murdoch made it clear he was in favour of Australia moving

in a new direction in her defence and foreign policies. He pointed out that Australia's traditional friends were preoccupied with their own problems and the time had come for Australia to take its own initiative. Australia was a European nation living on the fringe of Asia in a new, emerging region at the bottom of the Indian and Pacific Oceans. 'We cannot afford to live with illusions any more than Britain can,' he said.

In Australia, Murdoch argued, they had an overwhelmingly youthful population, many of them now the first generation offspring of the stateless post-War European immigrants who had contributed so much to the Australian culture. These people were now realizing that their future lay in finding a new rôle among her neighbours in which the 'only paramount force' would be the welfare and security of the Australian people themselves.

Murdoch feels it is Australia's fault they had not yet mobilized themselves and their money into developing their own national resources and said, 'Australians are no longer content that their country will go on being inevitably, irreversibly, or without protest, a metal quarry for Japan, a pastoral lease for distant investors, a province for Madison Avenue, or a South Pacific windbreak for French nuclear scientists.'

He said Whitlam had been given a mandate for buying Australia back and hoped this would be done by getting Australians interested rather than merely keeping foreign money out.

He ended the London speech with a rip-roaring, flag-waving piece of patriotic campaigning by saying these were exciting times for Australia. The new generation of young Australians had a different set of values from their elders. They were demanding from their politicians a different course, one that would mix the pursuit of material prosperity with the sort of idealism that demanded a destiny of its own. They were no longer content with a foreign policy based on security without initiatives.

'They are no longer content to be a pale echo of great and powerful friends, to be a second-hand society, a reflection of another hemisphere and sometimes another age. They are seeking a fresh, vigorous Australian identity of their own.'

Although this speech was conceived some time after the Labour landslide, it was a direct reflection of the mood he was in beforehand.

III

Unlike in Australia where Murdoch was a political force to be reckoned with he quickly found his direct political influence in England to be very limited. It is true, now that the *Sun* has established itself as a working-class force, his significance in London has grown considerably. But when he first arrived the *Sun* had not yet been born to his mould and the *News of the World* was traditionally true-blue Tory. He did have several meetings with both Heath and Wilson and probably treated them with as much reserve and caution as he did their Australian counterparts. Wilson went out of his way to get to know Murdoch when the Australian first arrived. It is not openly recorded what the prime minister thought of the tycoon but contemporaries feel that neither impressed each other to any great extent. Murdoch is traditionally suspicious of all politicians and feels their only real interest in flirting with a newspaper publisher is to gain his influential favours. Wilson's feelings on the press are well known and his relationship with Fleet Street has, for much of his career, been less than cordial.

Murdoch went down to Chequers a couple of times at Wilson's invitation and recalls he found one of these sessions 'terribly disillusioning'. But he feels that he is 'friendly' with Harold, if anyone is friendly with him.

Murdoch has never been politically involved with either party leader and has little deep feeling for Heath. A mutual friend arranged a lunch when Heath was leader of the opposition and Murdoch remembers they had a 'strange, stilted sort of conversation for a couple of hours'.

Murdoch feels Heath has very little knowledge of Fleet Street, and even less concern. He neither takes much interest in the personalities of the press, nor cares a great deal about what they think of him. Murdoch has been on Downing Street dinner party lists as a matter of routine and been to large cocktail parties at Chequers, at Heath's invitation. He says Heath is always polite and formally nice. The two sparred together, without bitterness, but with agility, over the 1972 miners' strike. Heath conceded that the Murdoch-Lamb stand in the *Sun* probably helped the miners win their strike. 'We certainly pushed public opinion very hard behind the miners,' said Murdoch with the same glint of self-satisfaction that he gets when referring to the 1972 Whitlam landslide.

Murdoch's first real political battle in Britain was the 1970 general election which put Heath back in power. To the general amazement of most people the *News of the World* told its readers, with some banner waving, to vote Labour. It was a bold stand, perhaps too bold. Dedicated Labourites were very pleased with Murdoch but there is little doubt the decision shook the readership by the tail. Before the first 1974 general election a very cautious Murdoch-Lamb stand veered 'only just on balance' back towards the Tories.

There are only a limited number of possible reasons for this apparent fence-sitting. I would suggest Murdoch, and in this circumstance even the staunchly Labour editorial director, Larry Lamb, were genuinely unable to come to a positive conclusion. Neither party exactly caused a flutter of the heart. British politics had come to a stage where the economic situation had become such a staggering problem it overshadowed the personalities involved. Consequently the essence of the first 1974 election was that neither side was really going to be able to do much about it. It was in many ways an impasse situation and as such it is perhaps understandable that Murdoch and Lamb felt they should not doggedly take sides for the sake of it. It could be that Murdoch's swashbuckling political days are over, though this is doubtful. But I do think he is now an experienced enough businessman (as against simply being an energetic journalist who likes to get stuck in) to have probably come to the conclusion it is not worth rocking the boat unless there is an issue really worth fighting for. Because of this both Murdoch London papers bleated weakly while the rest of

Fleet Street threw bricks at each other. With his eye on the circulation figures Murdoch rarely fights any cause simply for the hell of it. But it was still rather a shame because Fleet Street is more or less dominated by a staunchly Tory press which, whatever the issues, tends to back the Conservatives come what may.

Murdoch with his inbuilt sense of neo-socialism, based perhaps more on his dislike of humbug than his love for the working man, coupled with the deep-rooted Yorkshire dogmatism of Lamb and the textbook party gamesmanship of *Sun* editor Bernard Shrimsley, gave refreshing life to the Fleet Street political propaganda machine. The new *Sun* became a thrusting and even controversial voice of the working man. They did, indeed, campaign vigorously for the miners in a lengthy and powerful daily tirade which must have come from very near to Larry Lamb's heart.

The London *Daily Mirror* consistently backs the left, but its voice seems curiously middle class. Without taking its very excellent political campaigns away from it—their front-page editorials have, over a number of years, become classic pieces of journalism—it is fair to say that the *Daily Mirror* did little to really penetrate the thoughts or ideals of the British working man. Cudlipp and his colleagues would argue this furiously, but it is generally accepted in Fleet Street, and come to that, in Holborn Circus, that they over-rated their influence drastically.

Perhaps Murdoch has too, but at least he fully acknowledges that political influence is a fickle thing. What Murdoch did do, for a time, was to balance up the rather jaded right-wing attitudes of the *Express*, *Mail*, *Telegraph* camp and regenerate the rather soppy middle-class socialism of the *Mirror*, *Sunday Times* and *Guardian*. This was perhaps one of the healthiest things about Murdoch's visit to London. But, with the exception of his sudden enthusiasms which are normally short-lived, Murdoch is by no means a dogmatist and it is perhaps unfair to ask him to carry on backing an ideal which he feels no longer really deserves his support or attention.

According to rather guarded remarks by some of his executives two things seem evident. When Murdoch first arrived he was bristling to have a go politically and it took some highly diplomatic reasoning to persuade him that Westminster was not a suburb of Canberra. It is also evident that Murdoch has politically matured since leaving the gunslinging dog-fights of the Australian socio-political scene and this has had a far-reaching and generally beneficial effect on the rest of his newspapers. Murdoch's increasing knowledge of the two forms of government have helped him complement and criticize them both to much effect.

Murdoch's political involvement with Westminster was at one stage personally stage-managed by Lord Goodman. It is difficult, mainly because of Goodman's elusive nature, to pinpoint exactly whether Murdoch got closer to British politics via Lord Goodman, or vice versa. But it is certain that politicians asked Goodman to introduce Murdoch to them and it is equally certain Goodman readily complied.

This quite extraordinary solicitor, who has dallied with left and right with equal success, immediately made himself known to Murdoch through the offices of the Newspaper Publishers' Association (NPA), which he chairs. There was initially some mutual suspicion and sparring for position, but when both sides found places of safety they then quite happily went about the business of becoming usefully acquainted.

In the past decade of British public life Lord Goodman has become a living legend. Through the lives of various governments he has maintained a positive influence on the British political and social way of life. He is a peacemaker, a negotiator, a socialite of immense proportions, very obviously near to being a genius, and will certainly delight historians for generations to come. He has successfully manipulated himself into a position of legend by that difficult, but when it works, ideal pastime of hiding from the limelight. Knowing newspapers on a level of intimacy, Goodman has carefully stage-managed his complicated and intriguing involvements to keep a hungry world thirsting for knowledge of him. By tersely refusing to comment with anything but a three-sentence factual statement of nothing, Goodman has succeeded consistently in becoming the news story *par excellence*. The very fact that he is involved gives any situation an immediate cloak-and-dagger atmosphere of staggering proportions.

My favourite story, which Goodman confirmed, concerns former *News of the World* editor, Stafford Somerfield. When pledging his support for the old board, Somerfield had insisted he got a new contract which guaranteed him full employment for a number of years. This was duly done.

Murdoch later came back from having lunch with Lord Goodman and said, in passing, to Stafford, 'I think I've met someone who could break that contract of yours: Lord Goodman.'

Stafford said, 'I don't think even he could do that. After all, he made it.'

Any real assessment of Goodman is difficult because he only confides in confidential circles and then only that which suits him. My own meeting with him was incredibly disillusioning and I left his offices in Little Essex Street, off the Strand, feeling Goodman was the type of man who, when looking at an important work of art, would almost certainly look at the picture looking at him.

But he is of immense importance to the legends of Fleet Street, and several other aspects of the British way of life. As such, he has a secure place in the story of Rupert Murdoch.

Murdoch is a one-man band and by and large his attitude to people seems to be how deeply they appreciate that. It is probably correct to say that Goodman did not. At least it seems possible Goodman did not understand the fundamental difference between Murdoch and, say, Max Aitken, who remains one of his staunchest friends.

Murdoch is very capable of being influenced but it is practically impossible to manipulate the man. For this reason he has a natural suspicion of 'negotiators' and rarely feels easy in company which is still in liaison with his potential enemies. It is difficult to appraise what influence either man has had on the other, but I do not feel Lord Goodman has enjoyed as much influence in the Murdoch camp as elsewhere in the British press.

Lord Goodman delights in having a Johnsonian character

and it is almost certain he has kept some kind of private record giving intimate details of his intriguing liaisons. Proper assessment of him must therefore be left to history.

As private solicitor to a retinue of politicians from all sides of both houses of parliament and (through his thriving firm of Goodman, Derrick) to many hundreds of famous and important industrialists, businessmen and artistic characters, he has a fundamental finger deeply implanted in Britain's social and political pie.

He has achieved a position as a man of destiny by getting himself involved as a negotiator between Wilson and some of the prime minister's most difficult situations; by leading the Arts Council into a new era of influence; by his adroit manipulations at the NPA; by being called on spontaneously to settle disputes of varying kinds and by implanting himself deeply into what *Private Eye* aptly described as 'The Goodman Web of Influence'.

He is a robust man bristling with self-confidence. He has a powerful personality and tends to dominate the fantastically exclusive dinner parties to which he is continually invited. He is, in fact, actually far removed from the elusive behind-the-scenes character he loves to portray to the British public. On the contrary he loves the intrigue and sense of power that his particular and peculiar reputation affords him, and his belief in his own destiny is rampant enough to ensure he enters any situation completely convinced that he will emerge triumphant.

He has a Jewish sense of theatre and would have almost certainly become a leading player in the centre of any stage he had chosen. Deciding whether he would have had more influence at the London Palladium or Stratford-on-Avon is an interesting, but merely academic, exercise. For Goodman would have almost certainly dominated both.

But the essentially intriguing thing about Lord Goodman to the outsider is trying to understand who actually influences who. He is no one's fool and the game he plays to his own set of rules is locked deep inside himself. On the other hand it is a general view, if not an assumption, that bending Goodman's ear is an excellent way of getting your own views generally accepted, or at least put forward to people who might already be, or might become, your enemies.

Goodman is a contradictory character. He could be among the world's most able diplomatists, or else just a useful man to know in a crisis; a man of immense subtlety or else a man who has been lucky enough to be in the right place at the right time and to have made the most of his opportunities. Or maybe he is all of that, and some more, and manages to keep the complexities deep in his own personality. Lord Goodman is ruled by a sense of destiny. It might well be he needs and deserves a place in history. But it is an equal supposition he wants history to find a niche for him.

IV

After the *News of the World* takeover bid Murdoch returned to Australia to set his house in order before moving his operational headquarters to London. At the time there was a fierce office battle going on between Douglas Brass and 'Curly' Bryden. Both knew that whoever won the corridor war would rule the Australian roost while Murdoch was occupied in Fleet Street.

For a while a perturbed Murdoch let them fight it out. But he quickly saw if he left them battling without his control they could puncture much of the organization as they fought each other for power. He moved decisively and quite ruthlessly. He sacked Bryden and brought Ken May in from Adelaide.

Ken May was a loyal and trusted aide who could be counted on to carry out Murdoch's orders to the last letter, but he was an untenable choice for Brass who immediately resigned. This was a serious blow to Murdoch who begged him to stay. Bryden's departure left the editorial hierarchy weak at the top. Brass's leaving left a positively gaping hole. Ken May was a logical choice for Murdoch under the circumstances, but he does not enjoy the formidable reputations of Brass or Bryden and there was a large editorial gap between the top executive seat and the serious journalists.

Murdoch feels Brass was a very great writer but did not have the particular type of mind or character needed to be the top executive in a publishing house. 'I kept him there as much because he was a great friend as anything else. He had a very good influence on me. When I was getting lost in the detail of battle, and probably forgetting and letting myself compromise principles, Doug was always there to point out what I was doing. He was a magnificent influence in many ways.'

But Brass was a highly sensitive leading actor given, like many prima donnas, to tantrums, sulks, moments of acute depression—interspersed liberally with buoyancy and many brilliant performances.

Executives remember Brass could be very touchy. If Murdoch hadn't come in and said good morning to him by ten o'clock he would ask Murdoch's secretary why. Murdoch would send a message back, 'Go and tell him he hasn't said good morning to me yet either.'

'I could see,' said Murdoch later, 'that this kind of relationship could not be transferred to anyone else.'

The Barnum-and-Bailey atmosphere of Holt Street immediately prior to May's arrival was continued as the spotlight periodically picked up Adrian Deamer—the wizard or dragon of the whole show—depending on how you looked at it.

Deamer was able to 'brush Douglas out of his office', and was felt to be more in charge of the situation, or at least of the paper, than Brass. When Brass finally sacked Deamer he called Murdoch and asked if he thought he had done the right thing.

Murdoch told him he thought he had and advised him to put Neil Travis in charge of *The Australian*. But all that week both Brass and Travis were on the 'phone constantly asking Murdoch to reappoint Deamer. He finally agreed to this on the condition that Travis was there over him. The idea was that Deamer would be editor and Travis editor-in-chief—but really it would be an editor and deputy situation.

Murdoch said he felt Deamer was a good journalist and an extremely competent technician, but the real authority should rest with someone else. 'In fact I think Deamer was just too strong for Neil and within a week Neil had given up his office and had gone back to having an office next to Doug.'

Deamer did well for a while. But although he was very strong at keeping people out of his office he was not a strong editor. Murdoch claims he took on anyone who looked young and fresh out of university. He did not really impose a will on the paper and there were a lot of things on *The Australian* which Deamer did not agree with. 'He is not the extreme left-winger most people think he is. But he's got a large chip on the shoulder,' Murdoch said.

Ken May's actual function seems to be on two levels, one obvious, the other obscure. May had not expected to be made chief executive and is still not entirely sure why he was chosen. His day-to-day activities include major and minor decisions, but he refers nearly everything of any importance to Murdoch during his twice-weekly telephone contact.

Simmering just below him are Frank Shaw and John Menadue, an interesting corporate couplet if ever there was one. Both of them are keen, tough, self-assured, intelligent and ambitious.

The opinion in Holt Street is that John Menadue is the bright boy in the Murdoch camp. Not a lot is heard of him publicly and he seems to be a bit of a loner in Mahogany Row (the nickname for the executive part of the Holt Street building). He is a first-class and experienced in-fighter. Although he shows the customary loyalty to Murdoch, he is very much in command of his own tactics and claims he only refers to Murdoch on matters of great importance. He is not a typical Murdoch executive to be so high in the hierarchy. He is a new boy without the usual 'up through the organization' background. It was generally felt there that the 'Adelaide Mafia' were unsure of him.

Before joining Murdoch, John Menadue was in prime minister Whitlam's 'bright young men team' and had built a fair reputation in this field. He combines a bit of whiz-kiddery with cool political judgement. He is concise and precise as a business-man and is first class at managerial decision-making. Within the intrigues of Mahogany Row he is a central character.

He is smooth and dapper, soft spoken and a bit of a charmer. He oozes an aroma of executive power and is extremely sure of himself. He has shining bright teeth and one gets the feeling he cleans them with razor blades. He has extraordinary eyes which have a softness to them around the edges while at the same time a penetrating glint screams out from the pupils.

There is a certain style to top executives which distinguishes them from others. The fact they are well fed and expensively clothed is not really it. Fat executive faces can have a lean and hungry look. (I once thought it might have been the way they wore their braces.) It is really quite undefinable. But, whatever it is, John Menadue has it.

Frank Shaw belongs to the old Adelaide Mafia. He came up through the ranks by being a tough guy and is a journalist of the old school. He is a Sydney race fanatic who enjoys the good things in life and indulges in them with zest and enthusi-asm. It was said that at one stage in his long career he was out of favour. The story is obscure and not easily verified. Apparently he was sent to Hong Kong to look after the *Asia* magazine which was losing a lot of money. The two versions of the story are that he was sent there because he was out of favour. The other is that he was put there because he was a ruthless and tireless worker which is what the *Asia* magazine needed at the time. Whatever Invicta (the News Limited local pub in Surrey Hills) speculation says, Shaw quite brilliantly shook the maga-zine out of complacency, got it back on to a strong level of editorial content, slashed the costs and brought in a hefty profit figure. For whatever reason he went, he came back as company secretary—and a figure of strength.

Shaw keeps Murdoch informed, on an almost daily basis, of every last aspect of the company. He logs all the fluctuations, does a daily shares index, keeps tags on all circulation figures, and pinpoints, every twenty-four hours, exactly what is going up or down anywhere in the company. The Murdoch method of logging his company's daily undulations, was introduced by Mervyn Rich who was once boss of a large chain of cinemas. He invented a system which showed him, area by area and film by film, exactly how the cash flow was going every day. Although the situations might be different, the system could be applied to any company spread over a large area with daily sales. It was brought to News Limited, and with certain refinements, is still in operation today. Shaw reports directly to Rich in London who adds the Australian figures to the international concerns.

Ron Boland and Bill Davies are also on the Australian board. Boland is senior executive in Adelaide and Davies looks after all the company's broadcasting interests. Neither of them are serious contenders for the leadership of the company although with Murdoch around, you can never be too sure where anyone is going to end.

V

In Australia there is a large casualty list of people who could not keep up with the Murdoch dream. Between them Douglas Brass, Tom Fitzgerald, Maxwell Newton, Adrian Deamer, Rohan Rivett and 'Curly' Bryden, have what must be considered a formidable amount of brainpower and talent. But they have all fallen by the wayside over the years.

Murdoch says with a great deal of feeling that he was sorry to part company with them all. They, in turn, rage against him from the often lengthy diatribes of Max Newton to the slightly disappointed air of Douglas Brass. Both sides show highly justifiable reasons for each parting. But it can be said with certainty that these men have given Murdoch a ruthless reputation which is widely accepted by the Australian news industry.

It is difficult to assess this feeling properly. Most newsmen both in and out of Murdoch's empire tend to criticize him deeply. He is genuinely hated by some people, and in general is subjected to constant sarcasm in Holt Street. The situation is similar to Fleet Street but for different reasons. To the Aus-

tralian journalist Murdoch was not the upstart colonial boy
cheeky enough to play the Fleet Street game and win. He
proved himself years ago. But the Australian nature is aggressive
and hides deep in its bowels an inferiority complex which comes
to the surface in swaggering and loud-mouthed confidence. To
the Australian journalist the crime of sycophancy is the lowest
he can bestow on himself. He would rather be a rapist. He has
a positive phobia about it.

The phobia is so deeply rooted that the journalist will do
almost anything to prove he does not suffer from it. Therefore
it happens almost always that an Aussie journalist will attack,
rather than defend, those above him, however much respect
or liking he actually has for them. This makes it difficult to
get a constructive picture of Murdoch from his own Aussie
workforce. You could never be sure you weren't talking to the
chip on the shoulder. Most non-executives in Australia talk
about their relationship with Murdoch in a most peculiar
fashion.

They affect a certain contemptuous swagger. They swing their
shoulders from side to side. They sneer, puff out their chests
and point their fingers in the air. When mimicking Murdoch,
which, to a man, they all do, they affect a tough, hard line of
Murdochology where he is seen to slam his fists down on the
table profusely and insisting that the impossible is as easy as
eating fruit-cake. 'I told him,' they swagger, 'I told Rupert,
that's just a load of crap.' Then they gesticulate and pose out
Murdoch's reaction of slightly feigned horror at their outrage,
which turns to aggressive admiration and finally ends with
Murdoch agreeing in full with their point of view.

The Sydney cynics are led by a self-confessed arch-villain
called Harold Tilley, known by all in the news trade as Dr
Evil. Tilley is completely uncompromising in his condemnation
of everyone both above and below him. He sneers at his
superiors, bullies young reporters and has a very simple philosophy about humanity in general. Everyone, but everyone is
a 'rat-shit'—a phrase which Dr Evil enjoys spitting out with
gusto while sinking vast quantities of Invicta beer. Few people,
however, take Dr Evil seriously and after the first intense shock

of meeting him, agree he lends much colour to the Sydney newspaper scene.

But Dr Evil is by no means alone in his scandalous enjoyment of putting people down. The Invicta's favourite game is called 'monstering'. To 'monster' someone, in the Invicta jargon, is to be as rotten to him as you possibly can be. To bully unmercifully and break him down to size. Any newcomer to Holt Street has to be 'monstered' before he is accepted. The monstering process begins in earnest as soon as any visitor has his first jar of 'grog'. It ranges from simple swearing to full-blown accusations that one is a 'pommy poofta' or some other such ignominy.

Drinking becomes a monumental competition to see who will fall down first and seeing Aussie aggression at full belt is an amusing and interesting experience which should be first on the tourist's list.

The Holt Street game continues at 'Sweet Fannies' a pleasant wine-bar a few doors away and at around four in the afternoon when the day's work is done both places get packed with loud and raucous *Mirror* men.

At first the aggression is a little bewildering. But you quickly find that people who are being polite to you probably dislike you, those who go out of their way to be rude are, in fact, being friendly. A most peculiar ritual, but as soon as you get attuned to it, it can be a lot of fun.

Visitors from Murdoch's London office are treated with the utmost suspicion and until they have been monstered are treated as spies. This is in fact a quite valid reaction as Murdoch *is* capable of sending some seemingly innocent person to spy out the landscape while he is away. There is a famous story of a smiling Australian visitor who was interested in a certain department of the *Sun* in London. Murdoch asked the people in the department if they would mind showing him around because he didn't know much about things and wanted to learn for the Australian end of the business. Days later almost everything in the department was changed.

VI

Apart from his reputation for being ruthless Murdoch, in his flamboyant roustabout through Australian journalism, has been responsible for raking a very great deal of first-class muck. It was almost incidental that he should later take over the *News of the World*. Murdoch would have been happy buying any newspaper in Fleet Street. In Australia he has the *Melbourne Truth* which is a first-class fun read. It has some of the best girly shots in popular journalism. It has inventive headlines and tough little stories. It is thoroughly readable and perfect to pass an hour away with while having a glass of beer. Anyone who does not like it is a spoilsport. But many people in Australia *do* take it very seriously. They view it as being almost evil and certainly bad for public morals. But, honestly, who can really resist headlines like, 'Two old ladies locked in the loo', or 'A mistress in his bed, wife slept in a hen coup'?

When defending *Truth*'s reputation, Murdoch pointed out in his speech to Melbourne University that it is much easier to publish some newspapers than others. His argument was that *Truth* had a rôle to play in Australia and there should be a *Truth*-type newspaper in every society, however self-satisfied that community was. 'It is a knockabout newspaper, and it expects to be knocked about in return,' he said.

The truth about *Truth*, he claims, is that authority and officialdom rest easy when it is *not* campaigning. But when it is campaigning they want to close it. 'Sir Arthur Rylah, the former chief secretary, will know what I am talking about,' he added meaningfully.

Truth often deals with the seamier side of life, Murdoch claims, because there is, although *Truth*'s critics are not prepared to admit it, a seamier side to life. *Truth* deals with what happens in the courts—for that is where much of the humanity and the inhumanity of life is displayed and justice requires to be seen to be done.

'*Truth* grapples more persistently and more directly with crime and criminals—for crime and criminals are part of life, and there is nothing new about it,' he said.

Murdoch pointed out that in 1972 in Melbourne there were 216 rapes, for which 149 persons were brought to court; 557 robberies with violence with 131 cleared up; 138 robberies under arms with 56 solved. The figures are much the same for Sydney. These are the daily entries of the police stations. 'They are an ingredient of our lives. As such, they are reported and become the subject of front-page exposures and campaigns,' he added.

Murdoch goes on to claim an impressive number of things which have changed in Australia because of *Truth* campaigns. He claims that because of *Truth* tirades, scientology has been legislated against; misuse of government aircraft by ministers has been stopped; TV maintenance has been improved; the remand system has been speeded up; legal costs criticized; mental hospitals reorganized; there are tighter controls over private hospitals; new regulations over the tow-truck industry. 'Thuggery has been removed from the repossession hawks. And we all know what came from the famous revelations about graft and the abortion racket.'

It is an impressive record and even if the *Truth* was not directly responsible for all the things Murdoch claims for it, it has a very necessary place in Australian journalism.

He went on, 'In the so-called "quality" or "serious" newspapers, investigative journalism, sometimes called reporting-in-depth, is the trendy new thing. Recently, these newspapers discovered the sworn statement, the affidavit, and the confrontation. If they look back over the files of *Truth* they will find that it has been around for a long time—it is simply called reporting.'

Murdoch claimed that when people attack the press today it is usually the popular press which is the target. Such critics ignore that the serious newspapers for the past ten years have been moving more and more into the area of the populars—stealing their causes and their methods, if not their clothes.

He said the interests of newspapers and the public do not always coincide with those of the government, of business, of trade unions or, indeed, of rogue individuals engaged in particular pursuits at particular times. For when things go wrong it is the interest of those in power *to conceal*, and it is the interest of the press *to reveal*. 'The muck-raking tradition in popular journalism is an honourable one,' he maintained.

The *Truth* in fact has one of the most fascinating histories in Australian journalism. When delving back through its controversial past, one comes quickly to the conclusion it is but a shadow of its former self. During its heyday with the notorious John Norton, father of Ezra, it had a circulation in excess of a quarter of a million, was published in four cities and was never out of court for one libel or another.

Had not John Norton blackmailed the paper from another Sydney rogue of the time, Paddy Crick, a drunken lawyer-cum-MP every bit as sinister as Norton himself, I am sure the man would have invented it anyway.

Norton himself has to be the most fascinating journalist Australia has ever known. The illegitimate son of an English aristocrat, he went to Australia in the 1890s to carve his name in journalism, make a fortune, leave a trail of empty bottles and heinous crimes and to lash the entire world with a vitriolic and lucid pen.

Norton believed firmly he was either a reincarnation of Caesar or Napoleon and even in his incredibly few sober moments kept the line between genius and madness dangerously thin. His drinking bouts, in which he consumed between six and twelve bottles of brandy a day, lasted for up to three months. He was fond of urinating publicly every time he took his seat in Parliament and was charged in his varied career with rape, sedition, wife-beating, perjury, blackmail, habitual drunkeness, obscenity and 'improper conduct as a public man'. The Australians, with their unique love for those men who openly flout all forms of authority, treated him at all times as a national hero.

Norton printed tirades of abuse against everyone and anyone, including himself. He was particularly fond of giving pages of space to his enemies who were continuously lambasting him in one criminal or civil court or another. In his admirable book, *The Wild Men of Sydney*, Cyril Pearl says,

Norton was a fascist when Mussolini was a schoolboy. Climbing on the backs of a credulous, inchoate Labour movement, he assumed the title of 'Little People's Tribune' and by violent, skilful, and cynical demagoguery, persuaded thousands of Australians that he was their total champion. In some parts of Australia the myth still survives. People remember him as a fearless reformer; in fact, while he paraded as the defender of democracy, decency and truth, he lived like a power-drunk dictator, with a servile bodyguard of blackguards—bruisers, perjurers, stand-over men and pimps— the crony and accomplice of the most corrupt politicians that New South Wales has known. In some respects Norton's career resembled that of William Randolf Hearst.

Norton was the past-master of alliteration and future historians were to maintain that they could tell exactly how drunk he was when writing, by the number of alliterations in his text. No one was spared from his muck-raking pen. In the article which caused the sedition action he said of Queen Victoria,

Her chief claim to the remembrance of posterity will be that she has been the means of afflicting the English people with a most prolific brood of pestiferous German pauper pensioners who comprise some of the most physically and morally scabby specimens of the human genus extant.... Chief among these is her eldest son the Prince of Wales.

The future King of England is one of the most unmitigated scoundrels and foul-living rascals which the dirty Guelphic breed had produced. He is the chum of card sharps and horse jockeys; the consort to ballet girls and the houris of the demi-monde.

He went on to call Her Majesty 'this flabby, fat, flatulent looking scion and successor of the most ignoble line of Royal Georges' and '... to hesitate to grovel at the foot of the throne, and to refuse to lick the dust off the biggest of the two toes of the podgy-figured, sulky-faced little German woman whose ugly statue at the top of King Street sagaciously keeps one eye on the mint while with the other she ogles the still uglier statue of Albert the Good a few paces across the road, in the garb and posture that is suggestive neither of decency in attire nor decorum in attitude. In these degenerate days of political apostasy and slavish sycophancy, it is the chief pastime of the very "nicest of the nastily nice and nicely nasty people" to glory in the fact that they and their countrymen were ruled sixty years ago by a silly snivelling girl of sixteen and today by a semi-senile old woman of over seventy.'

He rounded off the article by explaining why he had called the piece *God Save the Queen*, '... if only to keep her rascal of a turf-swindling, card-sharping, wife-debauching, boozing, rowdy of a son, Albert Edward, Prince of Wales, off the throne.'

Age did little to stem the vitriol flowing daily from his pen. Four months before he died Norton wrote in December 1915, 'Winston Churchill is a witless wild ass ... a bulgy-eyed, frothy-mouthed, loose-tongued, leather-lunged, British-Yankee half-breed ... a demi-demented decadent ... the blatant, mad-brained bounder ... this sibilating shyster ...', and so on.

As I said before, the *Truth* of today, as a muck-raker, has nothing on its scandalous past.

Murdoch's critics also put him under considerable fire for his *Sydney Sunday Mirror*. It does not pretend to be anything else but a first class 'tit-and-bum' paper with a lot of good controversial Sunday-style journalism thrown in as well. Here again, it depends entirely how you feel about the subject. I have personally never been able to see that the naked posterior of a good-looking woman would convert anyone to sin, lust and depravation. But I will admit it is open to argument. The *Sunday Mirror* and the *Melbourne Truth* are both full of trivia. They do not attempt to educate their readers. They want to entertain them. For what they are they are both very good at it.

It is completely unfair to blame Murdoch alone for being a muck-raker. There are many popular newspapers in both Australia and England. Murdoch, it is true, has always made sure page three has a big-busted female smiling at its readers. He has always known the circulation pulling power of a thumping big scandal. But he was never the first to find this out and will certainly not be the last.

In his day Packer blasted away quite as fiercely as Murdoch ever has—sometimes against Murdoch himself. Packer's Rupert-bashing was a typical example of how Sydney newspapermen personalize their attack. They literally muck-rake about each other.

One Packer editorial had a good old dig at Murdoch during the Keeler affair in 1969, headlined, 'Suddenly the Porno Men Turn Pious'. The editorial went on to say,

> What a pitiful group of twisted little people they are down at the *Daily Mirror*, headed by Rupert Murdoch who seems to be seeking the title of 'Pornography King of the World'.
> The moment the *Mirror* team get beyond their normal day-to-day interests—nudity and veiled pornography—they become hopelessly confused.'

Murdoch himself is not averse to using his papers to blast at the opposition in a fashion which would horrify Fleet Street. A typical example, signed by him and Douglas Brass appeared in the *Daily Mirror* of August 1st, 1962. A huge headline said, 'We accuse' and went on to blast the *Sun* in no uncertain terms for printing misleading posters to boost sales. It accused the *Sun* of deliberately cheating the people of Sydney. It went on,

> The ultimate responsibility for this almost daily exercise in public deceit must rest with five men—the directors and general manager of John Fairfax Ltd, owners of the *Sun* newspaper.
> We do not make this accusation because we are worried by *Sun* competition. *Mirror* sales are steadily rising. We make it because we are sick and tired of flagrantly dishonest practices by a section of Sydney's afternoon press which tend to throw the whole press into public disrepute.
> We no longer wish to be tarred with the same brush as the *Sun*.

We make no apology for naming those ultimately responsible because they should be ashamed.

With some justification the opposition accuses the Murdoch press of not putting their morals where their mouths are and there are probably more misleading headlines in the *Sunday Mirror* than I have ever seen in any paper on earth. Even in the *Sunday Telegraph*, by far the more responsible and serious of the two, they recently had a headline 'Australian to be next Pope—says report'. The 'report' turned out to be completely unsubstantiated gossip, rumour and speculation of the variety 'undisclosed sources thought last night there may be a possibility that ...'

The *Daily Mirror* later that week carried a huge headline and an even larger poster for its first edition saying, 'Petrol Strike'. When one read the report, which was a correct report from their industrial correspondent, it said that at a meeting later on that day the union was expected to call for, among other things, strike action. The *Mirror* then suffered an embarrassing rebuff when everything *but* the strike was agreed on. The strike itself was called off but *Daily Mirror* posters all over town still reported the strike was on. The addition of one simple question mark to their headline would have averted this kind of incorrect journalism.

Murdoch's Aussie newspapers are by no means the only ones to take short cuts to sell more newspapers. Wherever there are tabloids there are short cuts in circulation battles. But muck-raking, if it is good and honest muck-raking, is a far healthier piece of journalism than a misleading story which gives the appearance of being honest.

Chapter 5

Tycoon under attack

I

When Murdoch felt the situation in Sydney was stable enough
he came back to London to take up his fight with Maxwell.
As we have seen he won the battle a few weeks later. Mervyn
Rich came over with him and as they whipped their new
acquisition into shape, both kept a keen eye on the leaderless
Holt Street.

It was not until much later that Fleet Street would start
to get bitchy about Murdoch. After the first throes of the
takeover he got very good press. Maxwell was seen to be the
dragon. Murdoch was given full marks for sheer cheek. Vincent
Mulchrone said in the *Mail*, 'He is the most promising young
hunter to have set foot in the Fleet Street jungle for a generation.'

Murdoch had arrived on the scene to appeal to the vanity of
the old hierarchy. He seemed like an oil-rich millionaire, a
bit heady on the sun, a bit drunk on power, and the sort of lad
you could pat on the forehead and tuck up in bed before you
got down to the serious business of running a newspaper.

It still remains, along with IPC's ridiculous plot to ruin him
by giving him the *Sun*, the most serious underestimation anyone
ever made of Murdoch. Certainly, in terms of Fleet Street, he
was not only cheeky, but naive as well and completely unused
to the games and gambits of the golf club, or to wheeling and
dealing his way through smoked salmon sandwiches with arch-
bishops and the Tory ministers. He was unused to the British
public. He was a total foreigner to the old-boy network which
thought it had him in the back and which, by its very complacency, strangled itself in front of his eyes. But he was a quick

learner. Murdoch was used, and at the *News of the World* the first feeling everybody had was that he was a prize chump. The view in the board-room—which quickly spread down to editorial level—was that as soon as they got him on the board they would chop him to pieces.

But Fleet Street itself lived up to its reputation for loving drama on its own stage. More than a million words got eaten up in newsprint telling us who the man was. Lovely phrases like 'challenge is his carrot' came floating out. In fact Fleet Street did a good job in assessing Murdoch and until the infamous Frost show, his reputation in British journalism flourished.

In the seven days after the first announcement of his bid the papers ran huge stories about him every day. Even the *Sunday Times,* which has since taken a clear anti-Murdoch stand, raved about the new boy.

Fleet Street found him 'cheeky with a naive grin; a swashbuckling hard worker; volatile and enthusiastic; practical; a gambler; impish; brash; disarmingly honest; ruthless; fantastically confident; an engaging battler; arrogant; frank; well-informed; a tough negotiator; a winner; a campaigner; a follower of hunches; a muck-raker; a working boss; aggressively competitive; direct but not devious; friendly but blunt; a great chatter-upper; breezy; a man-to-man approach; anti-authority; a radical; full of flair, dash, courage and bravado; lucky; an avid leader instant decision-maker; immediate likes and dislikes; immensely loyal to those he accepts; relaxed; egotistical; successful; tough determination; impulsive idealist'.

In one way or another most of these assessments have a lot of truth in them. But it shows he had very few critics in Fleet Street when he arrived.

Fleet Street's reaction to Murdoch was a strange mixture of incredulity, belly laughs, wonder, curiosity and sheer fascination. He struck an odd figure. To a great extent no one had ever heard of him before. Rumour immediately established him as a rich sheep farmer with more money than sense who ran a few giveaway papers as a hobby. There was little hope, ran the giggling speculation, that this young snippet and whisp of a cheeky Aussie could ever have a voice against the established publishing houses of Fleet Street. This feeling was amazingly still persistent when IPC gave him the *Sun*. It was certainly rampant when Fleet Street woke up to find Murdoch wandering around in its midst. It was probably this, more than anything, ironically, which had placed Murdoch in the position he is in today. The old *News of the World* board had been convinced Murdoch could be handled later. They would gently chastise him when the occasion arose and send him scuttling home from where he came. Maxwell was the threat—Maxwell had to be stopped at all costs. At the Savoy Hotel they patted their bellies, grunted a bit as they digested the roast pheasant, and decided Murdoch was very useful. He would be the ideal pawn in their game.

When he first arrived the media held him in some awe, and through this publicity a whole sub-culture, legend and aura sprang up instantly around him. It was short-lived, but people at the time expected to be meeting a giant. He is not a particularly large man and there is nothing to distinguish him from almost any other private citizen. It was with some disappointment then, that when he eventually arrived at Bouverie Street to take over day-to-day command, his new underlings were amazed to find a rather unspectacular man who, they rather unkindly remember, wore a slightly crumpled suit; seemed a little nervous; drove a particularly ordinary Fiat car (quickly changed for a Rolls); and sat at a desk which, until the day before, had been used by a middle-ranker's secretary.

He openly scoffed at Sir William's priceless antiques and said they belonged to a past era. One of the first things Somerfield remembers was that Murdoch admired six dining-room chairs in his office. A few days later, he 'borrowed' them. Everyone was amazed to find that the man who had somehow produced the sagas of romantic razzamataz all around himself, was in fact quiet-spoken, seemingly vulnerable and exactly the opposite to his aura-image.

But it was not long before Rupert made his presence felt at Bouverie Street. There was initially a great deal of general confusion and jockeying for position. Murdoch came into work at eight o'clock on his first morning and found the cleaning women sitting at his desk having tea. Those unfortunate ladies were the first in the whole organization to feel the wind of change. And it was a wrathful wind. They told Murdoch they had never seen anyone in the office before eleven. Murdoch scowled and sent them packing saying that from now on they would have to be out of the building by eight or they'd get killed in the crush.

In many ways the News of the World Organization when Murdoch took over was a great sleeping giant. It did not hum—it ticked slowly. The paper's political policy was often worked out at the golf club or the American Bar at the Savoy. It was not so much a matter of personalities. It was more that at management level the whole organization had dozed off. The *News of the World* had come to a rather dull patch after a bristlingly successful three-year heyday, but it is unfair to say it was editorially in the doldrums. The circulation of the giant Sunday was the cornerstone of the whole organization. But as the circulation kept rising, while other Sundays were losing or fighting hard to keep steady, the executive at Bouverie Street had got complacent and self satisfied. Success had become routine and the organization like many another in a similar situation had lost its impetus.

Carr was generally considered by his employees to be a difficult boss. Under his influence, the *News of the World* adopted an editorial policy of a fairly right-wing nature. When, during the Six Day War in the Middle East, I inquired as to our policy there as I would be covering it, I was advised wryly, 'Consider both sides as wogs.'

After taking over control of the *News of the World*, one of the first things Murdoch did was to sack Sir William's special mates on the payroll. People like Douglas Bader who was the 'air correspondent' and Henry Cotton who received six thousand pounds a year for writing a minimal golf column every week.

Carr's central idea had been that there was no real future in publishing newspapers. He felt the *News of the World* was safe and sound and had a great editor in Somerfield. He told Murdoch if he could hold it at six million circulation and put the price up a penny every year or so they would guard against inflation and give the extra to the unions. He said they should carry on like that as long as they could and then go into colour printing, and diversify as much as possible. It was not exactly Murdoch's idea of being a newspaper publisher. He claims the place when he came there was in a shocking state. The firm's paper-mill was literally falling down. All the machines had been built in 1900. They had had four fires in the year before he came and Murdoch says, 'The fools put every one out! We couldn't have given the place away.' He immediately poured in a million pounds and gave it a completely new management. In fact there was not an old management to speak of. The man who had been managing director could not even tell Murdoch how much paper they had made the previous year. The new management and an inflow of cash eventually started to work. The place is now making a steady, small profit. The old board had paid ten million pounds for it and then mortgaged almost everything in the company for it. 'It was a real cross to bear,' Murdoch added.

Today Murdoch is gradually getting the Bemrose subsidiary out of trouble and he feels it is an extremely wise back-up to have colour printing facilities these days. 'I don't know what we'll use it for, but we've got the capacity and know-how for a lot of possibilities.'

When Murdoch first came into the *News of the World* the board had just made a forecast that during the first year he was in the saddle, the company would make three and a half million pounds in England plus one million pounds in Australia. This was 'guaranteed', but they had put in some highly arguable assets like racehorses. In fact they made just under three million pounds. They had forecast a straight one million pounds out of Townsend Hook that year but Hambros had insisted that this be cut back to six hundred thousand. 'How the hell we got out of that year without a major disaster I will never know. We not only survived but we started the *Sun* too, so we didn't do too badly,' said Murdoch.

The main job he had to do when he arrived was to get rid of useless things. He sold an engineering factory which was making tiny engines for the aircraft industry. It was a million pounds in debt when he sold it to Lucas. There was another little factory he got rid of, employing two hundred women in Hove on the south coast. They were assembling tiny parts of nickel for telephones. It was making thirty thousand pounds a year but using up a lot of management effort. He did not know a thing about it and found no one else in the firm did.

The Carr board had bought a printing company in Acton, North London, which Murdoch says was quite hopeless. It had a contract for the GPO yellow pages advertising. They lost the contract when Thomson tendered three or four times as much as they did and burnt his fingers badly. Carr had decided to start his own yellow pages service on a local basis. It was called Winer's Green Guide and teams went round towns like Exeter listing all the butchers, bakers and candlestick makers and getting them to pay a fee to be included. They charged a fiver and delivered it to every house in the area. They lost one and a half million pounds just doing that because no one would pay their bills. The man who was running it was a fresh Cambridge graduate and he had graphs on his wall showing how he was going to make a million by 1973. Murdoch had to collect the debts.

Murdoch claims that, all in all, his first year handling the business and the Carrs was not a very happy time at all. Sir William Carr, who was very ill, had not been into the office for six months since Murdoch's arrival, and Murdoch decided, quite simply, that they would have to part company. 'I knew the situation was getting really hopeless. Carr was on the 'phone to someone in the office almost every day. The only person he never called was me. I suppose in a way it's very natural. He had been running the company for years and he found it difficult to give up just like that. But we just couldn't carry on like that.'

He went down and had tea at Carr's country place and told

him as politely as he could that he did not feel there was room for both of them in the firm any more and Carr would have to go. He pointed out that he had since bought the Jackson shares in a private deal and could now muster over half the voting shares.

'Carr said to me, "But you wrote to me saying when you bought the shares that it wouldn't change our relationship in any way!" I said, "That's right. I did. But I've changed my mind. I've got to face you and tell you you have to go. I'm sorry but it's got to happen and that's it." He told me he would fight me tooth and nail and I said if that was the way he wanted it, that's the way it would have to be.'

Meanwhile Murdoch's closest advisers and friends had told him he could not go through with it. They pointed out only six months before he had announced a partnership and that he would appear far too rough if he broke it up just like that. He thought about it for a long time and agreed they might be right. He said he would fight but would withdraw if it came to the brink. He was determined to go at least that far. The brink would obviously be the AGM three weeks later. It did not, in the event, come to that. The following day he got a call from the senior partner in Hambros who asked him to call later that day. When he went round they were in a bit of a state and he told them exactly what he had told Carr. 'For the good of the company he's got to go,' he said.

Hambros and Murdoch had a long and rambling conversation with Carr's bankers who tried to salvage something for their client. In the end the gist of what they told Murdoch was that they would advise Sir William to back down and asked Murdoch not to do anything drastic until they had seen Sir William themselves.

All the directors in those days had contracts. Carr had served himself with a particularly good one which was virtually unbreakable. It was agreed that he should keep his salary and his car and chauffeur and secretary and be appointed president of the company. But he was left in no doubt that the title was merely honorary and that he would not be welcome back in Bouverie Street.

The relationship between Carr and Murdoch was untenable. Murdoch showed contempt for the man and the way he was running the company. He certainly showed no sympathy at all. While it seems clear the old board captained by Carr was completely out of its depth, some critics of Murdoch point out that he was unnecessarily brutal in severing Carr quite so quickly and effectively from the family firm.

Carr still comes to the AGM every year and sits on Murdoch's right. At some stage during the meeting someone nearly always gets up and says how nice it is to see Sir William here again. Murdoch always smiles and agrees and says something about how healthy he is looking, then he sits down. The two men have no further contact although Murdoch has invited him to lunch several times. All the invitations have gone unanswered. Every year they hold a directors' lunch at the Savoy, but Sir William resolutely refuses to attend.

Murdoch claims, 'A lot of people tell me it was a very shrewd move to buy the *News of the World* as I did. But I used sometimes to wonder exactly what I had bought myself into.'

It was a period also which was rather publicly uncomfortable for him. A whole series of events followed one after the other. His fight with the Carrs was a prelude to sacking Somerfield. Then there was the ghastly McKay murder which naturally distressed everyone, and which had rather sinister overtones for the Murdoch family. Alex McKay is one of Rupert's oldest and most trusted aides. The affair threw them even closer together but it was a grim period for both of them. Wedged between this the ill-fated Frost programme came as a changing point in Murdoch and his relationship with Britain.

II

Murdoch has a surprising number of enemies and there are few people who are indifferent to him. People who have a genuine regard for him spring to his defence. Those who hate him will hear nothing which is good about him. With the peculiarly double personality Murdoch has sometimes shown, it appears that both sides and viewpoints can often be justified. Murdoch has been capable of being both nice and nasty. His enemies fall into two main categories, those men and women who bear him some kind of personal grudge because he sacked them, or was nasty to them, or had widely different editorial policies to them and had interfered with what they were doing; and those who don't necessarily know the man but dislike him by reputation and what they think he is doing as a media archangel.

It is difficult to be entirely objective about people who openly admit they have a grudge against Murdoch. Many arguments which appear trivial to those uninvolved might well have been of importance at the time and place to that particular person. But it is true to say that Murdoch, in his rampage through the world's media, has upset a lot of people. And the people who now dislike him on a personal basis have a bitterness towards him which seems unique to the name Murdoch.

Specifically, many critics accuse him of losing his integrity as a publisher and pursuing money and power for their own sake. They accuse him of interfering in editorial matters which they believe should be left to the editor, and of being dishonest in some of his dealings. They say he is ostentatious and a snob; he has trivialized all the newspapers he has touched and started a retrograde movement in popular newspaper publishing. Many are convinced that he only listens to 'yes men' and paid lackeys and that you will never get anywhere if you stand up to him. Many people think of him as being very ruthless and without sympathy for those who try to trip him up.

Even within the present organization many of his employees maintain he has got out of touch with them and what is happening in the rest of the world. The maxim of him being a boss whose door is always open has, they say, become a laugh. He is so surrounded by his own hand-picked buffer state of trusted aides many fear he knows little of what is going on down below and is often misinformed by people who would like it to remain that way. However true or false all these accusations are it must be stated that many people genuinely believe them and fiercely stick to them.

On the other hand executives faithful to Murdoch, most of them just as fiercely, can, and often do, put up counter-arguments for each point. Murdoch is the most accessible man they've ever worked for. He takes an interest in the business far below the level of most executives. He has no genuine regard for money or power and so on. The confusion then begins to set in. The name Murdoch, which in many ways is always an enigma, conjures up fierce argument whenever it is mentioned.

It is true to say that Murdoch enjoys knowing what he likes and where he is going. He wants other people to do it with him and gets highly frustrated if he feels people in his own organization are interfering with the natural progress he has set up. He can be quite petulant, and sometimes ruthless with these people, accusing them loudly of not knowing as much about the situation as he does.

However it must be pointed out there are a breed of people who always knock success. It is almost as if a successful man *must* be really bad for that reason alone. I think also, locked down in the depths of the British national psyche, there is a resentment that this brash young man can come breezing in from nowhere to start telling them what to do and then, very successfully, prove he is actually right.

There are also people who dislike Murdoch but have the intelligence or strength of mind to talk without malice. These profiles are invaluable and should be taken very seriously in any final analysis of the man.

On the turnover of editors Murdoch says, 'There may have been a lot of editors who I have parted company with. But I publish a lot of newspapers. The difficulty is that when you are driving and thrusting and trying to build a newspaper you tend to go for the more adventurous type of editor. The accident rate is slightly higher and there tends to be more casualties because you are taking more risks.'

But Murdoch admits to sharing some of the blame. His friends give him a kind of backhanded compliment by saying he is able to instil into new talent, when he gets it, a sense of purpose, challenge and idealism. (*The Australian* newspaper, throughout its ragged history, must be the best example of this.) Murdoch offers the dream and people succumb. Both sides are genuine about it all. They want to succeed. Murdoch is able to charge them with his own brand of enthusiasm. He backs this with generous portions of flair and energy. And for a time the mixture works. The trouble arises because few can actually keep up with Murdoch. They burn themselves out trying. At the end of around three years, they are exhausted. Then Murdoch bursts back—and not a drop of his energy seems to have drained away. He is able to milk a man dry. The man who can survive will survive to enormous reward. But the staying power is normally short. And there is a hollow feeling to the men who tried and failed—almost as if they gave so much in so intense a period that part of them died with the product they left.

The Murdoch drama is a veritable graveyard of dashed hopes and ruined dreams. It is of little compensation to the casualties that the miracle of his empire lives after them.

Although Murdoch has always been surrounded by much myth he immediately became subject to huge general controversy in this country. Before he took over the *Sun*, his year-long ownership of the *News of the World* established him as a ruthless buccaneer and the customary criticisms that he sacked everyone and cheapened the general standards of newspapers followed rudely in his wake.

At each stage of Murdoch's move from Adelaide to international publishing, he has surrounded himself with armies of talent. He has been remarkably successful in delving deep inside each man and plucking from him everything he could offer. He has used this talent to recharge often dying batteries. He has made them live and sparkle again. Murdoch is more proud of his ability to lead a sick concern to buoyant success, than he is with the end product itself. He argues that this method of operation must leave its casualties. In effect Murdoch uses people to teach himself all that can be known about certain aspects of his organization. Then, he not so much casts them aside as strides on to new ventures, leaving them, suddenly, leaderless and alone.

Murdoch claims he detests sacking people and gets very upset for days before he has to do it. He says one of his faults is that he often does *not* sack people he should and tells of many people who have remained in their jobs years after they should have gone. 'But when you have an editor or something,' he says, 'who has gone off beam and will not change, at some stage or other you just have to remove him. It has always been the worst aspect of being chairman of a large company with a lot of responsibility—not only to the shareholders—but to the rest of the employees.'

The word ruthless is normally used in a derogatory sense. There is no dispute about the fact that Murdoch has made many ruthless decisions. The dispute, if of any relevance, is about whether, under the circumstances, ruthlessness is a sin or a virtue.

In England this argument is based on whether Fleet Street was happy to get away from the ruthless age of fierce competition into an era of lesser, more complacent, newspapers, or whether ruthlessness was welcome back again. Certainly, before Murdoch's entrance on the British journalistic scene, Fleet Street sustained an awful lot of deadwood. And the *News of the World* had more than its share of brambles and nettles which very decidedly needed clearing. Rupert's ruthlessness was a scythe which effectively did more than clear the deadwood. As the choppers chopped and the saws hummed it was evident that the big trees were going to come down along with the nettles, the brambles and anything else which happened to get in the way. Murdoch savagely hacked the organization down to saplings. Only the young, keen and tough survived. The wood no longer had form or real structure. He had driven wide paths right through it. Gateways appeared which for years had been submerged in undergrowth. And the rest of Fleet Street felt the knife too, as other competing managements pruned their deadwood.

The controversy on whether Rupert Murdoch was right or wrong in keeping his axe so sharp and using it so swiftly and so effectively has raged on throughout his five-year visit to British shores. In the short term many people feel some of those old oaks could have been saved. Pruned a bit, perhaps, but not liquidated. But this is an unknown quantity. Certainly the new forest brought the whole countryside to life. It revived old rivalries, consolidated armies, ended a great deal of shuffling and confusion, and not least of all brought a ruthless energy and a healthy competition back to the Street, which had not been there since the 'good old days' of Beaverbrook and Northcliffe.

A great number of red noses suddenly stopped appearing at El Vino's and the Wig and Pen. Many a dusty desk tucked away behind the filing cabinets was shined up and given a new owner. The paunches of dozens of advertising men suddenly started losing their bulk and getting a lean and hungry look. The *Sketch* closed. IPC got a new owner. Editors were shuffled around along with front pages and new formats. A few lost their jobs. Many more were put upstairs.

But Fleet Street lived again. Before Murdoch the entire talk of Fleet Street had been the closing down of newspapers, the huge losses sustained by the great publishing houses and the general rotting of the industry. Lord Thomson, one of Murdoch's competitors, had said on regular occasions that only four daily papers could survive on a national level (*Daily Telegraph*, *Financial Times*, *Daily Mirror* and *Daily Express* or *Daily Mail*, the speculation went). Newspapers may still close down, but against this collective defeatism Murdoch has stuck his tongue well and truly out. As the rumours flourished he planned to revive a loser—or start a new daily paper. 'I made it plain very early on to my associates at the News of the World Organization that I wasn't going to sit around producing one paper a week,' he said. 'I wanted to print seven days.'

The ruthlessness with which Murdoch immediately went about putting his words into actions attracted the type of man he wanted almost immediately, men mostly in their late thirties who had got bogged down in other organizations. Some of them with talents that had been overlooked by the huge machines of Beaverbrook, Associated, Thomsons and IPC. Murdoch could not have merely bought them off. The type of men he was looking for were not particularly interested in an increase of salary. They were already at the point where more money merely meant more tax. They already had the car they wanted, the country house and the mod cons of modern living. But Murdoch offered them power in an organization which looked very shortly as if it was a winner. And that, in the climate of defeatism, proved irresistible to the middle-management men in the entire industry. As he cut and thrust through his new board and editorially obliterated everything which had existed before he arrived, he filled the gap with his kind of guys.

Murdoch is generally regarded as being ruthless because of his method of extinguishing anything which gets in his way; which he does not agree with; which insults him; or which loses money. In the main this means people are expendable. But it also includes any aspect of his business (with, I think, to date, the exception of *The Australian*) which causes any kind of blot on the wrong side of the ledger. Murdoch appears to have scant regard for people who fail him in any way at all. Generally speaking he does not like to take over the existing team when taking on a new newspaper. He prefers to replace it. But, rightly or wrongly, his system works for him. And it is fair to say many of his ground-floor critics would now be un-employed if he had not stepped so smartly into their lives. For Murdoch quite clearly stemmed a tide of newspaper failures which would have left Fleet Street with an army of jobless newsmen (as it is, there are probably three available journalists for every staff vacancy in Fleet Street). For a while at least Murdoch gave this downward spiral a new confidence and a breathing space.

II

People read the newspaper they want to read. The important thing about the free press is that every view and aspect should be *available* for perusal. The serious newspaper reader in the west will find himself conversant with a widely different series of viewpoints. If he wants to, he can keep himself exceptionally well informed.

But if he prefers the *News of the World* to the *Sunday Times* or *Telegraph*, good luck to him. It is his choice and why should anyone try to make up his mind for him? There is a huge and fundamental difference between the daily and Sunday press. The essential factor of daily papers, however frivolous their presentation, is the telling of new stories about the events unfolding in the world around their readers. Most Sunday newspapers do the same thing with more depth. In contrast, dailies are instant things which are born at dawn and die around midday. Sunday newspapers have a much greater air of time and leisure behind them, for obvious reasons. It therefore befalls the Sunday not only to inform, but to amuse and entertain. Because of this the essential character of popular Sunday newspapers is not necessarily *news*, but true fairy tales, titillating absurdity or shocking exposure.

Although both the *Daily Telegraph* and the *News of the World* are called *newspapers*, there is as much actual difference between them as there is between the *New Statesman* and the *Radio Times*. Therefore it sometimes seems ridiculous, and even frustrating, to find a great number of the British population looking at the *News of the World* as if it should really be the *Daily Telegraph*.

The *News of the World* is more of an institution than a newspaper. Its popular appeal is based roughly on its sports coverage, its court stories and its hard exposures. It thrives on naughty scout masters, rapes, murders and court cases about young men who steal female undergarments. It has also one of the toughest exposure teams in the world. People who read the paper leisurely after Sunday lunch will never really be aware of the drama played out every time one of these major exposures hits the front page. When a new scandal is being produced, the second floor of the *News of the World* building is like a maternity ward in a madhouse. Everyone shouts at each other and loses patience. Nick Lloyd, the assistant editor in charge of the department, flusters about like a nanny with a brood of unruly children trying to get the editor and the lawyers to agree on the headline. Everyone swears at the *Sun* because they are getting all the television promotion, and sentences are added or taken out of the story at the last moment as the lawyers panic. But at the end of the day tranquillity returns. The pages are signed and sealed and sent off to bed and by morning a few more undesirables are going to see their solicitors and another salacious titbit is consumed by sixteen million people.

Long before Murdoch hit the scene the *News of the World* had become supreme as a muck-raking organ. It worked out an almost watertight technique of exposure which is probably still the most professional in the world. Much of this technique was established and perpetuated by Michael Gabbert who was eventually sacked by Murdoch.

The *News of the World*, Murdoch quickly found, was a strange, independent animal with a loudly belligerent attitude to everything, including him. Journalists are similar creatures wherever they are found in the world, but Fleet Street breeds a special type. Fleet Street is aggressive, rude, drunken, hypocritical, disillusioning, bitchy, back-biting, sex mad and completely incestuous. It harbours a kind of man who drinks far too much, is amoral and often immoral, who is conceited, aggressive, theatrical, embittered, ruthless, rude, and whose status is normally based on exactly how much of an animal he is prepared to be in his political dealings with his colleagues.

There is a mysterious and strangely narcotic effect on those who produce newsprint. It is a hackneyed thought but there *is* an excitement to the front-page lead, to the noise and bustle, to the smell of newsprint and the gathering of stories.

All journalists secretly love the place however much they bitch about it. But probably the most important ingredient is not the love but the hate. They have to *hate* Fleet Street in order to survive. The aggression of a reporter is his most important attribute. His nerve and audacity in the field is fundamental to his success.

Fleet Street is a mistress few journalists can resist. She mocks them constantly, is forever unfaithful, and life with her is an endless and bitchy war interspersed with occasional but wild fornication. Fleet Street beckons with an evil glint in her eyes and journalists accommodate her vicious charms by abusing her in the most lascivious of fashions. They succumb to each other begrudgingly—sometimes like two dogs in a dusty street. At other times because, like Albee's backbiting anti-heroes, they actually desperately need each other.

Fleet Streeters in a pub drinking and talking together are a strange breed of creature found nowhere else on earth. Their talk is a mixture of raucous anecdotes about their exploits, moaning about whoever is boss at the time and brutal gossip about their colleagues and rivals. Oneupmanship is what the whole thing is all about.

It is when a man neither loves nor hates the place that his days are numbered. When he says, 'I simply don't care any more', you can guarantee he has lost not only the will but the chance to survive. When he stops hating the place he stops loving it too. And it is a sad day. For, however competent he may be, the sparkle will quickly fade along with any prospects he may have had left.

In this capacity Murdoch has not yet even begun to be a real Fleet Street legend in the same way as Beaverbrook. Fleet Street does not hate him enough. They bitch about him and even sneer, but he has not personalized his rôle enough for them to see a target they can positively hate. Most of his own staffers have seen only fleeting glimpses of him or heard through the grapevine that the chairman either likes or does not like a certain story.

In Fleet Street—unlike Holt Street where many of the journalists have grown up with him—a gradual indifference has begun to grow which, in terms of legends, is a certain killer. In Australia, of course, he is a major personality and anecdotes about his day-to-day activities in the old days abound. There they either love him or hate him or both, but there is not a single staffer on any of his papers who is indifferent. There he is a legend in his own lifetime merely because he has been exposed to them on a far more personal basis.

It is always amazing that journalists, who, in pursuit of stories, penetrate so varied a part of the world in which we live, can be such a bitchy, narrow-minded and bigoted bunch of humanity. In a world in which the *fact* is so sacred a religion it is amusing to see how much newspapermen thrive on myth, misconception, rumour and gossip when it falls to them to study their own lives and environment. In no comparable professional world is there to be found the vitriolic cynicism or the nasty-mindedness of the average newspaper office. When Murdoch stepped into this world he was subject to the best and worst it could offer. Few tears need be shed for him, for he cut, thrust and jousted his way to the top, oblivious of the tirades of abuse which followed in his wake. The point is that myth and mis-conception have tended to flourish around him. Some of it undervalues the real story. Much of it is clearly ridiculous. In talking to journalists about Murdoch, on all sides of the globe, you have to continually balance their views with the considera-tion that they are completely hamstrung by their own bloody-mindedness.

The world of the journalist is really rather sick. On the one hand you have the young and keen, bullying and elbowing their way with loud-mouthed and open, aggressive ambition to any position which has opened up to their trampling. On the other you have the men who have made it, many of them already beginning to fade, always watching over their shoulders for the stab in the back. Always insecure, taking their insecurity out on anyone who is weaker than they. Continually pushing their own self-importance with the blind hope that everyone will keep noticing. In the middle you have the ones without a real identity. The ones who are just beginning to realize they can go no further. And then finally you find the ones resigned to the absurd hope that no one will notice them.

Is there anything more pathetic than the Fleet Street has-been? The loud-mouthed drunk with the veins splitting on his nose, grey under his eyes, always missing his train home where the wife is bored to tears with stories of his past glories. The man who says with jaded cynicism, 'I don't give a damn.' But each large scotch is a large scotch into oblivion. Each glass drowns and numbs the truth just a little more. The once bright and agile minds which succumb to the glory of the front page, gradually going under with all the pressures the front page always brings.

As Murdoch sat astride this scene, it fermented far below him. He strode forth to manoeuvre and insinuate himself firmly into our lives. Far below, on street level, the myth and misconception began to flourish. Few people have ever bothered to look beyond the rumour and gossip. Even people who have purported to be studying the man. *Private Eye*'s sometimes amusing 'Dirty Digger' campaign has continually kept its antennae tuned to The Falstaff and El Vino's. The campaign has been based mainly on the ramblings of drunks, although, despite this it has been remarkably fair, in due course attacking Aitken and the *Sunday Times* in general.

When Australia's ABC television network attempted a serious study of him called *What Makes Rupert Run?* they felt it constructive to film half the programme in a Fleet Street pub. The forty-five minute show spent much of the time arguing about whether Murdoch tolerated beards or not. ABC used long excerpts in the crowded pub where a bunch of well-oiled journalists lammed into him.

Rupert-bashing has become great sport in Fleet Street. He is one of the easiest targets for verbal arrows to find a home, and he rarely hits back except in personal resentment. But if ever the 'sticks and stones' philosophy could find a living monument, it is Rupert Murdoch. He ignores personal abuse against him with a down-under gusto and, rather quietly, gets on with the job of getting bigger than his rivals while they are busy using up their energy attacking him.

Despite this, because of what and where he is, there are large areas of Murdoch's life which should be open to argument and controversy. The very nature of his rôle in our society means he should be criticized when necessary and the public at large must act as watchdog to his activities. His responsibility to us, through his media, is overwhelming and far too important to be left to his own personal whims and fancies. But while admitting Murdoch is fair game for attack, one must put all the arguments for and against him into some kind of perspective. Rupert-bashing is fine, but it cannot be taken too

seriously because so many of the real criticisms against him
have simply little or no real evidence to back them up. Murdoch's philosophy, anyway, is that if he actually offends people
they stop buying his newspapers. He is quick to point out this
is rarely the case.

Knocking Rupert has become, as it did at one time with
Beaverbrook, part of the way of life of Fleet Street. For instance,
if you look through the library cuttings on Murdoch you will
very shortly come to the tale of 'Murdoch the Tyrant' who
sacks people if they wear suede shoes to the office. You will
see how each journalist has gone to the cuttings library, read
the accusation and repeated it until it has passed from rumour
into fact and then into legend.

The incident actually referred to occurred in Adelaide several
years ago. Mark Day, present news editor of the *Sydney Daily
Mirror* was then a political roundsman of the *Adelaide News*.
'It was a very hot afternoon,' Day recalls. 'I had come in from
a political rally or something and I needed a shower. I was well
overweight at that time and my shirt was hanging out of my
trousers. I wasn't wearing suede shoes, they were more like
suede cowboy boots. When I think back I probably looked a
mess. Murdoch told Frank Shaw [then general manager in
Adelaide] that I should smarten up and he also made a comment about my cowboy boots.'

It could, and should have been, as simple as that. But a
chance comment in the Invicta Hotel in Sydney caught the
ears of a journalist. It was then only a matter of time before
it became added to the Murdoch legend.

III

The first major controversy to confront Murdoch in England
was the re-hash of the Christine Keeler memoirs in 1969 and
the resultant David Frost programme which was the first and
last time most people in Great Britain would see Rupert Murdoch in action. He came off exceedingly badly and now has a
positive aversion to public interviews.

Both Rupert and his wife Anna were bitterly hurt by the

programme. Anna was in a silent rage. After the show they went to what is called the 'hospitality room' at the studio. Anna turned on Frost and said, 'I think we've had enough of your hospitality.' His driver later reported that Murdoch had practically thrown up in the back of the car. He was very upset. Many people in Australia had a deep sympathy for him. They saw Frost as a brash Britisher getting unfairly at an Aussie. Most people in England rather cruelly enjoyed the slaughter. John Addey, Murdoch's PR man, was hopping mad although he was later to deny this and completely disagree Murdoch was crucified.

Before the programme started Murdoch had to stand in the wings while Frost gave the audience an anti-Murdoch warm-up. People were set questions to ask and it immediately became clear that the audience was full of Murdoch critics who could be relied upon to sneer loudly at the right time. After the warm-up, as they went on the air, Frost immediately switched to Cardinal Heenan who gave Murdoch a five-minute lecture on the sins of publishing muck-raking stories. But the crux of the matter is that Murdoch was naive and was seen to be so. Many of his own staff had misinformed him and Murdoch himself genuinely believed that the programme would be in the nature of a general late-night friendly chat.

Michael Gabbert claims he and Stafford Somerfield warned Murdoch very clearly what was likely to happen. Murdoch has since admitted that Somerfield, a great TV performer, would have put on a much better show than he did. But other executives certainly pushed Murdoch towards the programme with some glee. And it is doubtful whether Frost would have had anyone but Murdoch.

The background to the programme is that the *News of the World* originally bought the Christine Keeler memoirs several years earlier at the time of the Profumo affair and ran the story for eight weeks. In due course the contract had run out and Miss Keeler and an agent had worked out a re-hash of the story. Not a great deal of it was new and the first opinion of the *News of the World* executives was to turn it down. Keeler was asking twenty-one thousand pounds—a lot for any story, especially one which was five or six years old.

Gabbert claimed later than neither he nor Stafford was particularly keen on the story. He doubted very much whether they would have bought but for Murdoch's instructions. The ridiculous thing was, added Gabbert, that the new material, the only tenable excuse for republishing, was almost all deleted week by week as each instalment was discussed at top level. They got as much mileage as they could out of it, by generating controversy and stimulating criticism, but until the Frost programme they both looked on it as a bit of a damp squib, although Murdoch's own reflection of events are completely contrary to this account.

It has often been mooted that Murdoch had little realization of the peculiarities of the general British public. The buying of the Keeler memoirs was in fact one of his first major editorial decisions since he had come to London and the fact that the story appeared in the paper was largely Murdoch's doing.

Whether he was right or wrong in his decision has remained a talking point to this day and certainly many people hold the view that he was wrong. What cannot be denied is that, particularly after the Frost programme, the controversial series was a formidable reader-puller and developed into a best-seller as the series went on. The paper more than made its money back on increased circulation and foreign serial rights.

The essence of public criticism was that John Profumo was being unnecessarily hurt by the story. The argument ran that he had led a life of 'complete virtue' since the affair had broken and it was unfair to keep hounding a man who had made up for his past indiscretions.

Murdoch has often been accused of not worrying about the contents of a newspaper if it is putting on circulation. While this is not strictly true, he is certainly something of a circulation fanatic.

Independent Television blacked *News of the World* adverts as 'distasteful' and Murdoch reeled under a public outcry for which he had not been prepared. One way or another the whole incident proved to be the perfect target for Murdoch's new-found critics and they fired at him loudly from every direction.

While Britain argued about it Frank Packer, back in Sydney, was using the Keeler affair for a general editorial tirade against Murdoch in the traditional no-holds-barred style of Sydney journalism.

'Murdoch who ...' ran the editorial, 'runs a collection of papers which for sheer sensationalism and sex are perhaps un-matched in the world.... The *Melbourne Truth* is the most salacious of the publications followed by the *Sydney Sunday Mirror*.... The changes to the *News of the World* since Mr Murdoch took over have been remarkable. Nudity, scandal, orgies are now the order of the day, and make the former "sensations" of the paper look tame.... But there are limits to what the average Englishman will take.'

Much of this, of course, was pompous rubbish. Only time will tell whether Murdoch's handling of the *News of the World* has been wise or not. But the first changes he made were to make it slicker, tougher and more profitable. Editorially it is probably less smutty than it was before he came near the paper.

In Bouverie Street, Addey, as the organization's PR chief, was telling Rupert, 'Just go on and be yourself. They'll love you. Don't worry about a thing.'

Murdoch, in fact, had shown he was rather uninformed about many of the facts of the affair. Murdoch did not know, for example, that because of editorial subtlety Profumo's name had not yet appeared in the paper. So he could not use this fact against Frost when the interviewer set out to champion Profumo during the programme.

By the time it came to leaving for the studio, then, Murdoch had been led up the garden path by some of his advisers. He was 'going on a nice PR job' armed with misleading infor-mation and he was the only one who had no idea of what was about to happen.

It sometimes seems strange that a man of Murdoch's shrewd-ness could fall into such a trap. The answer lies in the fact that at that stage of the game in Britain, he was far more trusting than he is today. In Australia he was an old hand at battles and quite able to hold his own, but over there they call a spade a spade. Murdoch was quite unable to grasp that most people around him in London would say one thing and mean exactly the opposite.

John Addey, as Murdoch's PR man, was all for the programme. His idea was to expose Murdoch to as many people as possible, in the best possible light. Getting his newest and most controversial client on the Frost programme was a major coup.

Paul Hamlyn recalled later that he warned Murdoch against the Frost programme. He knew what could, all too easily happen, in such a situation in England. He claims Murdoch refused to listen to him. 'I honestly believe that with a different approach to things Rupert would have been loved in this country,' Hamlyn maintains. 'If he had been willing to admit exactly what he was—the new boy. But he couldn't, and he came off appallingly. After all, crucifying someone on the Frost programme is what that kind of television is all about.'

This lack of background knowledge apart one cannot really defend Murdoch to a great extent concerning the programme itself. He is not a good public speaker and was quite obviously uncomfortable even before the questioning began. As a piece of controversial television it was quite brilliant. Frost battered home question after question under which Murdoch was seen to visibly wilt. Rupert stuck to his guns and would admit nothing, but even this, in itself, was seen as a mistake.

Murdoch also claims Frost used every technique of television interviewing to the nth degree. It was brilliant but, Murdoch claims, unfair. It seemed to Murdoch that the cameras were switched just as he was about to speak, that he was interrupted, and that David Frost said on one occasion, when the unfortunate Mr Addey was picked up by the camera as being the only one clapping, 'I see you've brought your PR man along.' Disaster upon disaster.

The last word on the Frost programme must go to the intrepid

Mr Addey who, to this day, thinks of it in terms of public relations. His extraordinary assessment of the Murdoch-Frost confrontation was that 'all the world loves a loser. Someone who is seen to be vulnerable. They saw Rupert wilt and they loved him for it. I know they forgave him. It was the best thing that ever happened to him.'

IV

By now, after the Keeler affair, Rupert Murdoch was a target for controversy and criticism. This flourished around him for several years and a kind of 'personalization' set in. Whatever happened at the *News of the World* has always been Murdoch's fault to the critics—even if he was on the other side of the globe at the time.

But Murdoch seemed oblivious. After Keeler, he went straight into London Weekend Television with his knife sharpened. He sacked the *News of the World* editor, Stafford Somerfield, in a sensational bit of office power play. He started the *Sun* which immediately got a 'Dirty Digger' label and generally got a reputation for ignoring British sensitivity which ended with him, before striding across the Atlantic, leaving us with the Lambton scandal.

For a man who never gives interviews he causes an awful lot of headlines to carry his name. While his organization still smarted from the public spanking it had received, Murdoch stunned the media world by suddenly buying into LWT—in which Frost interests had a major shareholding. Fleet Streeters blinked at the news. Nobody, it seemed, could put this boy down. The television world immediately erupted with horror, and a gigantic panic set in at LWT.

Murdoch saw very quickly that LWT was in a very poor state. He assessed that, given the right management, it could get out of difficulties and make a lot of money again. The board there had got out of control. There were virtually two people for every job in the building. They were losing money fast. Major shareholders were getting extremely agitated about the state of affairs and insisting something should be done quickly. Murdoch, with his nose for such things, offered half a million pounds and said he wanted a firm hand in getting the company on to a healthy footing again. The board, under Aidan Crawley, admits it saw his offer as a present from heaven. Not only was there money to liven up the embarrassing bank account— but someone tough who could lick the company back into shape.

Murdoch moved in with a vengeance as temporary boss of the whole company. He was given, on a short-term basis, virtually complete control. He immediately reorganized the sales division, tightened up the whole operation, closed down losing concerns and manipulated the finances back to a healthy glow.

Few people deny that the most damaging aspect of the pre-Murdoch LWT was the huge excess of personnel. It was top-heavy with executives who had to try and make work for themselves to justify a living. They in turn had hosts of underlings, assistants, secretaries and the like, all doing the same thing. The unions had got completely out of control signing on people for totally unnecessary casual work. Someone who described the time when the sackings took place talked of Murdoch as a holocaust. 'One woman was literally sick with fear when she heard he was in the building one day. She went to the bathroom and actually threw up. Others ran out of the building hoping they wouldn't be seen.'

But Murdoch dismisses as completely ridiculous these stories that people were in such a state of panic and claims there was a huge amount of wrong and malicious gossip about the sackings. In fact he only sacked one person personally—Tom Margerison. Margerison had come to Murdoch to ask if he could sack Stella Richmond. At first Murdoch said no because he wanted to assess the whole situation first. He later agreed she should go. 'I thought she was a brilliant producer but she was misplaced as a programme controller,' he said.

The sales director was not fired by Murdoch personally and

he does not remember anyone else getting fired at the time. The head of light entertainment left. Murdoch thought he had been a very nice chap and regretted his leaving. The man had felt the company was changing. 'I thought it a bit unfair of him because it built up an atmosphere. On the creative side everything could have been smooth. Certainly in the sales side Bert Hardy did some pushing. It was in an awful mess. I put Bert Hardy in there at the top and he may well have pushed in different directions,' Murdoch added.

Murdoch maintains that the problem with his first few months at LWT was that he did *not* sack everybody. He thinks now he should have sacked a lot more people—or at least recruited people who would get a grip on the company. He feels the same about the *News of the World*, that he should have cleared the backlog of incompetence much, much sooner. He said wherever you looked in both organizations you saw people who were not up to the job. The whole middle management was inadequate to the challenge of keeping the thing going properly. 'We are still weak and vulnerable in some areas because of the legacy of the incompetence we took over.'

Some people have said that although Murdoch might only have sacked a few people himself, he did hire trouble-shooters to sack others for him.

On going back through press cuttings of the time it is certainly true to say that most people thought Murdoch was responsible for a lot of people leaving the company. There was something approaching hysteria from a dozen or so people picked up by various Fleet Street reporters. In one report he was referred to as 'The Axeman' and there was a great deal of public debate on whether he should have been allowed to buy into the company. It is a fair point of Murdoch's that many of the criticisms were aired in newspapers which had interests in other television stations. But Murdoch's LWT venture must at least be considered effective. London Weekend Television now enjoys not only a tough and busy existence—but a very happy and profitable one as well.

V

Murdoch rounded off his first busy and controversial year in London by taking over the *Sun* and revamping it as a tabloid. He and everyone else around him admit the first edition was a disaster. With his new-found British reputation as a trouble-maker and rabble-rouser his critics picked on the paper with glee. The *Sun* was almost certainly given to Murdoch—like the *Sydney Mirror*—as a load around his neck which was planned to pull him down to eventual ruin.

In early September 1969 Murdoch came out of the lift on the second floor at Bouverie Street after lunch when a *News of the World* executive showed him a copy of the *Evening Standard*. It was front-paged with a splash story of Maxwell making a takeover bid for the *Sun*. According to the executive, Murdoch's eyes immediately twinkled, and he said, on the spur of the moment, 'I'll have to make a bid too—just to spike his guns.' In fact Murdoch must have had a double twinkle in his eyes. He had been moving well in advance of the news and had already laid out his plans for his own takeover bid. Only a few days later Murdoch was virtually assured the *Sun* was his. In the interim period he had announced he was interested. So were the unions. It soon became obvious they were not particularly overjoyed at the prospect of having Maxwell as their boss. But unknown to most people at the time, Murdoch had made a crucial move at courting the unions, and this had proved to be the winning gambit.

The way Murdoch saw it was that IPC did not think Maxwell would get the *Sun* anyway. They had said they would part with it to him, but would be just as happy to see it fold. On the other hand, as they had offered it once, it was difficult for them to refuse to take up Murdoch's offer. Murdoch had been toying with the *Sketch* and had also considered the possibility of starting a completely new paper of his own. He was still undecided when the *Sun* deal came up. The crux of the matter was that Maxwell had been going around trying to get support from journalists and unions and had been rebuffed in almost every quarter. Murdoch had agreed he would have to get the unions on his side before the idea was tenable. With this in mind he flew out to Rome to see Richard Briginshaw, the NATSOPA union boss, who was on holiday there. His negotiations with Briginshaw proved positive and with this coup comfortably in his pocket, Murdoch flew back to London on an afternoon flight.

This flying visit was a typical example of Murdoch the 'chatter-upper'. Briginshaw was no youngster at the art of negotiation. The printing unions in Britain are among the most militant. Briginshaw and IPC had been a loggerheads over the future of the *Sun*. He was not going to give even tacit support for any new venture without being double-sure his members were going to be looked after. But when Murdoch has confidence in a situation of this kind, he is said to be difficult to resist. He cajoles and charms his way through the conversation. He is direct and forthright and goes out of his way to say he is promising nothing.

At the time Murdoch was staying with Lord Catto on the latter's Huntingdonshire estate. The two had arranged to meet with their wives at a country pub for a meal around eight o'clock that evening. Catto had suggested they relax and chat things over before gearing themselves up for action. Lord Catto remembers, 'I arrived a little late with my wife and Anna. As we went through the door I could hear Rupert's voice bellowing away on the telephone. It was typical of him. He couldn't have waited five minutes for us without becoming impatient and getting on the phone to someone.'

Murdoch did not relax that evening. He went out several times during the course of the meal to make 'phone calls. The bug, although it was literally only a day or so old, was working on him again. A new newspaper was in the offing. A country meal with his wife and friends could do nothing to take his mind off the events about to unfold. By the end of the week the unions had made it clear they would not work for Maxwell. Murdoch was invited up to Holborn Circus to meet Sir Hugh Cudlipp. It was a meeting which Lord Catto remembers with a certain relish.

By accident or design they were shown into a small ante-room at IPC. Cudlipp kept them waiting for some time. There was a chart on the wall showing the progress of the *Mirror* and the *Sun*. Murdoch looked at it for some moments with an evil glint in his eye. There were two pieces of cord. One went up for the *Mirror*—the other went down for the *Sun*. He simply couldn't resist it. His impishness came to the fore. He suddenly jumped up and switched the position of the cords so that they showed the reverse.

Catto recalls, 'I thought it was very funny but I had to persuade him to put the strings back in place. After all we were up there to talk business with Sir Hugh. I didn't want to start off with him thinking we had insulted him. Rupert was all for leaving it there. We both giggled, but in the end good sense prevailed and he put them back where they should be.'

At the end of the full negotiations Murdoch announced a triumphant victory. It was perhaps one of the easiest acquisitions of his life. It had happened through very simple gamesmanship —and because of Maxwell's unpopularity with the unions and with the staff of the old *Sun*. Murdoch's announcement came amid a flurry of other statements from all the parties concerned. Everyone got in on the act. And accusations came thick and fast. The three contenders in this particular game could not resist putting pen to paper.

A statement from Maxwell, carefully put in the third person, said, it would be a matter of serious regret to millions of Labour supporters and to all radicals in the country that SOGAT alone should have taken this unfriendly step. The full responsibility for the termination of these promising negotiations which had reached such an advanced stage was theirs. Mr Maxwell expressed his thanks and appreciation to all unions affiliated to the Printing and Kindred Trades Federation (other than SOGAT).

Cudlipp quickly added his grist to the mill. His announcement followed only hours later. He pointed out, 'This is obviously the end of Mr Maxwell's dream of being the proprietor of a national newspaper. He was, in my view, sincere in his approach to the problem, but the issues involved obviously were greater than he realized. The essential factors were that he could not arrange for the newspaper to be edited—there was some difficulty about that—and then printed and published.'

The statement claimed he had written to Murdoch in August explaining the position and informing him that if and when that position changed talks could commence immediately with the News of the World Organization.

Everything had happened within a matter of days. And it was the prelude to one of the fiercest circulation battles Fleet Street has ever known. It would quickly become Murdoch's newest and brightest baby.

Hugh Cudlipp spelt out the reasons why he arranged the sale of the *Sun* to Murdoch in an IPC inter-office memorandum. As there are widely differing versions for the Cudlipp-IPC motive it should be dealt with in this book.

'By spring 1969,' said the memorandum, 'the combined losses of the *Daily Herald* and the *Sun* over a period of eight years had reached a total of £12,702,000. The sale of the *Sun* was falling below the million mark, advertisement revenue was declining and newsprint prices were due to go up again in 1970.

'Two pledges had been made by IPC to the trade unions:

1. In 1961, to keep the *Daily Herald* going for at least seven years.
2. In 1964, to keep the *Sun*, as a successor to the *Herald* going for at least two years.

'Both pledges had been fully honoured. It was clear to the IPC board that a decision to close the paper could no longer be delayed. The decision was taken unanimously and announced on July 16th, 1969. Publication was also imperative at this stage in order to get the current negotiations with Robert Maxwell on to a realistic basis.'

Maxwell had approached Hugh Cudlipp in April 1969 with the proposition that if IPC decided to stop the *Sun*, Maxwell would take it over, free, in order to run it as a committed Labour daily, publishing in London only, with a smaller staff. It would be a non-profit-making venture, run by a trust. Maxwell's idea was to print on the *Evening Standard* press.

Maxwell stated that he would now push ahead with his plans. The attraction to IPC of the Maxwell plan was twofold: firstly, by keeping the paper alive it would reduce redundancies; secondly, IPC would be handing back to the Labour movement a daily paper which was a successor to the *Daily Herald*.

However, Maxwell's plan did not get very far. Journalists were sceptical, and he had trouble in finding an editor. (He was turned down by Robert Edwards of the *People*, Geoffrey Pinnington of the *Mirror*, Michael Randall of the *Sunday Times* and William Davis of *Punch*—in that order.) The printing unions were hostile, in particular NATSOPA.

On September 2nd, Maxwell withdrew his bid, blaming SOGAT which had said earlier it had lost confidence in Maxwell's plans. This was after Maxwell's failure to attend a meeting at Portsmouth with SOGAT's London branch secretaries. Richard Briginshaw of NATSOPA repudiated Maxwell's charge and accused him of 'public gimmickry'. Meanwhile, another bidder had appeared on the scene—Rupert Murdoch.

On August 26th, after a meeting on the previous day with Murdoch, Hugh Cudlipp confirmed that Murdoch had made an approach for the *Sun*, but had been told there could be no negotiations while talks with Maxwell were going on. When Maxwell withdrew his bid Hugh Cudlipp said IPC were ready to open talks with Murdoch.

Murdoch originally asked for the same terms as Maxwell— i.e. no payment. IPC however insisted that—unlike the Maxwell plan—this was a commercial proposition and eventually he agreed to pay about eight hundred thousand pounds. Agreement in principle was reached on September 26th. Board of Trade approval was given on October 20th and the first issue of the Murdoch *Sun* appeared on November 17th.

The memorandum goes on to point out that it was never feasible for IPC to turn the *Sun* into a tabloid. Commercially, it would have been crazy to set up a competitor to the *Mirror* within IPC. Journalistically it would have meant turning the *Sun* into a brash, sensational tabloid aimed at the bottom end of the *Mirror* readership. This was against the whole trend and recent development of the *Mirror* as an intelligent tabloid.

Another argument against this course was that without total replanting, the *Sun* could not have been printed as a true tabloid because of the 'bastard format' of Odhams' newspapers.

One major reason for not amalgamating the *Sun* and the *Mirror* was that when IPC took over Odhams' in 1961, it was understood that they would never merge the *Daily Herald* into the *Mirror*. It could be claimed that this pledge did not apply to the *Sun*, successor of the *Herald*, but this is at least arguable.

A merger would have been troublesome politically and over forty per cent of *Sun* readers at that time already took the *Mirror*. Amalgamation would not have appreciably reduced the redundancy problem.

Closing the *Sun* instead of letting it go to a competitor would have meant a further loss of two thousand jobs directly attributable to IPC's fear of competition and great union resentment, which would probably have caused heavy production losses to the other IPC newspapers.

In any case, the IPC arguments run, if Murdoch had not been able to get the *Sun*, he would have launched a new tabloid daily a few months later. He said so repeatedly during the negotiations over the *Sun*, and the economics of the *News of the World* plant made it imperative for him to do so.

When Murdoch later talked about the *Sun* takeover he said Fleet Street was a jungle on both the editorial and business sides and there were no holds barred. 'I suppose that's what makes it fun. Certainly I like the editorial side of Fleet Street, it's a constant battle. I think I have hunted successfully so far.'

When he looked back he knew that the original *News of the World* bid had been a strange and messy one. But the *Sun* venture was at the time considered completely mad. He needed a strong base in this country. He could have bought a printing press and started from there, if he had had the courage. He originally had long talks with Rothermere about the *Sketch* and thinks he would have paid more for that paper than the *Sun*. When the *Sun* came on the market he decided the eight hundred thousand circulation was worth having and wrote to Cudlipp telling him so. He told him to let the negotiations with Maxwell take their full course, but if they did not work out, he was firmly in the running.

'If they had written to me in the same way I would have said, "go and start your own newspaper",' he remarks.

'Then came the famous night of the first edition. We thought it was a disaster. It was late in production and God knows what else. The mistakes we made—everything. Cudlipp actually gave a party that night in his office, you know, with dead sunflowers decorating the room and other typically sick jokes.'

When he looks back now he feels they could have done it all in a much better way. He never dreamed he would succeed so far, so fast, and was unprepared for it all. He had always thought there was room for two popular tabloids in the huge British market and felt the *Mirror* was being silly about its market. It had not gone through the phase of being middle brow before being high brow, whereas Cudlipp's original concept was to chase the *Express*. Murdoch felt Cudlipp has been one of the most over-rated men in Fleet Street for a long time.

Towards the end Cecil King was not much better. He was a very big and interesting man, but did the wrong thing with the business. Murdoch feels that IPC originally had two invaluable properties in the *Mirror* and *Sunday Pictorial*. He argues if they had stuck to that the shareholders would have multiplied their money ten or twenty times by now. But King wanted to buy things and once he had got into magazines he started buying up everything. Some deals were good and some bad. But he ended up with something which fell down with its own weight. Murdoch agrees the paper increased its circulation by a million—but suspects only with the momentum which was already there from the 'rough and tumble' days of Bartholomew, Cecil King's predecessor.

'Cudlipp has never edited a daily paper in his life. He is purely a Sunday man. If you want to look at a good up-market tabloid, look at this morning's *Sun* as against the *Mirror*. We handle the news better, with more facts, more work, more attractively than the *Mirror* do. We do the same as their two pages with eight paragraphs, and cover the story in full.'

After the deal had been finalized Murdoch had to start thinking of who would edit the paper. Peter Gladwyn, News Limited's
chief of bureaux in London related that soon after Rupert
bought the *Sun* he 'phoned him and said, 'Find me an editor.'
Gladwyn was not very happy with the idea but checked around,
mainly with friends of his who had worked or were working for
the *Mirror*. Everyone came up with Larry Lamb first and some
of them said Bernard Shrimsley was also 'a pretty good operator'.
He reported to Rupert in those terms. John Addey 'phoned him
one day to urge that the best man available was Geoffrey
Pinnington (now editor of the *Sunday People*). Addey was told
everything Rupert heard, particularly the merits of Larry
Lamb, a thrusting and ambitious journalist, who had been an
assistant night editor at the *Mirror* and Pinnington's right-hand
man. Addey, however, was enormously keen that Murdoch
should chase Pinnington.

With Gladwyn's help Murdoch made up a short list of
about half a dozen men which was then pruned to Lamb,
Pinnington and Shrimsley (not necessarily in any order). It
was August and both Pinnington and Shrimsley were away.
'As a matter of fact, so was Lamb,' recalls Rupert Murdoch.
'But his secretary was smart enough to realize how important the
call was and got him to call me immediately.'

Lamb went straight to Murdoch's place and they had a long
and deep chat. He 'sensed' the man was right for the job almost
immediately. 'I signed him up there and then. We just seemed
to agree on almost everything.' Lamb intimated he had an idea
for his deputy and it just turned out by coincidence that he
was talking about Shrimsley. Murdoch never did meet Pinnington until the 1971 Labour party conference. He does not
think he ever knew he was on the shortlist. 'I doubt whether
he would have come over anyway. He still had a lot to gain
at IPC,' he said.

But Pinnington was not the only IPC talent they had their
eyes on. In fact in the early days they went on quite a shopping
spree for IPC middle-rankers. They got a night editor from
IPC and took another back-bench man at the same time. 'He
went back to the *Mirror* rather quickly because they only work

a four-night week over there and we rather expect our senior men to disregard hours and pressure. If you are going to be a top newspaper executive I think you've really got to live the paper and not bitch about the hours.'

Murdoch had bought the *Sun* for a cool fifty thousand pounds down and a further maximum of six hundred thousand over six years to be paid from profits. As Alex McKay pointed out later, 'This was a very shrewd move. We were not committed to more than the initial outlay unless it proved a success.'

Murdoch recalls he often used to tell his *Sun* staff, 'Look, the *Mirror*'s still got four million readers, don't congratulate yourselves too much until we've reversed this.' But he feels the *Sun* is a nice, bright paper now. It has come a long way in a short time and it continues to leave the *Mirror* for dead many mornings. However, during the last six months of 1972, the *Mirror*, to Murdoch's considerable surprise, was doing a lot better. It looked as though it had regained its energy and it was often better than the *Sun*. But it gradually lost the energy and slipped back again. 'I think Cudlipp thought we had hit our plateau and they could afford to go back doing the sort of things they liked doing. Three-page editorials and news on the back page and things like that,' he said.

Murdoch made it quite clear he did not have a great deal of confidence in the top management at IPC and he still feels it is suffering from a lack of morale and confidence. The *Sun* had lost IPC nearly thirteen million pounds over eight years. An unlucky thirteen which could have meant nothing to IPC—and Cudlipp in particular—but utter humiliation. As the old *Daily Herald* it had been the only paper in Fleet Street committed to the Labour party. The *Herald* was born out of the union movement, and was still supported by them, but the hard socialism of the post-war years had diminished into general self-satisfaction with the birth of the sixties. The paper had quickly become out-moded, old-fashioned and unwanted by all but the few die-hard working left-wingers.

Certain sections of the old IPC board had wanted to close the paper down. Some political pressure was brought to bear—the printing unions gnashed their teeth at the very idea. Cecil

King was not too sure. He was finally persuaded by Cudlipp that the paper could make money again—if its whole concept was changed. New name, new talent, new ideas, they tossed the adjectives around in a flurry of frenzied activity. King and Cudlipp gave interviews galore saying the new paper would appeal to the young, the fashionable and the go-ahead. 'The Pacesetters' was born as the 'most dynamic concept in modern journalism'—one of the few things originated by Cudlipp which survives in the paper today.

But the new broadsheet paper showed quickly it had little chance of survival; die-hard socialists found the paper far too frivolous; *Mirror* readers were out of bounds. The paper had to pitch at the *Mail/Express* and never really found its identity. The alternative Murdoch-Lamb-Shrimsley formula gelled and became productive faster than anyone had imagined. All three men are very hard workers, nearly always doing a twelve- or thirteen-hour day. Lamb comes from down-to-earth Yorkshire socialist coalmining stock and is keen to identify himself with the working man. He is an idealist as well as a good, practical journalist. It was his ideal of what a working-class paper should really be, as much as his reputation as a journalist, which first attracted him to Murdoch. He is, in the main, popular with his staff. He takes no nonsense but gives praise when it is due and has a sense of humour which normally keeps the staff around him in good spirits. He is soft spoken with an attractive lilting Yorkshire accent which can occasionally change to show the spit and fire of Yorkshire rage. He lives and breathes the papers he is in charge of and manages to keep very close to Murdoch thinking.

'We don't often argue,' he said. 'Most of the time we agree on the basic issues. I have had rows with Rupert about things, but they were quickly healed. He does not really interfere but we often discuss things and find we are remarkably close in the way we view them.'

VI

Shortly after the *Sun* hit the streets Murdoch jumped further into controversy when he sacked *News of the World* editor, Stafford Somerfield.

The sacking was as typical an example as one could find of a Murdoch dismissal. Somerfield got to his Bouverie Street office within a few minutes of eleven o'clock. He greeted his secretary Joan in his usual jovial manner and hung his overcoat on the rack in the corner. As was his habit, he hung his suit jacket on the back of his chair, snapped his braces with his thumbs once or twice and called for the morning mail. A few minutes later the buzzer went on his telephone intercom, and Murdoch's secretary summoned him to the presence. Before going in to Murdoch, Somerfield called on Michael Gabbert, until then his 'heir apparent'. (The two often fought like cat and dog in official matters but were on close personal terms.) He told Gabbert that Murdoch had called him in and asked what he thought it meant. Gabbert considered the formal nature of the summons and said, rightly, 'It will be the sack.'

In fact Somerfield had been expecting the sack for some time. He had always showed little but contempt for Murdoch, sometimes bordering on sheer rudeness. A colleague describes a scene where Murdoch found Somerfield having a discussion with Gabbert in the series department. Murdoch came in and told Somerfield he wanted a column on the front page for a *Sun* promotion. Stafford said, 'Why don't you take the whole front page?' Murdoch said icily quiet that one column would do. Somerfield went on taunting him and offering him the whole front page. When Murdoch left the room, Somerfield told Gabbert, 'I think I went a little too far that time.'

Somerfield was convinced Murdoch would not be prepared to pay the huge severance pay which Lord Goodman had arranged with Carr just before the takeover. In fact, Murdoch claims, it was *because* of the contract that he wanted to sack him. He accepts Stafford was a good working editor with a lot of flair. He could work under the exacting pressures of Fleet Street and always be relied upon to give the paper a lot of personality. But the contract made him feel too sure of himself. He was never willing to cooperate. Murdoch says he was sure Stafford felt he would never have the nerve to get rid of him and he openly defied his new boss whenever he could. It did not matter who was present. 'I was not very happy with some of his views and there were some rather odd people in the pay of the paper while he was editor. He constantly made things very difficult for me and for Larry Lamb. He tried to interfere in the running of the *Sun*. He would 'phone Manchester and tell them he was still the senior executive in the firm and everything should come through him. Generally speaking I thought the way he was doing things since I had arrived was detrimental to both newspapers.'

Had he not had that contract, things might well have been different. He might have been more amenable to cooperation and they might have become good friends. Murdoch was always willing to admit, 'He was a good editor for the *News of the World*.'

The last interview Stafford had with Murdoch was short. Murdoch smiled very slightly and said, 'I've asked you in here to tell you you are fired.'

There was a pregnant pause. Somerfield was not an excitable man. Then he said, 'Just like that?'

'Just like that.'

'I see.'

And the interview was quickly terminated. Somerfield left the room and went to see Gabbert. 'You were right,' he said. 'I'm now going out to get drunk.'

Gabbert said, 'No you're not. I'll take you up to El Vino's and buy us a bottle of champagne. But that's your lot. You're bound to be going on television this evening and you've got to keep a cool head.'

The two went and drank the bottle and Somerfield made a very good show of himself that night on television, uttering the now legendary Fleet Street remark, 'My mummy told me never to resign.'

Somerfield was a very good editor and a politician of immense subtlety. He got excited about good stories and no one can take his huge talent and ability away from him. However, he enjoyed the in-fighting of the executives of a large newspaper and handled it well. This jockeying for power caused him to adopt a policy of dividing and ruling his camp which could be detrimental to the running of the newspaper. As his executives were often at war with each other he managed two things. Firstly, they were all so involved with fighting each other that none of them could be bothered to try to oust him. Secondly, he was always able to play the rôle of the peacemaker.

It was a game of immense skill and audacity, a gambit often used by the shrewdest of leaders, but it can have disastrous effects if the thin membrane of order which controls it snaps. Somerfield had been supreme commander under Carr. Carr thought of him, perhaps rightly, as one of the last 'great' editors in Fleet Street. The two men had houses next to each other in the country and were socially on the best of terms. Somerfield lived his life as editor in a grand style. He loved luxury and expensive meals and he adored opulence.

Before the sacking when Somerfield went on holiday after Murdoch had taken over, Murdoch proposed several changes to the paper. Someone 'phoned Stafford in the South of France and the editor came rushing back on a Saturday afternoon to change back all that Murdoch had done. Like Deamer, Stafford's idea of being editor was to be in sole charge of the newspaper he was editing. Murdoch has never been able to resist interfering with his newspapers. When Somerfield stopped him, his days were numbered.

VII

The invigorating circulation battle between the *Mirror* and the *Sun* has, in several ways, plunged Fleet Street back many years to the great days when the big publishing houses were fighting it out fiercely to capture the popular reader. It has made Fleet Street an exciting place in which to live and hunt again. It hums once more with the singing buzz of competition—the healthiest sound in any newspaper jungle. Whereas before, the air was strangely melancholy, now it has a delicious bite and sting to it. Disenchantment and disillusion have been momentarily swept away across Ludgate Circus.

But two great newspapers in direct and fierce competition with each other are very unreasonable animals immensely subject to their own propaganda. Both camps sneer at each other across the circulation figures and refuse to concede little more than a wisp of praise for the other side.

The *Mirror* does not deserve the abuse it commands in Bouverie Street. The *Sun* does not deserve the contempt and ridicule it gets from Holborn Circus. Between them they are the best popular tabloid operation in the world. In their field they cannot be surpassed anywhere. They are both bright, tough, utterly readable and worth every bit of their cost. But there is no way in which you can get more than the odd individual on either side to admit this about the other.

The *Mirror* has for a long time been, quite simply, the best subbed, most professionally edited, neatest, tidiest, cleverest, tabloid of its kind anywhere. The *Sun*'s success does little to take the *Mirror*'s greatness away from it. The *Mirror* is so far the adult paper which has ironed out most of its faults, tidied up its dusty corners and settled down to a regular rhythm of good sense and spartan reading.

It has, locked within itself, a depth of feeling, a quality and a sense of experience which dominate every page. The paper has, in the main, better writers and better layouts. But somewhere along the line, the *Mirror* has lost the bounce, vitality and youthful aggression which springs from every page of the *Sun*. The *Sun* has a bright zing, an uncanny happy-go-lucky, holiday atmosphere which is difficult to pinpoint. The *Mirror* is often more satisfying to the mind and to the eye but the *Sun* runs away with the fun.

The staff of the *Sun* are very sensitive about their paper. In many ways this is understandable. Lamb and Shrimsley have sweated over every headline and every full stop in the paper twelve hours a day since it was born. They *believe* in it.

It is very much their product, their baby and their lives. And Lamb will not tolerate even a hint of criticism about the paper's policy or quality. When you question the *Sun* you are questioning Larry Lamb. It is this quality in a man—the ability to immerse himself completely so that the product becomes a huge and significant part of his very life—which Murdoch encourages and fosters in all his executive staff.

The *Mirror* has evolved, over many years of highly proficient technique, a certain mastery. Indeed, many of the top-rankers at Bouverie Street learned their trade in the *Mirror* organization. The *Sun*, on the other hand, is still a new baby, born, to a certain extent, from the frustration emanating from the heavily over-talented middle rank of IPC. It has had its bottom smacked and started to cry. Its umbilical cord was cut and it surged forth into the world. It has since cut its teeth and dried its nappies. It has stumbled forward, fallen over itself continuously, picked itself up and eventually rushed forward with the first childish delight of finding its feet.

It is now in the first throes of its belligerent teens. Brash and rude to its elders. Cocky and rather loud to those all around it. Conceited and arrogant, it struts around and shows itself off. Proudly boasting that it belongs to the takeover generation, it has a teenage spirit which cannot be broken.

Murdoch nurtures this attitude in his staff. He blandly dismisses the opposition as a pack of nincompoops. He can show utter contempt for the enemy which is both attractive and catching. His organizational self-propaganda is superb. But it does not necessarily follow he believes in his own game to the same extent. Murdoch is now clever enough to have a large conception of his own vulnerability. He covers his back with every step forward. His knowledge of the game and his ability to play it with his own set of rules, ensures he studies his enemies and, although he would rarely admit it, he has a healthy respect for them too.

The key to the *Sun*'s initial success lies very much within the personality of Murdoch himself—for he is a good and proud father. Stern when necessary, praising profusely when it is deserved, comforting when there are upsets and continually guiding, within the framework of his own image, the newest and fondest of his offsprings. The *Sun* was born from the womb of his organization. It was not Larry Lamb nor Bernard Shrimsley nor PR man, Graham King, or any of them, who were the paper's individual authors. It was born out of the essential Murdoch formula of finding them all; getting them together; blending them into a team under his tyrannical flag; waving this flag profusely in all their faces; beating the drum; laughing at the opposition; and, most of all, getting them, to a man, to believe in the 'greatness' of the product they were serving, while recognizing Murdoch as the creator of it all. The formula works. Murdoch has dragged success around with him as if it were a younger brother.

It is a well-voiced public view that the *Sun* is a 'comic strip' of a pop paper which treats very little news seriously and which has a highly light-hearted manner in its approach to current affairs. This comes about because of its TV adverts— nearly always based on the Pacesetters feature which is some- times vulgar, always light-hearted and often whimsical and flippant. And partly because the paper itself has a very bright and breezy approach to its presentation which gives the impres- sion of brashness. Larry Lamb claims this attitude is wrong. He says the *Sun* has more news, as often as not, than the *Mirror* and it is treated in just as serious a way. 'We might cut something down to only one paragraph—but it will be in the paper somewhere,' he claims.

In order to run a little test on this I went out one morning— April 17th, 1973, to be exact—and bought a copy of both news- papers. The experiment is not conclusive and the results cannot be taken too seriously on the grounds that there is a fluctuation rate every day between the content value of the *Sun* and the *Mirror*. But it does give an indication that Lamb has a point.

The most important fact was that the *Mirror* on this day had less news stories covering less column inches than the *Sun*. This means the *Sun was* giving more space to more stories. Both papers on this day had thirty-two pages yielding a total 3,136 column inches. Both had less than fifty per cent adver- tising, the *Mirror* had 1,251 column inches and the *Sun* 1,179 column inches. The *Mirror* featured thirty-four pictures covering 308 column inches while the *Sun* had allotted 330 column inches to only twenty-three pictures.

The comic-strip image of the *Sun* hardly lives up to the facts. The *Mirror* gives a daily 148 column inches to ten cartoons and six comic strips while the *Sun* has only 104 column inches for ten cartoons and three strips.

The *Mirror* carried fifty-two news stories covering 402 column inches while the *Sun* had given 549 column inches to fifty-five stories.

There were twenty-three sports news pieces in the *Mirror*, thirteen sports features and twelve general news features. The *Sun* had twenty-five sports news stories, twelve sports features and thirty-two general features (including several on such things as the TV page).

On this day anyway there *was* more news in the *Sun*, but I feel IPC would gladly concede this on the grounds that the *Mirror* had nearly a full page more advertising.

VIII

For many years the name Cudlipp has been synonymous with power at the top of the journalistic profession. A large part of the Murdoch story is the story of circulation battles. The particular battle between the *Sun* and the *Mirror* is one of the most intense of these. Until Murdoch moved into American journalism it was also the latest one, the largest one and probably the most important one. Cudlipp would obviously have fascinating views on the subject and he was, of course, approached by me with this in mind.

It became very quickly impossible to ask him a question. He refused to answer all of them and seemed over-defensive. If Cudlipp is not the author of the phrase 'the best form of defence is attack', he should have been. He brushed aside the first words of any sentence with an angry wave and forgot his polite letter of invitation. It is a shame because Cudlipp, more than perhaps anyone in Fleet Street, could have given lucid and concise criticism of Rupert Murdoch which would have found a significant place in this book.

He finally said he would only answer written questions and was then sent the questions which would have been asked verbally. A 'phone call soon after, in which he was the essence of charm, established apologetically that it had been an 'off' day.

Written questions and answers are highly unsatisfactory to the biographical writer as they leave the interviewer no leeway for intuition. It is also unfair that only one person out of the two hundred or so interviewees should alone have the advantage of this form of 'conversation'. However our agreement was made and the following answers were forthcoming:

Q: Murdoch has suggested that the *Daily Mirror* had got too highbrow for large sections of the British public. Do you agree with this?

A: He is right, of course. The natural journalistic urge, at any rate with me, is to enhance the content and standing of our newspapers. It was safe to do this when there was no tabloid *Sun* further down the scales to which the mentally under-privileged could turn. In pre-tabloid *Sun* days the *Daily Mirror* was enjoying its battle with the *Daily Express*.

Q: Murdoch has told me that, had he been running the *Mirror*, he would have chased the *Express/Mail* markets rather than compete with the *Sun*. Have you any comments on this?

A: The *Mirror* continued to chase the *Express* as its principal objective, but in my view it would have been utter folly to have ignored the *Sun* completely. I was not prepared to say to the *Sun*, 'You can have the next generation of young readers.'

Q: Lee Howard has been reported as saying he was very much in favour of dropping a million or more off the *Mirror*'s circulation if necessary, rather than go into direct circulation battle with the *Sun*. He has said he argued that the *Mirror* should keep its more intelligent approach to news gathering and presentation and be prepared to lose the 'bottom end' of the market. He maintains you personally disagreed with him and decided the *Sun* should be kept in place through a head-on process of circulation collision. His view is that your personal involvement with the *Mirror*'s place as the number one popular newspaper in this country, had become an obsession with you to the extent you were unable to accept any alternative. Is any of this an accurate assessment?

A: Lee may have held the views you attribute to him, but he certainly did not express them to me. I have discussed this question today with Sydney Jacobson, the editorial director, and Anthony Miles [now editor and in Lee's time very close to him]. Neither recollect the views Lee apparently now holds being stated by him at the time or being pressed by him in any cogent form.

Q: There are two widely differing theories concerning Murdoch's takeover of the *Sun.* One says IPC were more than happy for him to have it because they felt it would eventually cripple him financially. The other says IPC, and you in particular, were very much against him having the *Sun,* and that there was a very big row at board-room level about the situation. Which of these thories is nearer the truth?

A: Neither of these theories is true. There was no 'row' at the board. The reasons why the *Sun* went to Rupert Murdoch are set out in the attached memorandum. [Published in Chapter Five, Part V.] I hope you will find it helpful in assessing the situation as it was at that time.

Q: What do you feel about the *Sun* as a newspaper?

A: Bright and breezy, occasionally sleazy, but the *Sun* is unquestionably the Fleet Street success story of current times.

Q: Were you particularly angry to find people like Alex McKay going over to Murdoch, and were you surprised at the choice of Larry Lamb as first editor of the *Sun?*

A: No, Alex McKay is a friend of mine. He left IPC because of ill-health. No, not at all surprised. Larry Lamb was a first-class choice. He had been a big success on the *Mirror,* and had he stayed with IPC he would certainly have been given an editorship in a matter of years. Larry left the *Mirror* when he was offered the northern editorship of the *Daily Mail.*

Q: Are you happy with the *Mirror* in its present form?

A: Now that the pace of the *Sun*'s expansion has slowed

down, the *Mirror* is returning to its former standards, or at any rate moving in that direction. Tony Miles as editor is, of course, in charge of the operation.

Q: Do you feel Murdoch has been dishonourable in any of his dealings on the front-line of his circulation war with the *Mirror?*

A: No.

Q: Larry Lamb says that the pitch of the new *Sun* is based on the concept of the *Mirror* of twenty years ago. By this he means the *Mirror* in those days had a great reader-relationship which he feels is missing today. He says the *Mirror* has little real communication with young people. It is his feeling, backed by Murdoch, that the process by which you put special headlines on the serious parts of the paper has alienated the reader from the rest of the news. This is his view and his opinion and it is, of course, open to controversy. But taking in mind the comparative success of the *Sun*, do you feel any of these feelings are justified?

A: I think it is an interesting view, certainly a tenable argument. Newspapers evolve, and it will be interesting to see what the *Sun* will be like in ten years time.

Q: The last major promotion campaign which added considerably to the *Sun*'s circulation, was planned several months ahead. But Murdoch has contended to me that two months before the promotion was about to start they deliberately kept *Sun* promotion to a very low key so that the circulation rise had appeared to have stopped at around 2,700,000. Graham King said it was the first time in Murdoch's history that he had actively tried to keep circulation down. All sides in the Bouverie Street camp feel the 'ruse' was successful in that the *Mirror* felt the *Sun* had reached its top level. Suitably 'lulled' they feel you were completely unprepared for the promotion which followed. What truth is there in this from your side?

A: The *Sun* has consistently spent vastly more on TV promotion than the *Daily Mirror*. Since, rightly or wrongly, we have matched pound on promotion the extent of our 'surprise' and 'unpreparedness' is a Bouverie Street daydream, but daydreams—and even nightmares—are part of the fun of publishing.

Q: Murdoch's assessment of the situation at IPC is that: (*a*) the company has become far too large, and that the corporate tail is wagging the body; (*b*) that when you retire there is no one of your calibre to take over; (*c*) that the *Sunday Mirror* and *Sunday People* will probably be merged within the next two years. Do you agree with any of these statements?

A: I do not think I can comment on Rupert's view of us.

Q: During a 'World at One' programme [in 1973], you were asked what you felt about Murdoch and the rise of the *Sun*. I have so far been unable to get a full transcript of the programme, but you have been quoted as answering, 'Someone will always be around to scrape the bottom of the barrel.' With hindsight, do you honestly feel the *Sun* is really bad enough for a comment of this nature? What do you say to the comments of most Murdoch executives who maintain this is basically sour grapes on your part?

A: I said just that, or something very much like it. It's surely true. But I don't see why I should comment upon or dispute the views of Mr Murdoch's executives; after all, they may be right.

Q: The executive at Bouverie Street seem to be incredibly well informed about what is happening at IPC. Are you satisfied with your security there? Is this a two-way traffic?

A: It's a two-way traffic, not applying only to the *Mirror* and the *Sun*, but to all Fleet Street newspapers.

Q: It is the contention of both Larry Lamb and Murdoch that newspapers, before the *Sun*, had got too incestuous; that journalists were writing and producing papers for themselves and had lost touch with their readers. Have you any comment on this?

A: It has always been the danger. We have always tried to avoid it on the *Mirror*, but we may not always have succeeded.

Q: Would you have been happier if Maxwell had got the *Sun*? If so, why?

A: I think this is fully explained in the attached memorandum.

Q: Do you think the policy of the *Mirror* will change within the foreseeable future in regards to the *Sun*'s dramatic circulation rise?

A: I cease to operate at the end of the year. My successor or successors had better do the batting here.

Q: Is it true that on the day of the first edition of the *Sun*, you held a 'funeral' party and handed round dead sunflowers?

A: The story is utterly apocryphal and childish. Never heard it before. I might have a sense of humour, but I'm not a bloody fool. It must have been thought up by somebody who believes in witchcraft or black magic.

Q: Is it true, as Sheila Black describes, that you flung the first edition of the *Sun* down in disgust and said, 'Well, see for yourself. We have nothing to worry about'?

A: I don't recollect it. If Sheila Black says it, it must be true.

Q: Is it true that as a guest of honour at a recent Press Club dinner, you told the journalists that Murdoch had 'reduced Fleet Street back to the gutter' and 'brought down the level of the *Mirror*'?

A: No. I have never been guest of honour at the Press Club— I'm currently the president of the club and in this capacity have obviously not commented upon other newspapers.

Q: You mentioned when we met that I had not bothered to find any references to the nice things you have said about Murdoch. I have looked through all the cuttings again and can find very few 'nice' references. May I ask you simply what you think of Murdoch personally?

A: I praised Rupert's qualities as a businessman and entrepreneur at many press conferences in Australia at the end of last year. I—and many others—have also criticized the standards set by some of his newspapers. I have always liked Rupert personally. New blood, especially hot blood, is always an essential in Fleet Street. Murdoch is in the tradition of Beaverbrook and Thomson—rustling 'colonials' who could in fact teach their grandmothers how to suck eggs. There was room at the top for a new force in Fleet Street: Rupert's it.

Q: What do you feel about the *News of the World* as a popular Sunday newspaper?

A: The *News of the World* is the *News of the World*. What it sets out to do it does extremely well.

Q: Were you aware of the fact that, before Murdoch became involved with the *News of the World* takeover, he had got bankers to buy into IPC quite dramatically. I understand he had bought two million pounds worth of shares and was eventually aiming at ten per cent of the equity. It is, of course, a matter of conjecture that this would have given him any real power in the organization. But how would you and Cecil King have reacted to finding him a major shareholder?

A: There is no answer to this question.

Without getting into lengthy correspondence with Sir Hugh, it would be unfair to argue his answers. But it seems obvious Cudlipp has little love for Murdoch, while still managing to retain some diplomacy and humour when he is allowed to think about his answers.

It is difficult to say exactly how the personal rivalry between the two men has developed or how it affects their products. Although Murdoch was unlikely to disregard Cudlipp's danger to him, he shows little but contempt when discussing their rival concerns. Certainly Cudlipp has never hidden his dislike of Murdoch from many of his own workforce.

His only vague similarity to Murdoch is that at IPC very few people are indifferent to him. They either love him or hate him. He enjoys a fierce support from those who remember his great days and a quite vitriolic hatred from his detractors.

He is reported at IPC to get uncanny delight out of being rude and there is overwhelming existing testimony that he has been extremely mercurial in the last few years of his Fleet Street reign. He is a boisterous man and admits quite freely that most people who meet him find him aggressive and bad mannered.

During a recent television documentary on his retirement—

a fascinating piece of television journalism—he appeared at times rather waspish, and displayed, almost happily, a flamboyant aggression towards others. I don't think for a moment Cudlipp cares. He has never claimed he was in the business to make friends (although he was certainly in the business to influence people).

It seems he genuinely did feel that his life's work was to upgrade the reading material of the masses. It may have been a rather naive ambition, but it was sincere and one must admire his (and King's come to that) valiant intentions. To have three million readers suddenly plucked out from the bottom end of his own market must be the most frustrating and painful thing that can happen to any top newspaper executive. But it is no longer a matter of crying over spilt milk—rather that the cream at the top has gone sour.

How IPC as a whole would have handled its affairs if Rupert Murdoch had not come on to the scene is difficult to speculate. It always had the strength of its flagship the *Daily Mirror*. The *Sunday Mirror* has gone from being the most sensational of pictorial exposure-splashers to being a rather mundane, family-orientated, lower-middle-class woman's paper without a real identity. 'But,' said an executive, 'it's selling steadily and no one these days is going to rock the boat.'

There is little one can say nowadays about the *Sunday People*. From the hard-hitting, tough and swashbuckling days of the the great editor, Sam Campbell; when Gilbert Harding grumbled and groaned over our breakfast tables; Nancy Spain stretched her ski pants to sit down; Hannen Swaffer waspishly lashed us with a tongue of razorblades; when Duncan Webb invented the legendary phrase 'I made an excuse and left'— while putting the Messina brothers inside for a lifetime; and when the whole of Fleet Street groaned when they knew Arthur Helliwell was coming back from an assignment—his hat always cocked—because it meant the biggest booze-up they could remember since the last one ... to today where we find a rather pathetic little rag.

Without being intentionally cruel to the paper (although my

own year spent on the news desk there is a period I prefer to forget) it has lost its old spirit.

Campbell was a complete legend in his lifetime and when he died very suddenly a morose emptiness fell over the building and the newspaper itself. When they buried Campbell they buried the spirit of the *People* along with him. Never in a multitude of Sunday front pages would Bob Edwards, or any other subsequent editor, bring that sparkle, that humanity and that wry humour to grace the pages of what was then one of the greatest campaigning journals in the world.

Had Campbell lived on the whole Sunday journalism scene and the entire relationship between IPC and Murdoch would have certainly been very different. As it was, nothing but light-weights came in his wake. He had proved, if it ever needed to be proved, that papers are built on personalities—one of Murdoch's pet thoughts! When the huge corporate jungle of IPC—despite the undoubted talents of King and Cudlipp—swallowed Campbell's legend they left a vacuum which has never been filled. Undaunted, or perhaps even unaware of the significance of his death to the policies and politics of their camp, King and Cudlipp swarmed on regardless. The birth of the *Sun* on the death of the old *Herald* was to be the crowning glory of Cudlipp's spectacular life. With his shirt sleeves rolled up he spent fifteen hours a day on the back bench cajoling and encouraging his workforce. It was very much his baby and he washed its nappies every day. Cudlipp had a lot of sincere good feeling behind him. *No* journalist, however cynical, can bear the death of a newspaper and no one in their right minds felt anything but a bitter disappointment when the *Sun* showed early on it was flagging desperately. The initial surge of activity quietened down until there was a death wish hanging over the whole paper. Only one other newspaper this century—the *Daily Mail* —has ever been able to survive after the smell of death has graced its door.

It is said by many who know him that a large part of Hugh Cudlipp died with the *Sun* and he never really recovered. An executive in his organization recalls he used to be great fun and wonderful to work for. He took the failure of the newspaper quite personally. And God forbid anyone who dared remind him of it. He hated any suggestion that the paper was failing when IPC sold it. Not unnaturally he resented being reminded of it, as I found to my cost when I asked him about it.

Chapter 6

Running an empire

I

'Relationship' is probably the key word to the Murdoch method of patriarchy. It is certainly the most important governing factor to survival or downfall in the Murdoch hierarchy. The pattern has emerged through two main periods. During the Australian saga, people's relationships with Murdoch sometimes became jaded and Murdoch will not tolerate people who openly show him aggressive contempt. During the English period the pattern changed. Most of the people who made an effort to work with him are still around. Those who decided to fight him got quickly and decisively severed from the body of the organization with a bluntness which left many of them blinking and bewildered.

Rohan Rivett had a 'relationship' with Murdoch in Adelaide. When Murdoch knew he would not be around to carry on the 'relationship' in the same way, he felt it was time for Rivett to go. The situation was similar with Brass. In Sydney his 'relationship' with Brass could be mutually helpful. But when he was away he felt that, without the close and controlling relationship existing, Brass should not have the top seat.

Some people have found it ironic that the deeper their relationship with Murdoch has seemed to be during any of the periods of his rampage, the more vulnerable they are when he advanced to other things. Few editorial executives actually go with him.

Murdoch has said countless times things like 'at one time we were very close, but I felt he had gone off-beam' or 'I liked him very much and had a lot of respect for him, but I knew he could not be relied on to do the job if I was not there to control our particular kind of "relationship".'

But those who do survive and manage to get and stay close to Murdoch thinking live a surprisingly harmonious life. For with those he trusts and likes, Murdoch is a very free and easy boss. Granting often, and rather touchingly, perhaps, favours and rewards they would not expect from other bosses.

Murdoch's rapid growth bonanza has meant a lot of people have got bigger with him quicker than their qualifications or experience allow. And guys who started as juniors at Broken Hill have got so close to the hot seat so fast, they occasionally show a lack of maturity not particularly in keeping with the heavy, sombre hand of board-room politics.

This has one important benefit to the company but remains a severe handicap to many of the men themselves. The company is an aggressively young one. In no comparable financial organization are there to be found the vast number of thirty- to forty-five-years-olds who bustle the corridors of the Murdoch empire.

Because Murdoch has always been on the move the organization has never been allowed to get jaded. It has *always* had one fight or another on its hands, and people just joining Murdoch over the years have been thrown right in at the deep end. There has not been one year in the past twenty-two, when Murdoch has not bought something, started something or fought someone. His aides are all tough little battlers who enjoy their boss's avaricious delight in a newspaper punch-up. Murdoch newspapers are often immature and naive, but his youthful and aggressive tactics tend to show up the pomposity and senility of many of his more established rivals.

The drawback to the survivors in the Murdoch hierarchy is that they will always stand accused of being paid lackeys of the boss. This reputation is perpetuated by many of the people who lost their way to the top. They excuse themselves by telling everyone they lost because they refused to be sycophants. In journalism in general and Australia in particular this is a highly potent argument which enjoys much sympathy. But it is a very difficult factor to evaluate. Murdoch is supreme commander and is determined to stay so. To try and topple him from within the hierarchy is suicide. The first thing they have to accept is that Rupert Murdoch is Boss with a capital 'B'. It is then that the fun starts and the Murdoch hierarchy are sycophants only in the same way the courtiers at King James's court jockeyed for position of authority and influence next to their monarch.

King Murdoch would not tolerate someone who merely said 'yes' to everything he said. He constantly looks to his aides for advice and criticism of the organization and expects them to know every facet of the areas they control. Their discussions are lively and informal but aides are more than aware their influence on Murdoch is through gentle persuasion rather than direct confrontation. Because of this the sycophancy accusation is often without real basis. The men close to Murdoch are not so much arse-crawlers as military tacticians in a court where the King's word is total law.

Top newspaper executives are among the most interesting animals in the business jungle. They are tough, openly aggressive and unlike most other chiefs of such hierarchies, they love the theatre of it all. They act out the rôle of themselves with an exaggerated flourish of emotion. In many ways newspapers are show business. Most top journalists have a tremendous ego and they swagger through their jobs loving the limelight, the by-lines, the controversies, the heartaches and the excitement and razzamataz of it all. They are all frustrated actors who love an audience, as long as that audience is not actually near enough to throw rotten fruit, if the performance is bad. Quite famous Fleet Street names literally have rushed out of an important business session so they could get to the television in time to see Softly Softly's Barlow. They watch TV's most mundane spy stories completely hooked on the chicanery and intrigue. A newspaperman does not exist who would not like to be head of MI5. And yet no journalist could actually hold down that particular rôle because there are none who could bear to be that anonymous.

Because of the theatricals, the power games at the top of a newspaper concern always tend to be rather exaggerated and flamboyant. The knives appear to be sharper, the viciousness more intense, and the intrigue more conspiratorial. It is open to strong doubt whether they are actually more so than other concerns, but they are certainly seen to be.

The ousting of Cecil King by Cudlipp, for example, would have rated a one-day City page lead had it been an oil company —even if the politics had been as intense and as positive. Yet Fleet Street played it as a major story for over a week. It is doubtful if the audience were as interested as journalists thought they were. But stage-struck Fleet Street could not resist hoping they were. Murdoch's own arrival in Fleet Street and the consequent battles were another typical example. Only major cabinet reshuffles ever got so much notice from our press.

II

The corporate drama played out at News International, and, subsequently, down through the rest of the organization, is as intense, dramatic and vicious as in any other newspaper jungle in the world. One drama is enacted in Surrey Hills and another in Bouverie Street. The organization as a whole is like a theatre with a two-stage Barnum-and-Bailey type circus operating in the middle. Everything is there, the curtains, the lights, the stage-hands, the actors, the chorus girls, the promoters, advertisers, the heroes and the heroines. The only difference is that no one can actually *see* the audience. Across this stage dramas float and people make entrances and exits—sometimes with the frequency of a Brian Rix farce where one door has not closed before the other opens.

Essentially, as with theatre, corporate power is a story about people—playwright, actors, and impresarios and so on. The difference with this particular organizational power game is that the impresario pulls *all* the strings.

Murdoch's essential patriarchy over his performing circus is quite incredible. He takes on all the important rôles. He cajoles the actors, directs the stage movements, sells the tickets, produces the central drama and, in turn, almost becomes the audience as well. For many of the actual plays which are produced, are done so because the performers want him to clap.

The present News International board is Murdoch-orientated

from top to bottom. With the exception of Sir Norman Young, everyone else is there because they are tried and tested members of the inner-Murdoch fraternity. Sir Norman is there for several reasons. He gives Murdoch invaluable business advice and backing. He is a highly prestigious name to have as chairman of any board—with a lot of influence in the Australian business world. He also happens to be an excellent chairman, very able to run a board as it should be run. He pleases the shareholders and has caused Murdoch very little trouble.

Mervyn Rich is a member of both the boards of News Limited and News International. He is deeply involved in all aspects of this business. He is also a valued adviser to Murdoch. His power is not so much a direct power over people, but rather depends on his closeness to the functions of the company as a whole and then to Murdoch thinking.

Alex McKay must also be regarded as having much power in the organization. He is deputy chairman of News International, and as such, chief executive when Murdoch is away. He is an excellent negotiator, especially with the unions, and a champion of Murdoch's. He has also the invaluable experience of being a past IPC executive and, as such, is reported to be able to predict almost exactly what the opposition is doing (or more important—what they might do).

Lord Catto is also on the News International board. He is there as a banker and adviser to Murdoch and, like Sir Norman Young, as a prestige name. (He is, after all, the Queen's banker.) He is also sometimes responsible for putting a hand of restraint on a few of Rupert's more adventurous plans.

When, for instance, Murdoch recently wanted to acquire an Irish paper for News Limited, and not News International (which was already negotiating), Catto claims he pointed out that this would be quite unethical and Murdoch had to replan his strategy or face an embarrassing resignation. (The plan, in fact, failed because of Irish government restrictions.) Murdoch dismisses this as ridiculous. 'I thought,' he said, 'with the situation in Ireland being what it was, it might be politically better for an Australian, rather than a British company, to make the bid. It was as simple as that.'

It is tempting, when looking deep into affairs like Murdoch's, to be influenced by office speculation. When assessing how the actual corporate structure works one has to study things which fluctuate on a daily basis. People change and consequently so do situations. Everyone has different opinions about those around them. There is resentment, gossip, and a lot of bum-crawling. In order to say with any conviction that the power faction in this organization follows a particular pattern, we must be constantly aware of all the circus antics.

In the main the Murdoch executives do not feel they work for an organization. They can be counted on at all times to carry out Murdoch's instructions to the letter and to inform Murdoch about everything relevant. They are sometimes men who do not have particularly strong opinions of their own and have all been tested over the years for their ability to keep close to Murdoch thinking. Underneath this elite strata there are generally to be found rough, tough and ambitious men who are quite clearly after the top job. This is probably ordinary corporate politics and happens in most large organizations. These men serve a dual purpose. They keep the top man on his toes and they are ruthless with those underneath them—while Murdoch himself still enjoys the buffer of his hand-picked chief executives. At every level of the Murdoch organization there are at least two of those men to be found fighting it out for the top job—whether as managing director of one of the companies or as editor of one of the papers.

But there is no knowing who will or will not be appointed to a certain position for a given reason. People who thought they were close to the top have repeatedly stayed where they are while others have been plucked from relative obscurity and placed above them. There are several examples of junior executives, who thought they had reached their peak, suddenly being placed in positions far above their expectations. Brian Norris, presently managing director of Southdown Press in Melbourne, is a typical example of the Murdoch method of choosing his executives. Norris, a bright young man who is partial to floral shirts and flamboyant ties, was an ambitious advertising and promotions man who joined Southdown to gain experience of magazine publishing. He was not going to stay with the firm for long. Murdoch, very suddenly out of the blue, said he wanted to make him general manager at South-down Press. 'I didn't know what a general manager even did,' he said. 'But Rupert told me, "well come up to Canberra for the weekend and I'll show you".'

This kind of suddenness can work both ways. Vulnerability is as crucial a part of the Murdoch method as the rapid growth rate of the chosen few. Leading actors suddenly find the lights can dim and a bright young man is picked out of the chorus to play his understudy. He rarely remains understudy for long.

Murdoch claims that, through his own naivety, he is unaware of the vast complexes of games being played beneath him. There is little evidence to doubt him. Outside his own daily routine the central dramas of the corporate jungle do not really affect him. It is not so much a matter of him creating situations and then ignoring the battles, but rather of creating situations near to him which reverberate down through the pyramid until, on ground level, they appear to be earthquakes. While the base of the pyramid shakes, the top brick only just feels the rhythms of jungle warfare. Murdoch is quite hurt when people far below him criticize him as a boss. He does not realize that a chance remark made by him to an executive could have such fantastic-ally far-reaching effects.

Is it stupidity, naivety, good business, or genius, for instance, to have a massive crackdown on wages and expenses in London just before profits are seen to go soaring? It could be all four. Since Murdoch took over in London, it has happened five times and perhaps causes singly more discontent than anything else Murdoch does (or does not do). He could argue that the profits would not be as big if the cutbacks did not happen. (Murdoch does the same thing with headlines, when he thinks they are getting too big he has a cutting-down campaign.) On the other hand he simply might not even think about it. But his motives might be genius. One strong assessment is that Murdoch cuts all expenditure down before a big profit rise so that when it does come (and everyone starts demanding a share) he can let the figures slip up to what they were before. From a business point of view this is sound stuff and one sometimes gets a sneaking suspicion journalists and printers do get rather greedy. But then both sides see it as all part of the game.

With all this game-playing going on at every level of the organization by far the most interesting aspect is the 'fall-guy' system. This is by no means a Murdoch invention and Murdoch seems to be unaware it exists. It has probably developed in this case because of Murdoch's intriguing method of putting in teams of stablemates to watch over each other. It works from his point of view because he always has someone to take over—groomed for the rôle even—if the top guy at any level fails. But Murdoch simply must be aware that if you put a keen and hungry young executive next to another one, they will ferociously fight to the death—no holds barred. Murdoch and most of his executives point out this is corporate politics practised by all big businessmen. This may be true. However bankers I spoke to while researching this book admitted Fleet Street had a special atmosphere in its politics, and that although big business, in every sense, had similarities, the big business of Fleet Street was peculiar to itself.

The backlash of Murdoch's situation is that every executive has someone just below him who he can blame, agitate, or even fire. Someone to take the heat off him, or merely to pass the fire on to, when it comes to the crunch. The fall-guy system operates at the very top of the Murdoch ladder and it goes down through every rung to the very bottom. If you can handle your fall guy, you will be fine. In fact he will even act as a buffer between your vulnerable position and all the hungry men after your job. But if you cannot handle him, he will sting you and you will tumble. Murdoch's ladder is slippery with blood. And at the bottom there are a lot of guys who have slipped and broken their necks.

Because of the fluctuating fortunes of most executives in the Murdoch camp it would be most unfair to pick on individuals within the framework of executive control as examples of this system, but, in general terms, the pattern has the following structure.

Murdoch is 'The Boss' in every sense of the word. Underneath him is the buffer state which operates its own tactics. People vie strongly for positions next to him. Some go through periods of intense favourability—in which case the kaleidoscope tends to operate around them. For a while each of them has a deputy or a stablemate who could be construed as a fall guy. Poised below most editors there is an 'associate editor' who in theory is the link between the paper and editorial control. The editor has a deputy, the deputy an assistant editor, the assistant editor has department editors, who all have deputies, who all have assistants ... and so on.

III

By far the most interesting person in the present Murdoch hierarchy is Larry Lamb, editorial director in London. He has quite obviously had a great deal of influence over Murdoch's thinking since his arrival in London. In terms of the two national papers he is the supreme commander. For the moment at least the marriage has been very happy and most successful.

Lamb seems to enjoy his new and powerful rôle as head clansman of the Murdoch editorial team in London. There is no doubt he has the ability to create ideas in Murdoch's mind and then let them bounce back on him for execution. Murdoch often says things which are classic Lambisms, often without realizing they are. Lamb in turn is Murdoch-orientated and supplies an electric life-line of the chairman's current views and thoughts deep into the organization.

Lamb manages to handle the extremely difficult triangle of power which he has built up around himself. He has made himself the centre of the pyramid and can watch all the other points and manipulate them towards himself. All of the points are, in fact, as important to him as the other as long as he has the final say on how they look at each other. This is the fundamental essence of his power and, as such, he is as invincible in the organization as anyone can be.

On one level he controls the editorial and its executive with a clever and strong hand. Keeping most people happy most of the time but never letting them get too close to him, or come to that, to Murdoch. The other is the sheer power politics of such a position in terms of the board, the characters involved and keeping his finger directly on the pulse of the organization as well as the contents of the newspapers themselves. The third level is his relationship with Murdoch and how he interprets Murdoch to the others, and the others to Murdoch. As far as one can see he greatly enjoys the game and plays it to the full. He loves the feeling of hierarchy and the sheer theatre of Fleet Street politics. He plays the central rôle to the full, obviously pleased with his performance. Generally speaking he commands a hefty respect throughout Bouverie Street and is considered to be good at whatever he is doing. He also gets the same kind of cynicism Murdoch is subjected to, some of it just as bitchy.

He shares many similarities of personality with Murdoch, not least of all his impatience at wasting time. The two men, for instance, both drive cars, as a friend tactfully put it, 'like bloody maniacs'!

Lamb comes from Brighouse, a fiercely proud area of Yorkshire, just north of Huddersfield. There is a great tradition of Yorkshiremen in Fleet Street (surpassed these days only by the vast numbers of walkabout Aussies). He left Rastrick Grammar School as a fairly bright young man and started his working life in the Borough Treasurer's office. In efforts to relieve the boredom of officialdom and showing at an early age his left-wing tendencies—he started working on the NALGO union magazine in his spare time. He did not stay long as he had by now found the lure of newsprint. He joined the *Brighouse Echo* for a few months. But Ernest Sands, the editor, remembers he was too impatient to get to the big time to be a good weekly reporter. 'I must confess, I did not think he would get to where he has,' Sands related later. But Brighouse is a small place where the Lamb family home is still operating. Brighouse, being Brighouse, is fiercely proud of its former son.

People who have worked close to him have described him as being a man who works almost entirely by instinct. He is also an instant man given to quick 'yes' or 'no' decisions. He can be utterly charming when he is in a good mood and is described by women who know him as being 'extremely attractive'. He is happily married with three children, and friends of the family say the home is stable, happy and unpretentious.

Most people close to Lamb in Bouverie Street say he is often far more right than wrong in his decisions and his instinct for finding the right course instantly is almost uncanny. They accuse him of being over-sensitive about the *Sun*, getting terribly irate at the slightest criticism. He makes very sudden decisions on whether he likes someone or not and does not have grey areas about people. If he likes you he is a highly reasonable man with whom you can argue if you feel you are right about a subject. He is faithful to those he likes, making sure they have a protecting umbrella when in trouble. But he has been described as an 'absolute bastard' to those he takes a dislike to. Even those who are close to him and admire him admit they would hate to be his enemy.

After one of his rare rows with Murdoch, executives say he is capable of being sulky for days on end, being critical for little reason. He can have powerful and wrathful rages and in these moods is capable of severe ruthlessness. They say he *is* a powerful man and has guarded his power with a mixture of skill, ruthlessness, intrigue and an ability to keep close to Murdoch. When asked if he thought the day would come when he would be replaceable in the hierarchy, or redundant, he gave a quiet, but clearly scoffing smile. Clearly it seems Lamb has not got the same relationship with Murdoch as Rivett, Brass, Bryden, or any of his predecessors in the top editorial slot. It seems Lamb will go with Murdoch and in terms of similar close 'relationships' this must be regarded as a major achievement. He got himself deeply involved with the recent American expansion and obviously does not see himself as being merely editorial director of two London newspapers.

It is the feeling of people close to him that he has managed so far to keep close to Murdoch without compromising his position by being *too* close and dependent. His influence over Murdoch is well known and marked with a subtlety which I don't think has occurred before. The subtlety is based on his ability to gently place ideas in his chairman's head and wait until they come back to him. He also has a remarkably diplomatic way of arguing with Murdoch. Gently pushing his own point of view forward and nursing Murdoch to the point of agreement. At the same time he is careful to pass on to the editorial columns of the *Sun* and *News of the World*, general ideas and principles which he gleans from his boss.

The system being what it is he also manages to handle those just below him with a firmness which keeps them in their place, while still encouraging them to give of their best. For a coalminer's son from a humble home he has come a long way, and Larry Lamb intends to make sure it stays that way.

He is an expert on wines. Sometimes, say his underlings, to the point of boredom. Some people accuse him of being a wine-snob who goes through a great performance in the restaurant impressing everyone with his knowledge of wine. But when argued with they agreed they were probably jealous. It seems they did not think it quite right for a man from humble backgrounds to have an interest in wine.

One of the most widely versed criticisms of him is that he, a deep-rooted socialist—the man who vehemently fought for the miners through the editorial columns of the *Sun* for two years—should send his children to non-state schools.

In general terms though, it must sometimes be difficult for a man of deeply socialist principles and background, such as Lamb, to equate his position as a chieftain in a large capitalist concern. Consequently, he is not regarded as being the most expert union negotiator in the organization. Union leaders on the two newspapers say he seems to take their pressure very personally and gets rather offended as if they were having a go at him and not the management in general. He angrily refutes this and feels he has always held his ground with the unions on a specific level while still sympathizing deeply with the principles of unionism.

Although Bernard Shrimsley is very much in the same mould as Larry Lamb he has a different temperament which, in fact, tends to complement rather than clash with that of his boss. The two are old friends and allies from IPC days and Lamb has always seen Shrimsley as his natural successor. Shrimsley is tough and frighteningly dedicated. He is fastidious in his appearance, and page layouts, neither letting a hair on his head or a headline be too obtrusive or out of place. His diligence in ensuring that every last detail of his newspaper is as perfect as it can be is almost an obsession with him and he enjoys several intriguing nicknames from his production team. While they can occasionally descend into raucous blasphemy about his habit of causing earthquakes on a finished layout in order to rephrase a page-lead intro, in the main they express a deep admiration for him and his methods. As one layout man said, 'He can be murder to work for. He never gives you a moment's rest. But he never creates work just for the sake of it. When he tells you to change a page, however ridiculous it might seem at the time, he has an uncanny way of improving it when the change is made.'

The look and layout of newspapers is Shrimsley's particular speciality. His changing of the format when he was at the *Liverpool Post* was a classic example of exactly what a broadsheet should look like. Although he is proud of his period there because the circulation went up dramatically ('I have never worked on a newspaper where the circulation went down') he gained most satisfaction from comparing the old and new papers.

Staffmen in Liverpool describe his stay as a 'holocaust' but ruefully admit they enjoyed every minute of it. There is little doubt that what he learned in twelve years at the *Mirror*, and put into practice in his ten months in Liverpool, was a valuable forerunner to his success at the *Sun*.

He is essentially a creative ideas man who complements this talent by being also a draughtsman and technician. People who are close to him enjoy working with him. Those who work below him have mixed feelings. None question his talent.

He can brood about things that go wrong and gets very angry with people he considers incompetent. He charges in and out of every department of the paper he edits—changing types, approving pictures, up-paging stories, cutting others, consulting with his staff and generally moving at such a pace it makes many people weary to be near him.

But staffers at the *News of the World* remember when he

came for a short visit before his editorship. 'He was like a breath of fresh air,' one said. 'He took such a keen interest in everything you did.'

Another told me Shrimsley instilled a sense of enthusiasm in the job he had rarely felt before. One man who normally sloped off at four in the afternoon stopped each night until eight to work exclusively for Shrimsley.

His kind of management has its casualties and he is a hard man who takes no arguments when he thinks he is right. Journalists and junior executives who have worked directly under him say he has a brilliant attacking technique which is both frustrating and biting. Frustrating because a man of lower rank engaged in an argument with him can rarely win. Biting because he has an amazing ability to pick out and use to its best advantage any point of vulnerability he can find in his victim.

Shrimsley is thrusting, ambitious, tough, a tabloid man through and through, he is a classic Murdoch choice. He keeps a tight hold on the *Sun* yet his ambition is checked. Within his field he is straining at the leash. Below him directly are the team of ambitious younger men plotting quite openly for his job. It is a classic Murdoch method situation.

The relationship between Lamb and Shrimsley is one of the major talking-points among Fleet Street philosophers. The original situation was simple. When the *Sun* started Lamb and Shrimsley headed a formidable team of crack newspaper executives raring to go. Murdoch, they, and about six other key men were the spirit behind the *Sun*. A former news editor under Lamb said the success of the *Sun* was held in the hands of a very few people who became immediately engrossed in it. At one stage, during a strike, a dozen people produced the whole paper.

Another executive told of how in the beginning Lamb and Shrimsley were thrown into the battle and did not have much time left for politics. But as Lamb got closer to Murdoch, Shrimsley became more frustrated with his position as number two. Murdoch was in fact aware of this frustration and put Shrimsley into the *News of the World* to 'broaden his wings' before eventually appointing him actual editor of the *Sun*.

The relationship between the two men could be considered almost an accident. Both men were on the Murdoch short-list. Had Shrimsley got to Murdoch first their positions could have been reversed. But both utterly repudiate any rivalry, despite this being one of Bouverie Street's favourite subjects.

It seemed inevitable their paths should cross, though at one time events appeared much to the contrary. Lamb was well and truly in the Cudlipp camp at IPC while Shrimsley became a King favourite. When the two gladiators bust up and King left, Shrimsley was left rather high and dry, destined not for the editorship he wanted but for the group directorship. The two had known each other at Holborn Circus and both shared the same kind of burning ambition very early on. Both played middle-rank politics at the *Mirror* with a furious ardour. Both left within a short period of each other (Lamb to Manchester as *Mail* northern editor, Shrimsley to Liverpool) but neither kept their eyes off Fleet Street.

Without identical natures both men were remarkably close in their respective careers eventually coming together under the Murdoch flag. As political animals they are an immensely interesting team. They are very definitely the new breed of Fleet Street executive. The essence of their talent and ability lies on the production side whereas the old breed normally came up through front-page leads and headlines. They both got to the top of their professions by their fortieth birthday and both are thirsting for even more power.

IV

Deep down in the organization, minor executives sometimes complain about being intellectually frustrated, often not so much by the editorial involvements, but rather by the process of executive power itself. They claim the fall-guy system can work in reverse. In other words the man below is obliged to sound out the man immediately above him all the way up to Murdoch. The system means they are virtually unable to use their own judgement on anything but minor points and that if anything *is* important it quickly gets out of their reach. The ultimate decision is made high above them. This often means a breakdown of communication on major judgements. Each person adds or detracts from the available information until the process reaches its own executive level. Then it comes down again through the ranks—again at each stage drawing interpretations until it reaches the middle ranker who actually has to handle the problem. They have expressed frustration that the scene at ground level, and the opinions which are expressed above them, are often badly connected.

However far up you go, the same process exists. For instance, if you are a budding news editor or assistant editor, you have to convince associate editors, deputy editors and editors themselves. But even if you become one of the high rankers, there is still always someone above you—or right alongside you—watching everything you do. Therefore it means that in true terms, editors do not really exist. They are still answerable to others. And at the very end, in the highest position in the organization, you still have to deal with Murdoch himself. Therefore to be ambitious in the Murdoch organization you have to realize you will only be replacing whatever hang-ups you have at one level, with even larger ones when you go above them.

Apart from Murdoch there is no actual figurehead. From Murdoch himself right down to office boys there is merely a hierarchical process of inter-relating power. Inter-relating because each watches the other. Each rank is striving to become a rank above and each one above is trying to keep those below firmly in their place.

At the top is the only invulnerable factor. A palace coup in the Murdoch camp is impossible. The Murdoch family are held tightly together with a terrific feeling of kinsmanship. They own Cruden Investments which in turn owns the majority of News Limited—which in turn owns fifty per cent of News International. This gives Murdoch a unique position of strength and responsibility—and also almost unlimited power over every last man in the organization.

Murdoch does seem to have something of an obsession about

the number of hours a man works for him each day. Most of
his top executives work a twelve-hour day and gradually they
get the same obsession. Murdoch himself works mainly between
eight in the morning and eight in the evening and expects
his top executives to be available if he should want them.

It was pointed out several times by middle-rank executives
that the number of hours on their own could often be irrelevant.
One said, 'I have known men working under pressure who
could put two hours into one. But when things got slack they
hated sitting around doing nothing.'

He also felt it was counterproductive to expect a man to
work too hard too long. The very nature of newspaper publishing means he is often under pressures and after about eight
hours the average man does not give his best.

Every few months the London executive of Murdoch's newspapers go off together for the weekend to a country pub for a
'constructive booze-up'. Here they spend two days swapping
ideas and getting to know each other on a more informal basis.
Murdoch has his senior men, and their wives, out to Coopersale,
his country home near Epping, for the weekend for informal
get-togethers.

Against this background of major executive power the full
drama of corporation politics is played. The game has several
levels. On the one side, probably the most important, is Management *v* the Men: running a competent organization and
persuading all employees to produce as much as possible for
as little cost as possible. This equation is, of course, the major
task of any board and the end result of how they play the
game is profit or loss. Murdoch's management are very good
at keeping the equation very much on their side—despite the fact
that they pay—over the whole spectrum of the organization—
as much as anyone else in Fleet Street, although this not the
case in Holt Street.

Secondly, the area has its purely journalistic level of operation.
However far you go with the figures you must still come back
to the basic product—newspapers. And this produces its own
set of military tactics. There are constant wars over journalists'
expenses. Fights over who should get what television advertising

on what story. Policy decisions and battles to get controversial stories in the paper. It is in this context that the Murdoch organization is a little different to others. Murdoch, as supreme commander, will leave most decisions to the chain of command below him—but they can come up again through the ranks direct to him personally with surprising speed. He probably makes more decisions at more levels than any other managing director of any concern of comparable size. Certainly a lot more than any other newspaper proprietor.

Probably because of Murdoch's direct involvement deep into the organization. News International is in the main, tough, hard-working and generally harmonious. Few people who, in any way, disrupt the harmony, last for any length of time on the second floor. And this has led to some interesting sidelights to the Bouverie Street drama as a whole. Not everyone fits in with the Murdoch method of operating.

Since Murdoch's arrival in London—and his subsequent breaking into America—executive control in the organization has begun to take on dramatic changes. Generally speaking the executives of past years have been people who knew Murdoch when he was in Adelaide. Now, although the Adelaide influence is still strong, a new breed of executives is being carefully bred up from the bowels of the company. Murdoch has a very keen eye on anyone with potential. Now that he has begun to consolidate his forces he can look back through the organization to tomorrow's men. I predict that in terms of management there will be something of a free-for-all war very shortly. The second strata of executive power (advertising and promotion managers and the like), has a lot of ambitious talent lurking in its midst— men who are ready to pounce when they feel the time is right and a lot who are quite convinced they are heading for the high spots.

From the editorial angle the position is a little different. The organization is getting so large now that journalists with little management experience are going to find it far more difficult to get into Murdoch management in the future. Unlike the past when they could bridge the gap overnight, now they will find themselves confronted with a new breed of men, emerging from

other divisions of the organization, who did not necessarily
come up through editorial ranks.

But News Limited is, after all, a publishing company special-
izing in newspapers. And there will always be editors and
editorial directors. And this is where the new Murdoch con-
solidation is gaining ground fast. A young journalist who gets
spotted doing well on one of the Australian provincial papers,
for instance, will find himself with a highly constructive ladder
in front of him. If he can make it, the sky's the limit.

Mark Day, news editor in Sydney, is a typical example of the
many up-and-coming young journalists of middle rank who are
being bred by the organization for future executive possibilities.
Day was spotted when he was a political roundsman in Adelaide.
He broke several important exclusives and was pointed out to
Murdoch at an early age. They sent him to Broken Hill, the
proverbial training ground, and he continued to show promise.
Broken Hill, small though it was, was the first rung of the
ladder. His experience there gained him a visit to New York
where he was legman and general dogsbody to the major staff
there. He was seen to blossom out and broaden and was brought
back as editor of the *Adelaide Sunday Post*. Each of the steps he
has taken have so far been carefully worked out and watched.
After experience as an editor on a small weekly paper he was
brought into Sydney as news editor. This was to give him experience of competitive daily journalism and to see if he could
stand up to the tough boys on the *Daily Mirror*. If he is successful he will be brought to London to be put under the scrutiny
of Lamb and his colleagues for a couple of years on both the
News of the World and the *Sun*. On going back to Australia he
will probably become an editor.

'If he doesn't bust a gut trying,' Murdoch told me, 'he will
almost certainly go far in the organization. The trouble with
Day is—he wants my job.'

There are many Mark Days hovering around the middle
orders of News Limited. All of them are being carefully watched
and nurtured from above. Murdoch wants them to get a completely all-round experience. As it stands they can get this
within the organization itself. 'With a lot of them the only

trouble is that they try to go too far too fast,' he said.

But Murdoch likes aggressive ambition in his young potentials. In fact it is an essential ingredient. Day said, in all seriousness, 'I started off knowing I would get to the top. I have never doubted it. If I haven't got very close to Murdoch's job by the time I'm forty I shall go into politics. I'll go for the top job there too.'

In Britain the situation is a little different. Murdoch does not have the daily provincial press he has in Australia and little chance of spotting a youngster who has potential. To a certain extent by the time a young journalist has made it to the *Sun* or the *News of the World*, he has already proved his potential on other people's newspapers.

V

As pure circus the Rupert Murdoch–Paul Hamlyn marriage simply cannot be beaten. It is a cameo of top executive fun and games. By looking directly at Hamlyn, one learns a lot about Murdoch. Not so much by what Hamlyn actually says about him—more a matter of studying the interaction of the two forces.

Like many of his books Hamlyn is an instant man. Like many of his books too, he is highly successful. Hamlyn is a whizz-kid publisher who sold the 'Paul Hamlyn' publishing concern to IPC in exchange for a small fortune and a job. He was not very happy at Holborn Circus, or come to that, in Bouverie Street. He now runs 'Octopus Books' from his opulent offices in Grosvenor Street, Mayfair, and is 'very happy' again. He is a very quotable man producing in conversation more usable words than any other similar person. He may not know Rupert as intimately as others claim to, and much of what he says may well be the coloured flamboyance of his own opinion. But he gives a great illusion of intimacy. You certainly *feel* he knows Murdoch as well as most people.

Despite a slight speech impediment, which he ignores with gusto, he breezes confidently around obviously very pleased with who and what he is. He has the sort of charm reserved by naughty children which is both characteristically irrepressible and irresistible. He is outwardly distinguished, very rich, spoilt and public-schoolish. He is trendy, fashionable, lovable, intimate, fun-loving, expansive and extravagant. He is a belligerently tasteful playboy who nearly always gets what he wants.

He is given to throwing 'fun' parties where he delights in arranging meetings between bitter enemies. He rarely runs out of new ideas to entertain his guests. Before his recent marriage he was one of the most eligible bachelors in Europe. He spoilt his girlfriends madly and is spontaneously generous to everyone he knows and likes. He also happens, in passing, to be a brilliant publisher. Hamlyn is very much one of those tubular steel and glass people dreamt up by *Vogue*.

Hamlyn and Murdoch made a most unlikely partnership. Their friendship is remarkable on its own, but they must have made the strangest bedfellows ever in publishing administration. Hamlyn's days at the *News of the World* were rather like an operatic farce within a farce. Here were two irrepressible prima donnas, both used to the limelight, with Alex McKay (the impresario?) trying to create the sort of tranquillity which would enable both of them to share the same top of the bill.

Clearly it was impossible. And both later claimed they knew it would be before it started. There is a slight discrepancy concerning who exactly did what when one looks at all the available versions. Murdoch and McKay claim Hamlyn told them he would never join the board unless he had a big title and lots of responsibility. McKay said he wanted to be a senior executive or managing director. 'Well, of course, Rupert would never agree to that. There was no way in which it could happen. So he said he would settle for joint managing director. Rupert told him emphatically that it would merely be a title. To all intents and purposes Rupert would still be managing director—full time.'

Paul Hamlyn counters, 'Rupert 'phoned me up one day, out of the blue, and said, "I want you to be my joint managing director". I said, "Don't be fucking daft". You know, before I ever really thought about it I knew it would never work. But

Rupert was adamant. So I said I'd give it a try. It was doomed to failure from the start.'

Alex McKay, of course, was a friend of Hamlyn's at IPC, and he probably knew him even better than Murdoch did. McKay wanted the marriage to last, in the beginning anyway. He took the tension out of the situation more times than most people can remember. The Hamlyn–Murdoch affair is a very typical example of the McKay intrigue and diplomacy which is so well known on the second floor at Bouverie Street. In effect Hamlyn wanted to play a much bigger part in the running of News International. But Murdoch is very much an early starter. By the time Paul Hamlyn strolled in for elevenses, most of the day's major decisions had been made. His main function at News International was to look after Bemrose newspapers which, in fact, are a very important section of the organization responsible on their own for a large profit every year. 'But I am essentially not a newspaper man,' Hamlyn admits. 'In fact I think the only really important contribution I made over there was to convert one of those awful dismal offices into something worth living in.'

Hamlyn and Murdoch met in Singapore when they were both there on business. The two struck up a friendship and Hamlyn met Murdoch again several times in Australia. The two publishers had discussions long into the night at Yass, Murdoch's home. There was something in each which appealed to the other. Neither describes the friendship as particularly deep, but they were attracted to each other. Hamlyn could never master finding a word when trying to describe how Murdoch acted. Instead he would fall off in mid-sentence and gesticulate in the air wildly throwing his hands around in every direction and lifting both legs right off the floor. He would say, 'Murdoch's so [gesticulation]. You know what I mean.'

Of their friendship he says they have always been good friends and still are. He has a tremendous respect and liking for Rupert as a person. But does not think Murdoch is the type to have really deep friendships. He goes through periods of great intimacy with people and then a general repression sets into the relationship. He thinks his greatest friend and ally in the world is his wife Anna. She has a wonderful influence over him. Rupert, according to Hamlyn, is very much a one-woman man, who does not feel comfortable with women as a rule.

Hamlyn went on to describe the type of 'relationship' he had with Murdoch. 'I think he needs people like me around. Someone who doesn't owe him a living. I am very rich in my own right and I don't need him like many others do. I can tell him what I feel about him and I often did. He did the same to me of course, as well. But that's what he needs and he doesn't get enough of it. People like Murdoch are vulnerable to becoming pompous in their middle age if you spoil them too much. Alex McKay is the only one who can really handle him. Alex does a lot more than even Rupert realizes. He keeps a tranquillity at Bouverie Street and I think the whole thing would work a lot less well if that tranquillity wasn't there to form a buffer between Murdoch's [gesticulation], you know, and the rest of the organization. Alex is someone who can calm everything down when it gets too heated. Rupert tends to come through everything like a whirlwind. Someone has to be behind him to settle the waters and start implementing it all. Alex is a father figure and all the younger men find they can come to him when they get het up and he will give constructive sympathy and advice. He is an immense diplomat and more than Rupert's right-hand man. He reads Rupert like a book—but only ever takes advantage of that for Rupert's own good.'

He added he had a different kind of relationship with Murdoch, agreeing neither of them could serve under the same flag. Both of them are far too used to being the boss. They are both temperamental. 'I love to run things my way and I am basically motivated by a sense of fun. Murdoch is far more serious. I love to *love* business. And rightly or wrongly my way works for me.'

Murdoch and Paul Hamlyn were involved when Hamlyn was at IPC. Hamlyn wanted Murdoch to try for IPC, and says he would certainly have gone in with him in a very big way.

IPC certainly would have been a better proposition for the marriage of these two unlikely characters in a business which had so many different areas to it. It must be open to opinion whether the flirtation at this time was ethical or not. Cudlipp and Hamlyn parted on less than amicable terms. When Hamlyn finally resigned and told Cudlipp he would probably be joining Murdoch, Cudlipp was hopping mad. He told Hamlyn that he and Murdoch would never hit it off. 'You'll last under a year,' he said. In fact the two got on for two years.

But Hamlyn, like Alex McKay, had a unique opportunity of seeing at first hand the corridors of power in the rival camps. With the two of them in his stable Murdoch was able to predict almost anything IPC would be doing next. Hamlyn maintains the *Sun* will inevitably take over from the *Mirror*. It could be next year or it might take ten years but it will happen. It will happen because Rupert is a better newspaperman than anyone else around, and he still has so much to offer. Hamlyn's own attitude is very simple. He backs his judgement with hard cash and still leaves more than two million pounds in the company because of two basic reasons.

'If newspapers *do* have a heyday, Rupert will have ten per cent more of a heyday. If they don't Rupert will have ten per cent less of a hard time,' he says.

Hamlyn maintains that thinking of the Murdoch organization as a one-man band is a misconception. Too many people think that. But there are a lot of people around. He thinks all the various sections of the organization could run themselves without him. But the huge difference between the way Murdoch runs things and what happens at IPC is that Murdoch knows everyone and everything about his organization. He can meet an advertising department junior on the stairs and say 'Hallo Bob. Congratulations for getting those two pages from Woolworths.' Nothing is too small for Murdoch to notice. And no one is too junior. At IPC, he adds, nobody really knows what anyone else is doing. Editorial would know very little about advertising or promotions. And very high up there on the top floor there is a board which stays on the top floor. But Hamlyn also maintains that someone has got to give way in the circulation war between the *Sun* and the *Mirror*. Both of them are spending money out of all proportion to the situation. He thinks the *Mirror* would like to stop if Rupert would. But he can't see Murdoch stopping.

Hamlyn accuses Murdoch of sometimes not seeming to be really aware of the shareholders. It is not that he is contemptuous of them, he just seems not to worry about them. Hamlyn wanted to produce a really nice annual report, for instance. He thought the shareholders deserved something attractive. 'The report they have been getting is atrocious. I thought a couple of hundred getting a really nice design and display would have been worth bothering about. After all, it's not even a second of television time. But he voted the idea down.' Murdoch countered, 'It's the figures inside the damned thing that count—not what it looks like.'

Hamlyn feels the really interesting period of Rupert's life is still to come. The organization is now on a very sound business and financial footing. The company will make a lot of money and it is one of the best long-term investments in this country.

Murdoch has never, in Hamlyn's knowledge, made a bad business deal. Every aspect of his Australian concerns are built on brilliant moves. His getting into London Weekend Television was equally brilliant. His *Express* deal (where he bought and sold several million pounds worth of shares at large profit) was very brilliant all on its own. 'That, by the way, was as typical as you will ever find of Rupert being cheeky.' Murdoch counters, 'I could tell Paul of a few awful business deals. Real humdingers. I wish I could be that infallible.'

Unlike many Murdoch confidants Hamlyn thinks Murdoch is socially and politically ambitious. Anna is very socially ambitious for him and this will make a big difference.

Hamlyn complains that he finds Murdoch very much a person who listens to the last one he spoke to. He is very definitely impressionable. You often find you talk to him at ten o'clock and come to an agreement. Then he has lunch with someone else and completely changes his mind. By six he's had a drink with someone else and as likely as not he comes round again to his original theory.

Many other people do not agree with this assessment. It is a habit of Murdoch's they point out, to ask everyone he meets their opinion on certain problems. He listens to them all. He will ask almost anyone, whether it be journalist, director or outsider. It is probably true that he is momentarily moved by an argument. But it seems also true that he can toss it around in his own mind—building ideas with the help of other people— before he comes to his own final conclusion.

Hamlyn once held a surprise birthday party for Murdoch which was typical of his generosity to friends. Without Rupert knowing it he had sent over to Dame Elisabeth in Melbourne and had dozens of pictures of Rupert the child flown over. These he blew up until some of them were six foot by eight foot. Several of them were of baby Rupert lying nude on a rug. All Rupert's friends and acquaintances were gathered together for Murdoch's arrival for a 'quiet drink'. The champagne flowed freely. When Rupert got there he was flabbergasted to find massive pictures of him adorning every wall in the house. I asked Hamlyn if Murdoch appreciated the stunt. 'I never did find out,' he said, 'but I think he had to. There were so many people around.'

VI

There are two main tactical ploys newspaper proprietors use to influence the papers they own. The first is to work out the general editorial policy of their newspaper and its attitude to current affairs. If this is not abused, and his editorial executive gets a fair hearing, it is generally a healthy thing for that newspaper. The second ploy is when newspaper owners insidiously promote or suppress news and views about their influential friends. All newspaper owners to some extent practise the former. Most owners, to greater or lesser degree, practise the second.

In Fleet Street, generally speaking, it is the more establishment Tory newspaper journalists who find their news stories being suppressed on personal orders from the board-room.

Lord Thomson alone in Fleet Street claims he never uses his influence at any level except financial. This is hard to believe but

there is little testimony to challenge him. Very few stories have
filtered through the grapevine, which is virulently attuned to
such things, about significant Thomson pressure. Editorially,
the *Sunday Times* is probably more opinionated in all sections
of the paper than any other, but this seems to stem entirely
from the journalists themselves.

Murdoch makes no secret of the fact that he believes in his
divine right to influence his newspapers editorially, and he
does so often and with gusto. The line between the two widely
differing sorts of influence has occasionally been drawn very
thinly by Murdoch. His own personal loathing of Menzies, for
instance, dominated his newspapers for many years. But no
testimony has been provided that he ever unfairly suppressed
a story because of a friend and Murdoch strenuously detests
any man who tries to get editorial favours out of him in return
for political ones.

His sternest critics claim he interferes far too much. But
none have suggested this was to gain him political influence
or advantage. There is a strong rumour that he asked for
political favours from Gough Whitlam but the story simply
does not stand up to scrutiny. A story that Murdoch was to
accept a title from Harold Wilson in return for his support
just before Heath romped home in the 1970 election is emphatically denied by both sides. One eye-witness account insists the
offer was made and the *News of the World* did certainly come
out strongly Labour.

A more authoritative source, however, said Murdoch made
it clear almost before Wilson spoke, that he was going to plump
for him in the election. Wilson intimated if he did he would
find him appreciative. There was no mention of any specific
reward and Murdoch did not ask for one.

It seems Murdoch keeps a healthy eye on the world around
him and lets his editors know his feelings loudly whenever
he meets them. Most of the time he lets them evaluate his
feelings themselves. Beyond that Murdoch fiercely detests 'news
management' and it seems unfair for his critics to infer that his
involvements are politically devious.

But because this, with ruthlessness and muck-raking, constitutes the main areas of controversy connected to Murdoch's name, the charge must be viewed from both sides.

He is quite forthright on the subject. He believes in the right of a newspaper owner to make his own views felt in his own editorial columns.

In 1973 he inaugurated a long series in the *News of the World* called 'The Strife Makers' which exposed militant union 'trouble-makers'. This came out of a discussion he had with Larry Lamb who also liked the idea of such a story, but everyone who worked on it knew full well that Murdoch had wanted the story done. It is clear when he does get a bee in his bonnet about something, he lets everyone on his staff know about it. But his responsibilities as a publisher now keep him often far above the day-to-day wrangles of editorial policy.

'Of course I intervene,' he says. 'I intervene because I am the one who is responsible—not only for the paper that is produced, not only to the law, not only to the shareholders and to the banks that have staked us, or the mortgages, or whatever, but also to the people working for the newspaper— and that means everyone depending on it for a living.'

He claims the whole existence of a newspaper organization— its viability—depends on the product it turns out. It is nonsense to say that the man who is going to be held responsible— physically, financially, legally, and in every other way—must not be seen or known to exercise that responsibility.

Running a newspaper organization, he maintains, is not something done by stealth. Clearly, when you are operating inside the glass palaces of newspaper offices the closer the rapport between a newspaper proprietor and a newspaper editor, the better it is for all concerned. Sometimes this rapport is instantaneous; usually it evolves. Either way, it is fundamental. A publisher, he goes on to claim, cannot abdicate his responsibilities to an editor. Practical considerations compel him to delegate many of them, and this can only be done on a basis of mutual trust and understanding.

During an interview he extended his analysis by admitting there was editorial interference all the way but claimed there was nothing sinister in it. If he was interfering in a narrow manager's sense he would consider it very bad. On the other hand, newspapers would suffer if owners did not interfere in any way at all. All successful companies are personalized. They are the work of someone building them up. He says the idea of committee management doesn't really work. 'I like to run the business like a corner grocery. I find it very difficult to grow out of this. If you can't show you can do the job yourself, or be intelligent about it, or take an interest in it, it's very hard to get others to do it too.' He agrees you have got to delegate responsibility everywhere, in the editorial sense, but that doesn't stop you from going up for twenty minutes for a briefing with the editor before you go home. 'I don't ram ideas down his throat. But I'm certain we influence each other. I spend every opportunity I can with Larry or his people and he's entitled to disagree with me.'

Murdoch says he stays close to the job rather than interfere with it. He likes to know what is going on and dashes around in a 'rather Dylan Thomasish sort of way'. The effect of this—apart from making the very major decisions in business—is to give some impetus and surprise. 'As long as you can do that, it's fine,' he adds.

VII

Murdoch is the kind of man who rarely questions himself or what he is doing. He tends to take it for granted that what he is doing, and how he is doing it, is correct. Under criticism of a direct nature he tends to get hurt and he rarely forgives someone who has hurt him. When he reads something nasty about himself he does not get angry so much as incredulous. A rather bitchy profile of him written by the *Sunday Times*, hurt him very deeply. But his attitude was 'look at this, how *could* they write things like that'. He was genuinely perturbed that anyone could dislike him so much. When told of criticism he shrugs in a sort of helpless way because the person who has had a go at him has probably never met him. He rarely tries to justify himself to critics rather letting his executives fight in his defence, which, to a man, they ferociously do.

It is difficult to know whether he has ever really thought about what he is doing. Policy meetings are few and far between in the Murdoch organization. Everything is kept informal and 'Australian'. Where the paper stands on abortions, for instance, will invariably be worked out beside the swimming pool at Coopersale over an after-lunch chat. He does not drop little notes to his staff like so many of his predecessors have done and there are few records of his thinking. He is a telephone man. He is impatient with writing because it wastes time. (A good job too. He writes so fast and with such nervous energy it is rather difficult to read.)

He is a showman but only within the confines of his castle. There are therefore extremely few sources of information about his thinking and philosophy available to the biographer. No historical miles of writing like Beaverbrook or Northcliffe. He is on record, in the main, only by word of mouth and that often suffers from interpretation. He does not like making speeches and is generally regarded as being a poor speech-maker, although, on paper, his words are articulate and readable.

Many people have likened Murdoch to the other colonial press barons, Beaverbrook and Thomson. But really the only discernible similarity is the fact that they are colonials. They are all as unlike in character as any three people could be. Beaverbrook was a political animal using brilliant techniques of journalism to further his political aims. Thomson is a businessman using different types of equally brilliant journalistic techniques to add to his bank balance. Murdoch is interested in politics and money, but never to the same extent. He sees no similarities whatever between any of them. He feels Beaverbrook was a merchant who became a brilliant adventurer and got into politics. He agrees the late press lord had immense flair and gave his newspapers a great deal of personality. 'I admire the technical expertise of the *Express*,' he said, 'but I didn't much admire what Beaverbrook stood for. In some ways he could be a wicked man in the way he manipulated people and broke them. He could corrupt people. Yet there are others who are devoted to him and say he was a wonderful and great man. It's hard to say.'

Murdoch recalls how Beaverbrook used to buy off the communist *Morning Star* editors (the *Daily Worker* in those days) and put them on the *Express*. He would take them down to the South of France, put them in luxurious conditions and bring them back and call them the 'Bollinger Bolsheviks'.

Murdoch's image outside his organization seems to worry everyone but his wife and himself. He seems oblivious to it. Anna dismisses as completely unimportant the fact that her husband is surrounded by unfair or unjust popular comment.

Paul Hamlyn assesses it by saying he is the most misunderstood man he has ever known. It got to a stage once when people would not invite Hamlyn to dinner if Murdoch's name was mentioned.

Trying to assess his reputation truthfully causes more difficulty than any other single thing about him. This is mainly because most people persist in believing the myths and any defence of Murdoch brings immediate distrust. When people actually meet him they find he shows himself to be very open and extraordinarily frank about himself and his activities. He rarely ducks questions and, on the contrary, elucidates even more than is necessary.

There are many people who talk of him as being sensitive and highly conscious of his responsibility to the public. It would be both pointless and boring to print all the quotes of this nature, but one in particular is representative of the pro-Murdoch lobby and should be put forward. It is the short statement of John Freeman who believes that, 'Rupert is the most misunderstood person in the public eye. The absolute central paradox of the man is that he is the exact opposite to his public image.'

Freeman is a good pro-Murdoch barometer because he has nothing to win or lose by liking or disliking Murdoch. Although he has not known Rupert for as long as many, there are several other reasons why his particular assessment of the situation should not be ignored. While critics could argue that people in the organization are biased in Murdoch's favour—not so Freeman. Firstly, he must be one of the most eligible managing directors in London. He took over at London Weekend Television, where News International has a large block of non-voting shares, on the understanding he would enjoy a completely free rein. He has done this—often implementing ideas which Murdoch disagrees with. In short, he does not need the job at LWT. He could find a place on almost any board in the country.

Unlike many others he is a highly trained observer of human beings. In his own right, before he leapt to the top of the British diplomatic profession, he had led current affairs television into new realms of subtlety and imagination. His 'Face to Face' interviews of the sixties have never been improved as pieces of evocative television journalism. Freeman's shrewdness and ability to pluck out of people parts of their character which had hitherto been hidden from the public eye, made weekly compulsive viewing. Always polite, yet firm, he led well-known public figures from every walk of life, into argument and eventual confession. Since then, life as ambassador in India and later Washington, has added wisdom and depth of experience to this subtlety and shrewdness. So that now he has a unique experience of summing up people and situations which must be regarded as formidable.

He admits he first approached Murdoch very warily. He had known him virtually only through reputation and that reputation was hardly flattering. He was not at all sure he would ever be able to work with him.

Freeman had been involved in the very first discussions with David Frost and others which eventually led to the formation of LWT. Because of his position in the diplomatic service he then dropped out. But he always retained an interest in the company and knew many of the people working for it. He had often toyed with the idea of joining it after he left the service, but when Murdoch became involved he more or less put the idea out of his mind. Then, out of the blue, he got a 'phone call from Sydney. Murdoch asked him, just like that, if he would join LWT. He said he would have to meet him first and this was arranged as soon as he returned. 'I found I was meeting someone completely different from my picture of him,' he said.

'Since then I have developed an affection and trust for him which is quite sincere. The central paradox of his life is that he

—a man who is completely trustworthy—is not entirely trusted
by the community in general. I honestly believe him to be a
man of deep and warm honesty, great kindness and generosity,
who reads books and collects paintings and is generally very
intelligent, well-educated and cultured. I would leave my last
nickel with Rupert. He is a straight dealer who hates double
talk. I have no doubt that in the middle of a fight Murdoch
can be as crafty as the next man—but never dishonest.'

VIII

Murdoch does his daily work behind a huge antique desk. He
sits on an executive's swivel chair which is rather like a pogo
stick. It is never still. On it he can move in any direction or in
circles and he does both all the time. On this chair he hands
out instant decisions at the rate of about twenty an hour, eleven
or twelve hours a day.

The decision-making process is perhaps the most important
saleable commodity of any tycoon; the way his mind can assess
facts, compare them with others, shade it all with experience,
surround itself with expert advice and then come to the actual
decision.

Murdoch has a great capacity for decision-making. Because
of this it is easy for him to be a gambler and, in terms of
business, a highly successful one. He rarely puzzles about the
odds. He sees what he fancies and he goes for it.

Only a gambler with his youthful aggression, his shrewd
ability to stake the cards high and the total self-assurance to
offer, unblinking, odds higher than he can afford, could have
got away with the bluff needed to dominate Fleet Street as
quickly, as effectively as Murdoch did in just five years. He does
have his little idiosyncrasies some of which can annoy people.

Paul Hamlyn said the most annoying thing about Murdoch
he could remember was he got so bored so quickly. He said he
could be talking away nineteen to the dozen and Murdoch
would suddenly pick up a letter and start reading it right in the
middle of the conversation.

Sacked assistant editor Mike Gabbert put it another way. He

said Murdoch could be as elusive as a grasshopper in conversation. You would go to him with an urgent request—say for money to advertise a particular story on TV—and he would say, 'You know, I got another puncture on my Rolls today?' So you would tut-tut about that and say, 'Well, about this TV money?'

Murdoch would interrupt, 'Have you seen the colour planning in my new women's magazine?' So you'd look at that.

Then, in desperation, you'd say, 'We really must make a decision about TV.' And Murdoch would look at his watch and tell you, 'Sorry, no time to discuss it now. I'm due at a meeting.'

Murdoch is not actually particularly mean. He has, on the contrary, often been very generous. But there is something frugal locked up somewhere in his Scottish ancestry. His own lifestyle is extremely comfortable but hardly extravagant. He can be sometimes quite obsessed by the most trivial unnecessary expense.

Murdoch tends to be really friendly only with people who work for him. Certain people who profess to know him well say his only real friend is his wife Anna. One man in particular maintained although you could like Murdoch a lot, it was almost impossible to get really close to him. Murdoch himself does not share this view. He points to a dozen people with whom he considers he has had a deep friendship and association beyond the call of business. Although ironically all of them were associated with him through business.

It is very difficult to assess. Many people claim deep friendship with Murdoch which is clearly wishful thinking or ambition. Others hold him in awe. Many say he is a likeable man but after knowing him for many years they have been unable to penetrate his thinking or emotion. Murdoch can be rather like an iceberg with a hot geyser in the middle of it. At the core he is warm-hearted and soft, but he shields this with an infinite coolness some people even term as callous. People can go in and out of favour with Murdoch very easily and are therefore often wary of the depth of their friendship. When they are in, they are very, very in, but when they are out they are finished. This does not mean to say that Murdoch's friendship and liking of someone is not deep and genuine at the time. But it is possible for him to suddenly get 'feelings' about someone, and although they *can* win back his affection and approval, it is a rare occurrence.

Some older associates of Murdoch have a rather paternal interest in him. Many of them were around when he was a green postgraduate and have retained a sort of fatherly benevolence towards him. These people are interesting because they have long since stopped trying to impress him and no longer hold him in awe. Some of them in the company openly admit they have been kept on at their jobs well past their prime, and offer this as an indication of Murdoch's loyalty and kindness.

One admitted that he knew times were changing in the company and that he could go no further. The particular section of the business he was controlling was losing money. He began to feel a bit useless and obsolete. He spoke to Murdoch frankly about his fears and Murdoch told him there was no question of his being forgotten. He had been with him since the beginning and told him he would always hold a secure position in the company.

Murdoch enjoys an extraordinary loyalty from his general executive despite the fact he is a formidable taskmaker. One managing director in the organization told me, 'I like Murdoch to be at the end of a telephone. To keep his distance. I like thinking I am working for him personally and not just the organization. But I like him to be nice and far away. It is a constant challenge to myself to decide whether I could take the sheer heat of him working in the office next door. When I am honest with myself I really don't think I could.'

Murdoch's infinite self-assurance—where he remains very much in command of his own position—is based very much on how people treat him. He probably does try to make a truthful assessment of how he stands with them. But in terms of his empire he stands on a high pillar and is the first to admit he resents people trying to rock it. It does not seem to be primarily a pillar of conceit. He is not so much self-righteous, but rather self-right. Because his way has worked so successfully for him he is convinced his way is best. He is forthright and shrewd,

able quickly to assimilate his immediate relationship with whoever he meets. After the initial humbleness wears off he likes to
take command. He has scant respect for anyone he does not
immediately trust, but with those he does he can be charmingly,
and very quickly, straightforward and friendly.

Murdoch can, on occasions, seem to be obsessed with money.
He will talk about it as a commodity and defend the last penny
he feels is being taken from him unfairly. He admits that
high finance is a deadly serious game which he enjoys but there
seems to be something of a gap between his attitude to the game
and money itself. He has a definite 'thing' about profits. He gets
positively angry about losses. He takes them very personally
and they niggle him endlessly.

Yet, when all is said and done, he has a quite genuine disregard for the stuff. It is as if the figures of his companies are
an end in themselves. He likes to see concise balance sheets
showing clear and neat profits. He is far more content fiddling
with figures on the back of an envelope than he is handling the
paper money itself. Money, as such, is of little interest or use to
him. His pleasures are simple and relatively inexpensive. He
does have lovely properties, but even on the farm at Yass he
cannot resist the temptation of saying with a great deal of pride,
'It is very useful at the moment as a tax loss. But when I've
done everything here I want to do, it should bring me in about
twenty or thirty thousand dollars a year which will be four or
five per cent return on my capital outlay.'

His relationship with money is very similar to his relationship
with power. It was put forward to me time and again that the
motivation behind his infinite drive was the pursuit of money
and power. But I firmly believe, although he will pursue both
with outrageous ardour, it is the game of getting them rather
than the beauty of having them, which really drives him on.

IX

Murdoch appears to have little personal ambition yet cannot
resist aiming higher and higher. This is one of the many, many
inconsistencies in his personality. He is, for instance, close to

politics, yet never lets politics get too close to him. He is keenly
intelligent but rarely intellectual. He loves artistic things but
has little knowledge of or interest in abstract arguments or
even the theory of art.

Murdoch's inconsistencies become an important part in any
assessment of him. Gradually, as you look at all the arguments
behind his rise to power, two clear patterns emerge. On the one
hand, there is a highly complicated set of theories which are,
by far, the most attractive and to which it is easy to succumb.
On the other hand, there is a single 'uncomplicated' argument,
strongly expressed by many people, which appears too easy for
so complicated a man, but which is probably nearer the truth.
Many people who claim to know Murdoch well, expound deep
theories on the vast and dark mysteries surrounding his psyche
and lifestyle. They maintain he is a highly complex individual
and his basic drive is motivated by very definite and intriguing
factors. This argument goes on that he was overawed by his
father, academically humiliated at Geelong and Oxford, and
has spent the rest of his life proving he was not the dunce
they thought he was. Pundits of this argument insist he had
an odd relationship with his father which resulted in the
twenty-two-year-old postgraduate arriving in Adelaide with a
burning desire to outdo the paternal image in every way. Murdoch cynics extend this reasoning by adding he is greedy for
money and power and everything he acquires is merely a new
toy to amuse himself with before adding it to the main power
structure of his empire. Certainly, at times, Murdoch's behaviour
adds credence to this speculation, but although none of this is
without some kind of truthful foundation, it does bend and
exaggerate the truth.

The diametrically-opposed argument is that Murdoch is not
deep enough to be so devious or have such intriguing complexes.
They say he is, in effect, a man of simplicity who is essentially
a fidget. A man with a massive energy drive who cannot sit
down for a minute without looking around for something to do.
Power and money mean little to him. He has, they say, simply
got too much adrenalin in his blood stream. He is not deep but
superficial and is driven through nerve. He certainly *is* a fidget,

but the notion that this alone drives him on through so many powerful successes is something which is hard to believe.

Murdoch can change from self-assurance to sudden indecision where he wants immediate response from his executive. He is given to quick moods of anger which can pass just as quickly. In the main a row the night before is forgotten in the morning, although Murdoch will harbour a deep resentment for someone who has really offended him. He can be sulky and a little petulant at times and occasionally feels the need to be a bit spoilt by his closer associates. He can on occasions be very arrogant. He is used to dismissing conversations, however short, if they are not to the point and dislikes people who interrupt when he is talking. He likes getting his own way and can get quite piqued if things go wrong. But he will change his mind quite graciously if someone puts up a reasonable argument and he nearly always apologizes if he feels he has been unfair. He can be highly considerate. A typical story of his humanity is the one about the reporter he kept late on a story. He personally spent twenty minutes trying to get a mini-cab to take the man home.

I do not mean to overplay the major character split in his life. In most circumstances Murdoch is basically a rather unspectacular man who runs his life coolly and efficiently without a lot of fuss. He is not troubled by much, works very hard and with a great deal of energy, and lives a fairly reserved life. He is a domestic person and very much of an ordinary human being.

The inconsistencies in his nature only come out from time to time. These indicate that underneath the image of the simple, hard-working life he likes to lead, there could be a highly complex person with a most intriguing nature.

Murdoch can call upon a wide breadth of maturity with which he can hold his own against the most formidable of brains. And yet, conversely, he can be petulantly childish or attractively boyish in the most disarming of fashions. Murdoch has proved he can move among politicians, bankers, businessmen and other such top professionals, with the utmost diplomacy. And yet can suddenly be clumsy and make a hurtful comment to someone without ever realizing the implications of his remark.

He has shown, over the years, quite extraordinary kindness and generosity to people throughout his organization, yet is able to be quite ruthless with someone who he believes to have wronged him in, sometimes, the most insignificant of ways. He can memorize infinite details of the most complicated sort, yet forget some stretches of his life within which much of importance occurred. He can be cold and apparently devoid of feeling, yet can get emotionally upset and very depressed at the death of someone with whom he was only vaguely acquainted. He can niggle over pennies, yet spend millions at the wave of a hand. He can bellyache over the price of an executive lunch, yet, days later, send the same executive halfway round the world with the wife at the expense of the organization. Murdoch is suspicious of anything which is way-out or trendy, but is deeply fascinated by new ideas and the Left. He can be set in his ways and ideas—to the point of stubbornness—yet is impressionable and can suddenly change when he has met an intelligent argument.

He needs the cut and thrust of politics almost as if it were a drug; yet likes nothing better than to wander around his farm in the moonlight. He can be incredibly evasive about very small points but suddenly expand in infinite detail about things of a highly personal or confidential nature. He can be devious in the political sense, immersing himself in intrigue, yet be naive about something very simple which everyone has warned him against.

He can be quite brazen about serious critics but get incredibly hurt by a chance remark pointed against him. He is unpretentious in his private life yet can be suddenly highly flamboyant and splash out in every direction. He dislikes snobbery, but can succumb completely to the atmosphere of the landed gentry.

He can rush around one of his newspapers, charming everyone out of their seats and be highly complimentary about what they are all doing. He will suddenly instil around him a great sense of good feeling and importance. Yet the following day he will storm around ranting and raving about a front-page layout.

He can puff up the confidence of a cadet reporter by asking him important questions about the paper he is working on; yet bring a top executive down to complete humility by countermanding his simplest order.

His behaviour follows no real pattern and one must take Murdoch as one finds him. There are, of course, many consistencies to his nature. Yet it must be confusing to those close to him never to really know what will be happening next.

The quirks and undulations of Murdoch's mind react to sudden impulse and impression. He is moved by mood. Yet there is a something locked within him which always strikes a cautious note. Somehow he speculates and gambles with a brashness inconceivable to less adventurous minds. But at the end of the day there is a decision which is quite definite.

Most people who know him say that deep inside Murdoch he has inherited the reserved shyness of his father. I think it a fair assessment. He is slightly awkward with people he meets for the first time and is a firm believer that he should be on highly intimate terms with those who work for him. Yet Murdoch can show a boisterous confidence and exuberance which is the antithesis of shyness.

He can be boyishly humble yet aggressively arrogant. He can talk about himself in a deprecatory fashion, yet sometimes show a spring of egotism from which he will bounce higher and higher in his own esteem. He believes completely in his own judgement yet will ask advice on the most mundane of points. He loves underlings who argue with him and yet gets annoyed when they disagree with one of his sudden enthusiasms.

He has a suspicion of 'yes men' but surrounds himself with a buffer state of men who have nearly always said yes. 'The point of surviving in a Murdoch camp,' said one managing director, 'is to know exactly when to stop. You can raise a point and if you know you are right you can argue your point fiercely. But you must have the sense of timing to know when Murdoch has made his mind up one way or the other. You are in serious trouble if you continue to argue beyond that point. He will listen to you, argue with you, even be swayed by you; but then suddenly you know that the decision has been made in his mind. He will immediately become bored with the subject and to continue raising arguments will niggle him beyond repair.'

In fact Murdoch is very much of a typical Piscean. It amused me, after getting confused with the two sides of his nature, to remember that the sign of Pisces is that of the two fishes swimming in opposite directions.

Murdoch has a remarkable memory for detail and a huge ability to concentrate. His mind is not over-objective nor scientific but almost psychic. He has a unique gift of being able to 'feel' something out rather than simply 'think' it through normal channels. It often seems, to close observers, that Murdoch has access to a secret fund of information available to him alone. He is adept at the art of lateral thinking, and can strip a problem down to the bone so that he knows how to deal with it. His mind can grasp around all four corners of it and under and over it rather than tackling it head on. He has often made very definite statements for which, at first, there seems little source or proof. It appears as if he has plucked ideas right out of the sky.

There are also rare occasions when Murdoch can be subject to fantasy. Not in any serious sense but enough to affect his attitudes. At other times his creative imagination can be extraordinary. His mind puzzles the average person. When thinking something out he seems to be reasoning in an abstract fashion. Yet when put to the test it is his intuition and common-sense which prevail. This confuses a lot of people because it often looks as if his actions are different from his ideals. There are occasions when it seems as though Murdoch is completely non-operative. But it is at this very stage that he is deepest in creative thought. The depths of his subconscious are fermenting and the results are always formidable. This is an important period of mental gestation for Murdoch in which he can cram a long thought process into a few moments. Murdoch the Piscean is highly sensitive to his surroundings and to the people he is mixing with. If he feels uncomfortable he is inclined to keep quiet and become reserved. When he meets people for the first time he affects a roll to his walk and a nervous smile which clearly indicates his discomfort. There is nothing Murdoch dislikes more than to be surrounded by affected women chattering to him at a cocktail party.

On the other hand, when he is in company he trusts and likes he can go to the other extreme and be very much the 'king of the kids'. He is fluent but sometimes careless in his speech. At heart he is something of a romantic with a subtle and artistic streak which is not sparked so much by virility than by sensitivity. He is highly receptive to outside influences and this could make him vulnerable to long periods of stress.

But, with all this, one must not foster an unfair picture of the man and his way of life. His behaviour pattern is not normally erratic to the extent described. He can be changeable and he can be most certainly unpredictable. But Murdoch, more often than not, wakes up in a good mood and stays that way all day. By pointing out the converse structure of his nature one is dealing more with the extreme than the normal.

There is a side to the Murdoch nature which is immediately appealing. He generates a warmth which in turn demands friendship. You start off with 'the big ruthless boss' image and end with the human being. And the human being is surprisingly vulnerable, frank, open and sometimes even insecure. Here is a man who is saying to you very openly that he has a need to be liked but at the same time probably without ever realizing it, he generates an atmosphere in which you also feel the need to be liked by him.

He has the ability to relax but you are never quite sure whether it is a pose or not. He slouches back in his chair, speaks much slower than when you first met him, and is apparently at ease. But, very suddenly, the chance question will bring him quickly back into nervous gesticulation. It is very difficult to decide at which point the Murdoch mind changes. At one stage of any conversation the whole mood will change. You are plunged again, and very immediately, into the business world which is the bastion of the Murdoch self-defence.

X

Murdoch is a robust man who sometimes seems fastidious and

yet slightly crumpled at the same time. He is of modest appearance. Sometimes allowing himself the slight garishness of a bright, spotted tie, and he is always soberly suited and generally well groomed.

In his early forties he now has deep jowls to his cheeks which become tanned and wan depending on whether he is in Australia or England. He is not a handsome man in the photogenic sense. But because of his soft brown eyes, rather cheeky grin and impish countenance, he is considered attractive. Although his wife Anna beseeches him to exercise (mainly swimming, walking and tennis) as frequently as possible, when he does so the 'desk habit' causes him to be a little short of breath rather quickly. He is soft-spoken and his accent is attractive in a peculiar fast sort of drawl. It is a Melbourne accent occasionally lending itself to some Sydney harshness and a sprinkling of London cockney and Oxford English.

He fidgets endlessly and doodles on the backs of envelopes when talking or listening. His politeness is never exaggerated but well-mannered. His door is always 'open' and endless cycles of executives pop their heads round during the course of any working day. His hair is just beginning to recede at the temples revealing the tell-tale worried forehead. When thinking deeply, it furrows into three or four deep lines which fluctuate up and down as something captures or surprises him.

Although Murdoch has a chauffeur-driven Mercedes, he comes to work by the ordinary underground railway. His 'runaround' car at home is an average family four-door saloon. He did once try and save journey time by coming to work by helicopter. But he found the journey from the heliport, south of the Thames, to Bouverie Street, took almost as long as Epping to Bouverie Street by car. The roads out of East London are perhaps the most inadequate in the capital and Murdoch found he could be stuck in traffic jams for hours on end. For someone who likes to hang his jacket up on the back of his office door by about eight o'clock, this proved highly frustrating for him. Apart from this, Murdoch suffers from travel sickness and he found he could not even read on the journey. 'By tube I can get a seat early on at the departure point, get whisked to within two hundred yards of the office within half an hour, and read all the morning papers at my leisure,' he said.

He added that he is not exposed to the British public enough for him to be made uncomfortable by staring fellow passengers. Anna, however, is reputed to have said in one of her humorous moods that Rupert only goes by tube because he likes ogling the young secretaries and shop assistants who flock into central London by underground every day.

Coopersale, the Epping mansion and farm, is a delightful and desirable property. It milks about a hundred Channel Island cows and is a neat, trim, businessman's farm yielding a small, but tidy, profit.

The sprawling, spacious house itself commands a view over rolling, meticulously landscaped mini-downs which flow down over grassy ridges to a rippling lake.

A short way down the road from the farm is a huge, very English wood full of oaks and elms and possessing that gorgeous leafy, musty, rustic smell which can be found nowhere else but in dew-soaked and shaded English woodland. Murdoch takes regular weekend strolls for a few miles across the moulding glades. Although 'stroll' is probably the wrong word. Murdoch strides and marches at a terrific pace, puffing heavily as he charges up hills and almost running as he descends the other side. He walks nearly every Sunday afternoon after lunch and comes back to tea in front of the log-fire and a romp with the children. There are very few Sunday lunches without a lunch guest or two and they are invited, in the winter, to walk with him (scampering after him as he charges across fences, streams and anything else which gets in his way). Or, in summer, a game of tennis or a swim in the half Olympic-size pool which can be inside or outside at the press of a button.

It is a comfortable, airy place, rather unpretentious and full of the Murdoch personal art collection. It seems 'lived in' but tidy in the sort of disorganized way in which *au pairs* might leave it. Yet it has an uncanny feel of temporariness about it. As if the decorations had just been finished after they had moved in, yet the suitcases were still packed and ready for the move out. It did not have that sense of permanence which most mansion houses have because of their ancestral qualities and 'feel' of family dynasty. Maybe it was because Murdoch *is* always on the move one sees it in that way. But the place—all Murdoch 'places' come to that—has its share of dust-sheets very near the top of the chest of drawers.

There is always an *au pair* ('only non-smokers should apply') to help with the three children (Murdoch's oldest girl from his former marriage goes to boarding school). The Murdoch family also have, apart from the general farm workers, and the chauffeur, a housekeeper-cook, a butler-handyman and a gardener. Murdoch also has a personal couple working for him in his suite in Bouverie Street. Mainly employed cooking and serving his office lunches ('they're cheaper to run than most restaurant prices these days'). It is true to say then, that, although the Murdochs remain basically family-orientated, many of the tribulations which beset typical families are looked after by some seven or eight paid employees.

Murdoch sometimes seems a little incongruous in his traditional English surroundings. He is never too sure of the English custom of male servants. And now and again, especially when he breaks out into typical Australianisms ('that old poofta'), it seems out of place in the environment of delicate bone china teacups in front of the farm-house fire. He appears much more happy and buoyant when charging across the outback at Cavan, than he does in the rather drizzly, dull days at Coopersale. In England he seems as serious as the sombre grey sky and the tragic wet oaks. At Cavan he appears excited and youthful (I do not say childish, but, certainly, he treated everything we saw on the ranches almost like a child would show off his Christmas toys to his best friend).

At Cavan the lack of 'permanence' is obviously very understandable on the grounds that, at the very most, the family can only spend about two months a year there. Yet it is more simply and conveniently furnished with big heavy old-fashioned tables and chairs in the dining room and comfortably deep sofas in the living room. The Murdochs seem to belong to Cavan, even though it has to be their very temporary home. Murdoch does, in fact, want to go back and live there per-

manently 'as soon as it is feasible'. But few people seriously
think this will be before at least another ten years.

Murdoch stops fidgeting at home. He is quite clearly able
to relax when in the company of his family. He does try and
take weekends off completely from work so he can 'recharge
batteries' and, although I suspect that without a telephone,
television and constant visitors to keep him in touch with the
outside world, he might find it difficult, he spends as much time
with his children as he can.

The Murdoch children are not spoilt in any particular way;
nor are they crushed as individuals. They are noisy, boisterous
and full of impish naughtiness. They have lots of toys to play
with and lots of wide open spaces to play with them in. Anna
remains quiet and serene while the baby cries and the other
two pull at her skirt. Rupert is more impatient. He growls at
them now and then and does the stern father glare when they
make too much noise while he is speaking. But in reality he is
very soft with them, probably in the same way that Sir Keith was
with his children. I think he is probably a very good father,
when he has time to be, and there is no doubt at all he is very
proud of being one. He takes an active interest in their welfare,
schooling and home life although he leaves the day-to-day
running of the family very much to his wife. The after-Sunday-
tea few hours with the kids is a Murdoch ritual. He does not
share the traditional British distance from children with his
rich and influential counterparts on this side of the world.

You are immediately aware from the whole atmosphere of
the Murdoch family—despite the informality—that the tiny
and defenceless child being fed by the *au pair*, is very much
heir to the Murdoch throne.

Anna Murdoch is pretty, fashionable, witty and excellent
company. She gently chides her husband when she thinks he
is being a little boorish ('Gently chides me—she tears me to
pieces!') He values her opinion and asks for it often. They keep
an excellent table in a pleasant family atmosphere.

Anna can hold her own with all the guests who flock to the
Murdoch homesteads for Sunday lunch. And there is no doubt
that she enjoys it. She has a gentle quality and an English-rose

complexion which does nothing to hide the keen intelligence hidden beneath it.

She is ambitious for her husband and deadly in his defence. She is utterly unpretentious and I suspect pompous people who meet her might find the tranquillity of her countenance hides a rather sharp tongue. Little daunts her and she has a rather roguish sense of humour.

At a party in 1973, given to celebrate the *Sun* turning three million circulation, someone pushed Rupert into the swimming pool. It was typical of Anna that, seconds later, fully clothed, she should jump in and join her husband.

XI

Under the owlish countenance of Lord Goodman, the Newspaper Publishers' Association forms the central stage whereby the various clan chieftains of Fleet Street show their strengths and their weaknesses. Although the NPA gathers mainly to deal with unions and strikes it is where all the central characters from the board-rooms of Fleet Street collect in one place at one time.

There is evidence to suggest that there have been moves among the members of the NPA to discredit Murdoch at a high level. Obviously he does not belong to the old stock of newspaper proprietors and is certainly treated with caution by the old guard. Despite his great talent for negotiation most other newspaper owners would love to see Murdoch lose his battles, even with his unions. There is also a certain amount of jealousy at this top level. After all, only five years ago many of them were planning to close up because they felt there was so little future in Fleet Street.

Murdoch did not take the manoeuvrings at the NPA too seriously. He is as good as anyone at playing the game although he is sometimes isolated. He claims he had learnt early on that in Fleet Street people often shake hands on an agreement while they are with you and conspire against you as soon as you have turned your back.

The circulation war between the *Sun* and the *Mirror* was

being fought as fiercely at the NPA, in one way or another, as it was in Fleet Street itself. In between this particular game other publishers bounced from side to side as the scores mounted up between opponents. Within the framework of the game it seems evident there is something of a conspiracy against Murdoch on several levels.

On the news and features desks themselves Murdoch has incurred the wrath of a faction of journalists who call themselves the free communicators. Murdoch's attitude to them is on public record. He thinks they are dangerous and impractical. Like most left-wing organizations dedicated to one form of agitation or another, they get highly indignant at criticism. A lot of what they stand for is highly attractive to the working journalist, although many people feel their ideas are unworkable. The essence of their movement is that editorial and management policy should pass into the hands of the journalists themselves. They plan a 'workers' council' of themselves to run virtually every aspect of the newspapers they work on. Their enemies accuse them of wanting to abuse the power and freedom of the press by dominating free expression with their own minority viewpoints. Be that as it may, the free communicators are scattered liberally around Fleet Street and are slowly beginning to dominate the National Union of Journalists at chapel level. The *Sun* itself has a fair share of them and the militancy of that union is an obvious result. But with the exception of obviously left-orientated periodicals like the *New Statesman*, the largest faction of free communicators can be found enjoying a great deal of influence at the *Sunday Times*.

The *Sunday Times* is one of the strangest and most interesting newspapers in Britain. It breeds a weird species of reporter who is radical, opinionated and has a very high regard for his own newspaper. These reporters manage, through their own self-confidence, to wrap sometimes speculative stories in a cloak of respectable, deep, inside reporting which has a veneer of authenticity and credibility. While many people accept the *Sunday Times* as the best newspaper of its kind anywhere in the world, others also often resent its sheer arrogance.

The majority of journalists at the *Sunday Times* share

with the free communicators the same frothy indignation at criticism and are firmly convinced they are the only ones in the world who are right. The free communicators and many people on the *Sunday Times* see Murdoch as a right-wing dictator who has not only plunged the editorial level of Fleet Street down the drain, but has reintroduced to sleeping managements the interfering hand of an active proprietor. (In fact, under the rural socialism of Larry Lamb the *Sun* has consistently been deeply socialist orientated.)

It is fair to say that the free communicators are after Murdoch's blood in any possible way and have succeeded on a minor level in striking several successful blows.

Up at Thomson House, almost incidentally, they also enjoy the undoubted influence of Tom Margerison, sacked by Murdoch from London Weekend Television, and it was made abundantly clear to me by several *Sunday Times* reporters that Margerison was pushing very hard against Murdoch. One told me, 'I don't think Murdoch realizes how many enemies he has scattered around Fleet Street. And they are gaining the ear of a lot of people.'

The campaign from the *Sunday Times* culminated in 1974 in a profile of Murdoch by a reporter on the paper called Peter Dunn. The story was written three times, each time, despite a cautious note from editor Harold Evans, more strongly anti-Murdoch than the last. When Murdoch read the article it upset him quite considerably and at one stage he was planning to issue an injunction against the paper to stop it being printed in the colour magazine. In a letter to Evans he pointed out thirty-seven separate mistakes, all of which he claimed could be proved and many of which were libellous. The final version actually printed had little of the original in it.

In the middle of all this activity the free communicators were also obtaining some News International shares, so they could attend the AGM and attack Murdoch from the floor. At the same time, a huge union attack on management was being waged—mainly at the *Sun*—which resulted in many long and heavy sessions of the NPA.

There was then a consolidated effort on several levels to take

pokes at Murdoch. And in one way or another, they could be
seen to be threatening the Murdoch camp. (Although Murdoch
seemed to be the only one oblivious to it all. He felt personally
hurt by many of the things said about him but shrugged
suggestions of conspiracy away as irrelevant.) Into this atmosphere then, dropped from the very heavens the actual morsel
of propaganda a lot of the rest of Fleet Street had been waiting
for. The Lambton affair burst upon an unsuspecting public
through the columns of a Murdoch newspaper itself.

Another facet emerged at this point on the 'personalization'
of Murdoch. For example, early in the same year the *Daily
Express* made one of the biggest and most stupid journalistic
blunders by printing the Martin Bormann story with incredible
claims of 'conclusive new evidence ... fully substantiated'. When
the whole thing was exposed as a fake no one went around
saying, 'Aitken's done it again. What a blunderer the man is.'
But when the Lambton affair hit the headlines everyone, including the *Daily Express*, personalized it by directly blaming
Rupert Murdoch. It is not an exact parallel but demonstrates the
simple point that his critics never blame the paper but the
man himself. Murdoch somehow has been personalized and
it is a habit which has caught on throughout the media. During
a recent 'What the Papers Say', for instance, it was interesting
to note that the *Guardian* journalist mentioned every other
newspaper by its name but, when he came to the *News of the
World* and the *Sun*, said, 'Down in Bouverie Street, Mr Murdoch
felt it wise to print ...' The formidable Jean Rook even fell into
the familiar trap only two weeks later. After having a go with
her waspish tongue at every *newspaper* in Fleet Street, she then
picked on a front-page story in the *News of the World* and
asked why *Murdoch* had 'sent him to cover such trash'.

So it was that when the Lambton affair was at its height
everyone in Fleet Street was going around saying things like
'Murdoch's done another Keeler'. The *Express* campaign, under
the auspices of Jocelyn Stevens, attacked the *News of the
World* with regular daily snipes and was only stopped when
Murdoch 'phoned Aitken and told him if they continued the
News of the World would hit back by printing the rest of what

they knew concerning the affair. He pointed out that the only people who would get hurt by this would be the *Express* and Lambton. The *Express* quickly shut up.

The Diplock Commission set up to investigate the scandal was exceptionally disappointing and is still considered by many people to be remarkably inconclusive. It answered virtually none of the questions that the Lambton affair had thrown up.

Trevor Kempson of the *News of the World* was perhaps more versed in the intricacies of the affair than any other man alive, but according to him the Diplock Commission submitted their findings without ever approaching him or any other member of the staff. The essence of their complaint was that the *News of the World* had handed back to the potential vendor pictures they had taken at Norma Levy's flat, leaving the danger that they might be used to blackmail Lambton.

Throughout the proceedings, Chief Superintendent Bert Wickstead of Scotland Yard and Kempson had had varying formal and informal liaisons. Norma Levy and her husband Colin had been interviewed several times by Wickstead and the Levys became convinced in their own imaginations that MI5 might try and dispose of them surreptitiously because of the scandal looming. It was in this kind of panicking mood that Levy and his confederate, a man named Goodsell, had ventured into the *News of the World* office. They wanted someone else to know about it in case they were, as they put it, 'rubbed out'.

It was only after this point, when Lambton had been positively identified and the full realization of the unfolding scandal had become apparent that the story went upstairs to Larry Lamb and then Murdoch. It is not clear at this stage how much actual information was available to Murdoch when he was asked for his advice. The information had gone from Levy and Goodsell to Kempson, to Nick Lloyd, assistant editor, on to the editor, Lear, on to Lamb, editorial director, and finally to Murdoch. It is felt in some quarters that Murdoch was not given the whole story as told to Kempson, but this is unclear. Murdoch was to say later however, 'If I had known what I know now I would have printed right away on that Sunday.'

Larry Lamb's view was that it was an extremely important story but he advised Murdoch that they should not be compromised by paying these two men money for what amounted to clear violations of the law. Murdoch was persuaded by this argument and ordered that under no circumstances could any payment be made to Levy or Goodsell. The general feeling now is that the *News of the World* came under such attack anyway for *not* paying them *and* for handing back the pictures that they might as well have paid them and been done with it. Murdoch's view is that they owed no allegiance to a couple of 'dishonest pimps' and should have printed anyway on the grounds of national security.

Assistant editor, Nick Lloyd, said, 'I felt once we had started the investigation and found it to be substantially true we should have printed the whole thing in full on the first Sunday—payment or no payment.'

Kempson added, 'I had worked closely with the two men for a week and I had given them my word that, if the story proved correct, we would only use their direct evidence if we paid them. If we had conned them I would have been put into an impossible position. I had agreed with them that all the material evidence they had cooperated in collecting would belong to them unless we bought it from them.'

One of the most widespread misconceptions is that Kempson handed back the relevant photographs when no payment was to be forthcoming. In fact Mr Levy, who was not completely unintelligent, had followed photographer Brian Thomas into the darkroom and grabbed the negatives immediately they were developed. 'He was convinced we might con them and he took the stuff immediately. We did not mind at the time because we still believed we would be doing the story together,' an executive remembers.

Later the Press Council again singled out the *News of the World* for criticism in such a way as to make even Murdoch's sternest critics blink at the seeming unfairness. One criticism of the censure on the *News of the World* was that it appeared to bear little relation to the bulk of the evidence and reasoning

printed in the rest of the report. Larry Lamb's editorial the following Sunday was a classic piece of writing in every sense of the
word. It coolly and logically appraised the situation from the
beginning to end, including the Press Council's findings. And
then, just as coolly, dismissed them.

There is little doubt in most people's minds that if the
Sunday Times had broken the first story about Lambton it
would have been accepted very differently by Fleet Street, and
consequently, by the rest of the country.

Feelings in Bouverie Street ran high, and they angrily pointed
out that Murdoch's involvement with the scandal was merely
to say, after considering the version of the facts before him,
that he would not be party to buying the story. They felt that
the relish with which his critics, for their own motives, had
moved the general censure away from one kinky government
minister on to the head of Murdoch, was a piece of Fleet
Street dishonesty of the first order. The drivelling about his
'serious involvement leaving him cowering under a cloud', was
nothing short of absurd.

The Lambton affair was the last serious chapter in the long
confrontation Murdoch has had with the Press Council. They
have never exactly seen eye to eye and Murdoch's resentment
is tied up with the fact he thinks a captain should be master
of his own ship.

Certainly there is a growing feeling that the Press Council
has had its day. In the early sixties, newspapers were in a
bit of a dilemma. There were no concepts of reportage apart
from 'always tell the truth and look after your contacts'. There
were many sides to journalism which were unhealthy. *Daily
Express*-type journalism was notorious for sending too many
men on the same job and discrediting the men who missed.
Consequently journalists were spending a great deal of time
trying to out-do their own colleagues. The *People* and the *News
of the World* perpetuated a system of 'foot-in-the-door' brashness
which was sometimes highly questionable.

The Press Council, in its heyday, did succeed in establishing
a code of conduct for newspaper reporting and publishing which

had a generally healthy effect. But most people agree with Murdoch when he says few people listen anymore. And few care. The Council is acting like an annoying flea to be slapped as conveniently and as often as possible.

Murdoch came out vehemently against an Australian Press Council and used the British one as an example of 'useless interference'. Certainly his well-known views were not at all likely to enhance him with that particular body. He told Melbourne University that the British Press Council was manned by 'failed editors and retired schoolmasters'.

Murdoch's argument was that, because editors did not want interference, official or otherwise, they regulated themselves. 'Is not this what any good editor does when he edits?' he asked, and went on, 'If the critics of the press knew the extent to which an editorial executive will go to check a story, to exercise restraint when in doubt, to throw out what is in questionable taste—if our critics, in short, could sit there night after night until the early hours of each morning and participate in the lonely and irrevocable decisions taken on our behalf, there would be far fewer critics.

'The Press Council was invented as a fig-leaf by a frightened British press establishment at a time of genuine concern. Surely we do not need such hypocrisy in Australia. Certainly much of the picture snatching and foot-in-the-door journalism which used to be indulged in was curbed by the press itself before any council was invented—by the journalists and news editors of a new generation coming into Fleet Street.'

Referring to the Keeler affair in his argument against the Press Council Murdoch claimed it was alleged that they were hounding the former minister involved, but asked, 'Or were certain forces in British society coming together to try to stop us because they did not want the public reminded of the events of 1963?'

Murdoch rounded off his views on the Press Council by saying the Council was ineffectual compared to, say, television or radio criticism and claimed very little time was spent in any British newspaper office worrying about whether a story would result in a complaint to the Council.

'On the other hand, a great deal of time is spent in worrying whether a story might bring a newspaper into court. This is the essential difference—a difference between illusion and reality,' he added.

Chapter 7

America—and after?

I

Rupert Murdoch went to America because it was there. He went for the same reasons that mountains are climbed. It was the last hilltop in the world, and Murdoch, approaching middle age, was itchy to test himself on the biggest challenge he could find by climbing it. In 1975, a year after his arrival, I think it safe to say Murdoch has found a place which is big enough for him. His muscles are flexed and he has his teeth bitten hard on America's newspaper collar bone—but at last he has met his match. There can be no doubt he is enjoying success. But it is hard won, expensive, time consuming and competitive.

In a land positively dripping with rags to riches stories, no one in America is particularly impressed by the Australian tycoon. In fact, if they have heard about him at all in the States they mention it with a sort of kindly indulgence.

Judging his success is difficult because there are several sets of figures which show what various people want them to show, including Murdoch's rivals. But morale in New York is high, though Costello's Bar off Third Avenue, the haven for hard-bitten veteran Fleet Streeters, sports the same kind of bitchiness to be found any opening time in The Tipperary. He is making money in the States, lots of it. And I think most of the time *The National Star*, which Murdoch began with a huge fanfare in 1974, is a jolly good, tough, professional little paper.

A few months before Murdoch's weekly newspaper started hitting the news-stands he bought the morning and evening newspaper in San Antonio, Texas. Few people (unless they knew Murdoch) could understand the purchase. Those who knew him realized at once that it was the Murdoch method of getting a foot in the door. His foot, any door, so long as it had glass windows so he could look around for further purchases. (Parramatta and the *News of the World* were both typical foot-in-the-door purchases.) The Texas papers are both money-spinners and will certainly make extra profits for the international company, but I suspect Murdoch bought them for their strategic value as much as anything else. If his past record is anything to go by (and it must be) Murdoch will cover himself east, west, north and south, with distribution points, printing presses and money-making newspapers.

One of Murdoch's original ideas was that the big glossy monthly magazines had become far too subscriber-orientated. They were economically vulnerable because their readership had become unfeasibly large for the price they could charge. He wanted to cut out all subscriptions and sell directly through supermarkets or on the bookstalls themselves. He reckoned that, with the attraction of Fleet Street style front pages, he could compete with a distinct advantage.

His final plan carried on directly from this idea. By setting up a plant in New Jersey and starting a weekly British style newsmag he would by-pass the stranglehold of the main distributors and sell direct through supermarkets. A plan quickly written off as yet another example of Murdoch's formidable cheek, and his never-ending love of a newspaper punch-up.

Everyone felt 'Star' was a very American word. It was at first considered by most people, in and out of the company, to be the riskiest gamble he had ever undertaken. It cost a fortune and it has a rather high chance of failing. But Murdoch cannot ever resist a gamble and the higher the stakes the more the attraction. He put as much into the fight to succeed in New York as he has done in anything before.

His first efforts immediately showed reward. A senior executive coming back from New York reported, 'He's completely lost in the battle. Right now he can think of nothing else. He is totally immersed in winning.' Within a few months the circulation had soared beyond anyone's expectations. The formula, again, was at first exactly right. Overnight Murdoch became, as in London, a force in American journalism.

In 1973 the *Sun* had topped three million circulation and was obviously heading for the stars—spawning the now legendary exchange between Murdoch and Cudlipp in which Murdoch said, 'I think we may just reach four million before you Hugh,' a reference to the fact that most new *Sun* readers were snatched from the *Mirror*. But Murdoch felt it was time for a change.

It was five years since he had hit the Heathrow tarmac clutching his thin file of takeover papers. Five years is a long time for Murdoch to stay anywhere. There was no real reason to go to America. Murdoch was rich, famous in his home country and in England and fabulously successful. He told me some time before going to America that from now on he wanted to concentrate on what he had and build it into something greater—rather than just go on acquiring new assets. But the lure of that vast, untapped new market was simply too much for him.

His power in the European and Australian communications industry was immense. His organization was running smoothly and he had by now an undisputed reputation as a formidable and successful businessman. The new market in his life was born from fidgeting. He had become somewhat jaded by Britain. Trying to beat the economic problems in London was rather like beating your head against a brick wall. He had become disenchanted with the massive union power, by the bickering of the Press Council. He had become fed up with Fleet Street games. But, more important to any Murdoch watcher, he had become terribly bored.

As the success of the *Sun* seemed to become a simple fact of life Murdoch went into his play safe policy. They were winning, why rock the boat? For another of the central paradoxes in Murdoch's life is that once he has set it all up and it works, he likes to keep it that way—yet that is the very point at which he becomes disenchanted with the product and looks around for new ventures.

For nearly two years a break into America seemed to become almost an obsession with him. He made several forays there.

The Americans either seemed unimpressed by him, or wary of what he might do if they let him in. Larry Lamb went over to America several times to find out the feasibility of broadening the Murdoch empire.

At one stage he was offered, in separate deals, both *Look* and *Life*. He toyed with the idea but felt, in the end, that they were not for him. The one paper which fascinated Murdoch was *The National Enquirer*. He guessed it had fantastic potential, not only as one of America's fastest growing newspapers— but for him. He felt he could make it grow faster with his own personalized style of packaging a paper.

He emphatically denies ever making a bid for the paper. But there are certainly many witnesses to the fact that he visited Florida where *The Enquirer* operates, and people in that office insist he was very keen to buy and offered a record sum. Several of Murdoch's top executives also confirmed he had bid for the paper.

Murdoch's reaction to the situation was typical: he decided to start his own newspaper. The original plan was that he would start a similar tabloid, but it would be different and better. He reasoned that news-stands were the most underexploited distribution for a thrusting new tabloid. He also argued that newspapers in America practically never linked up with television advertising. After a year of operating in a typical *Sun* versus *Mirror* situation, *The Star* now makes no bones about the fact that it apes *The Enquirer* story for story.

The National Enquirer is now what the *Mirror* was to the *Sun* in Fleet Street in 1970. It has a tried and tested formula and a highly professional team working it. In 1975 it is the fastest growing publication in the States. It is the brainchild of Generoso Pope Jr., who lives and breathes his paper twenty-four hours a day. In the old days it was a blood and thunder crime paper which sold about a quarter of a million copies to gawkish people who got some kind of mental stimulation out of reading the sordid details of a rape case or looking at the bloodstained corpse of a murder victim. A typical front page contained a gory picture of a severed head. Few people will disagree with the fact that it was a dreadful newspaper.

Overnight, Pope, who came from an immigrant family who had started a successful Italian language newspaper in New York, changed the entire format and contents of the paper—dropping all the crime and gore and concentrating on a 'good family read'. It took off immediately as America's *Reader's Digest* in tabloid form and by the time Murdoch hit America it was compulsive reading for some fifteen million people.

There is no doubt that beating the *Enquirer* is Murdoch's present goal. He is doing with the *Star* what he did with the *Sun*. He has a ridiculously low budget; a small key team of top aides; he openly apes his rivals in a bid to cut off the lower end of their market. He pushes bare boobs and light reading as far as he can. He concentrates on brightness, but not necessarily lightness, and he neatly packages this in a fanfare of self-stimulated 'soaring success' jargon all over the front page.

There are two points where Murdoch is vulnerable. The *Star* is not dealing with a de-personalized IPC like the *Sun* was, Pope is to the *National Enquirer* what Murdoch was to the old *Adelaide News*. He counts the paper clips, crosses the 't's and dots the 'i's. He pushes the paper forward into new realms of battle on a daily basis. He demands and gets, quite ruthlessly, superhuman efforts by everyone from his top executive down to his assistant gardener.

While not accepting fully Pope's complete contempt for the *Star*, there is no doubt Murdoch will have to pull several strokes of genius before going on the soaring success wagon he has been used to in the past. The *Enquirer* is there and it intends to go on. Pope's goal is to beat the *TV Times*, a small format supermarket magazine which, because of habit buying, sells twenty million copies a week and has some sixty million readers. Pope wants to beat it and he pursues his goal with a single minded determination bordering on obsession. In my opinion, to beat Pope at his own game is going to take a little more than even Murdoch has got.

The second stumbling block is that Murdoch has not yet succeeded in courting the huge distribution combines into getting his new newspaper into the heart of America. Because of this the *Star* is New York-orientated and neither Murdoch, nor his team, has yet completely understood Middle America, where the really vast circulations can be had.

It is still far too early yet to predict doom for Murdoch. This man who has been so full of surprises in the past, is by no means likely to let things rest as they are. Challenge is, indeed, his carrot and it will be interesting to see where his particular kind of dynamic pushing will take the *Star*.

II

Rupert's entry into American journalism, in his now customary dramatic and flamboyant way, made it evident London has been but a staging post to bigger and better things. It belittled Murdoch's own statement: 'Now I've got to this stage [London] the thing I really want to do is go back into the company and start reinforcing all its weak points—rather than continue break-neck expansion.' The move confirmed to many that he would never be satisfied and that he must always continue higher and further. It must now at least be a relevant question to ask whether he will ever be able to stop.

When Murdoch moved to America the general criticism of him changed. During 1974, when it seemed he was going to make it successfully in the United States, a whole new emphasis on how people interpreted him emerged. By then most of the former criticisms of him had become obsolete or unimportant. In the past, individual criticism of Murdoch had built up gradually into a confused mêlée of gossip, fact, fiction, spite, anecdote, jealousy and plain animosity. But as his rampage speeded up and began to broaden the individual criticism could not keep up with him.

Adrian Deamer's thoughts began to get *passé* and almost ridiculous because issues became so much broader than the function of the Australian newspaper alone. Everything had begun to get empire-minded, and although it is possibly difficult for any journalist to see a great deal farther than the newspaper he is working on, a gradual awareness of the sheer size of the organization began to take over. Then the basic pattern of criticism changed radically. It became general and concerned more the ideals and methods of Murdoch, rather than personal swipes and gripes from low-levellers who wanted to grouse about the boss.

The American move makes assessments of him increasingly difficult because even in the two years leading up to it Murdoch has moved so far so fast that every conclusion about him has had to be revalued every few months.

But there is a mood in his organization which has been growing continuously and is still prevalent. The American saga crystallized this mood of frustration which, at the end of it all, is much more significant than all the other general criticisms put together. His strident and overriding success has begun to make the old feelings, i.e. that he was ruthless, decadence-orientated and circulation crazy—rather jaded. It no longer matters. True or false, the arguments have been overtaken by his overwhelming success and they begin to seem very spoil-sport and childish.

The frustration has always been there, perhaps not as deeply felt as it is today, but it has been a fact of life for most Murdoch employees for most of the time they have worked for him. It has gradually come about because the rather wonderful corner grocery shop where Murdoch was the almost Victorian, kind but frugal patron, is now a glossy supermarket, twelve storeys high, with tinsel in the windows, and the boss is only glimpsed from time to time rushing to open a new department.

In the early days the postgraduate Murdoch once caused objections because he was too hard on a junior reporter on the family newspaper where he appeared early every morning. He managed to dismiss most resentment against him by rolling up his sleeves and getting down to the serious and essential business of running the daily news. Resentment now snaps and snarls at him from the depths of an organization where a vast majority of employees have never seen him and where the 'grocery' philosophy brings nothing but calculated cynicism. These sneers, wherever the Murdoch media penetration can be found, are extenuated by the professional opposition who have been left reeling by the rather extraordinary way in which Murdoch has suddenly come and gone out of their lives. The only way in which much of this criticism could be balanced was by listening to people who had joined the Murdoch team and decided to go all the way on his bandwagon of success. But neither side can rationally be expected to be without self-interest.

Critics who moan because Murdoch has vetoed their expenses are now no longer taken seriously. The issue is much broader. In a nutshell he is able very successfully to pop up somewhere, create a highly saleable product, and disappear leaving the floor managers to carry on selling it. And the floor managers, talented and efficient though they are, have to conform to the policy of the giant store as a whole. No one is going to rock the boat and the colour of the tinsel in the window must never clash with that of the department next door.

Right back at the very beginning in Adelaide, Murdoch caused considerable controversy in that sunny city. But you will not see many upsetting banner headlines in Adelaide today. His onslaught on Sydney was similar. While he sat by his telephone dictating headlines, or rushed down to the sub and put some more guts into a last-minute story, the rough and tumble of Sydney's cosmopolitan news readers blinked at the stones and boulders he managed to overturn. But now he has gone and the day's news is carefully contrived to be utterly readable and well presented, but never to take a chance.

The Sydney scene was different to the London one in that his Australian newspaper wars were fought on the streets. It was tough, terse, controversial headlines which attracted the casual reader and gradually built up his coveted circulations. It was a poster in the corner milk bar which decided that day's figures. And the Australian newspapers are almost completely geared to a twenty-four-hour circulation figure.

The fundamental change which took place when Murdoch reached British shores was that his war became a 'product war' in which a carefully conceived package was sold through advertising. The *News of the World* was a useful acquisition, but it was never Murdoch's baby. It already had a circulation bigger than any in Europe. There was very little Murdoch could actually do to the paper and he was itching, after the stimulation of the takeover battle, to roll up his sleeves and get 'involved' again. Murdoch simply has to create his own impetus and although it must be admitted he put some fireworks well and truly up the Bouverie Street backside, he became bored very quickly with twenty-four pages a week.

The immediate answer, of course, came with the *Sun*. Here again he was able to show what he was made of. He sat in the middle of the new-found razzamatazz clearly enjoying every second of it. Emotionally he was back in Adelaide, with his shirt sleves rolled up getting a daily paper on the streets and pulling every stop out of the book to make sure it appeared with a bang. Here was the true Murdoch: the impish post-graduate with his new toy showing it off to everyone who would look. And the paper crackled with life.

The essential difficulty with all his newspapers comes when Murdoch goes on to new things. Once each of the papers he has been involved with becomes a steady and victorious seller there is little left to satisfy the Murdoch ego, impetus, or imagination. So he moves on.

He takes an interest in every newspaper in his organization. But gradually, as his world broadens, this interest becomes more superficial. It is simply impossible for him to create his own special brand of atmosphere in three very separate corners of the world all at once. Once he has moved on his interest becomes inevitably one of managerial decision. He will be consulted on a price rise. He will bark at a circulation loss. He will praise a profit figure or he will comment on an editorial.

The accusation that he delves too deeply into editorial policy becomes ludicrous after he has gone. In fact he is not able to be involved enough. Those he has left, both in Australia and England, are unable or unwilling to put the essential impetus into their respective papers that Murdoch himself managed when he was there. This means that eventually the paper loses its real teeth. There can be no doubt that the formula he has left them with is successful. And if the circulation stays where it is, or, more important, goes up, along with profits, no one is going to complain. But when he is not there no one is going to rock the boat either. The newspaper immediately becomes a carefully contrived marketable commodity which in many ways is sold like a packet of soapflakes. There is little anyone—even Murdoch—can do about the situation, but it is a shame.

It is strongly argued that the Murdoch management could well keep the circulation of its newspapers up by spending less on direct promotion and risking more on its libel fund. A controversial argument but the point, if not the subject, is valid.

Murdoch did, in fact, admit in an exclusive interview, 'I think it is a fair criticism to say my main fault is that as we expanded I became more of a businessman and devoted less time to the creative side of my newspapers. If you're head of a company you have to take an interest in everything. Whether it be union negotiations or newsprint. There's always something.

'But I still firmly believe that the great thrill of publishing is that you are making a new product every day. Every edition is a new creation. The problem is forever trying to get enough time to spend on the creative side of your newspapers once you've become a big businessman.

'My original ambition was to be something bigger and better than the publisher of a weak evening paper. But I can be criticized for sometimes forgetting my original motives. You build a big business in order to publish good newspapers. But once you've built that big business you are on a treadmill. You are trapped by it. And you can be in danger of losing touch with your journalists.'

This is one of the most significant things Murdoch has said because it shows that he is deeply aware of the one thing which is becoming most dangerous to the function of his empire.

The ingredients of the *Sun* are just right for these times in Fleet Street. The idea has worked. The circulation is rising, the management is tough and, within limitations, highly imaginative. But without Murdoch's personal, direct involvement, the paper tends to have a body without real soul; a personality without character, and a cockiness without guts.

There can be no greater example of this frustration than with the *News of the World*. Whatever its reputation in the

old days, it had fire and it roared. Nowadays, although some
of the traditional magic can be found in its pages, it is gradually
becoming a Sunday *Sun*. This is not so much a mistake as a
great shame. For the real and very personal guts of the paper
are being gradually eroded. It is becoming another product on
the production line of a large organization.

Within Fleet Street there is no sight of another Arthur
Christiansen to roar like a prophet at the disciples of his god.
Nor the earthy wisdom and cackling good humour of a Sam
Campbell to whom all humbug was a mortal sin; there's no
Northcliffe on the horizon. They've all gone and left the roaring
headlines, the character and guts and the fire and the glory to
production-line journalism dependent not on reputation, but
on advertising and stunts. In fact, there was only Murdoch
who was able, for a while, to instil that old magic. Now he
too has gone, in most senses of the word, and taken most of
Fleet Street's remaining razzamatazz with him.

III

Business-wise, the Murdoch empire has never been healthier.
Murdoch's now famous winning financial formula is little short
of mind-boggling if one considers how he could expand in the
future if he keeps to the same takeover pattern. Through his
system of reverse takeovers he manages to double his company's
assets every seven to eight years. Look at the pattern. He holds
a major shareholding in the home-base company (Cruden
Investments). This company owns a large holding in News
Limited (Sydney), which in turn owns a major shareholding in
News International (London). By offering a major slice of his
company for fifty-one per cent of the new company the pyramid
process goes on. News International would have cost in the
region of sixty million pounds if someone had wanted to take
over every share (and lock and stock). Murdoch's pyramid
theory on paper gives him enough power to take over a majority
shareholding in a company worth about one hundred and
twenty million pounds. Although Cruden Investments itself
only has a limited say in the new company, the spiralling

process gives Murdoch the ultimate power at source. Simple paper mathematics on the Murdoch/Mervyn Rich formula indicate that this pyramid could grow to unlimited proportions. With speculation, in five or six years time, when the company has steadied after the American expansion he could, in theory, go for a company worth more than two hundred million pounds and still have the ultimate personal power in the organization at ground level.

It would still be impossible to unseat him through this process. For the major company would have to go to its shareholders. Fifty-one per cent of these are owned by a Murdoch company which would have to go to *its* shareholders, which in turn ... as I said, the mind boggles.

This is the theory. In fact Murdoch had made it work for him so far on an even more incredible scale. He didn't offer one hundred per cent of News Limited when he took over the News of the World Organization. He offered a small fraction of his assets—and a rather small amount of ready cash. This is good business, but essentially the Murdoch dreams go on because of his own kind of bravado and aggressive self-stimulation.

IV

Murdoch is deep down, as we have discovered, an 'Australian' Australian. He reflects in many ways that country's burning desire to prove itself to the rest of the world. He has the deep-rooted inferiority complex which is covered by the customary brashness and nervous cheek of the Australian nature. His action is a kind of cocky, yet somehow self-defensive, show of aggressive brilliance.

America was, in fact, a logical step. It put the fourth chapter to his astonishing life-pattern. It completed the final part of the first half of everything he has done. It must be true to say now, geographically speaking, he simply *can't* go anywhere else of relevance. The 'breakneck expansion' must at least be held within the confines of what he already has. Yet these 'confines' are now literally straddling the globe.

Murdoch broke into America less than a quarter of a century after he stepped off the plane to take over in Adelaide. The whole thing was a natural progression. The brash and cocky youngster who first took on and beat the deep-rooted Adelaide Victorianism had now gone through the tough battles of Sydney, grown up and matured in London, and was an established, and, in American terms even more important, a 'winning' newspaper tycoon of international reputation.

His arrival in America was as different to his arrival in Adelaide as anything could be. Even his first appearance in Sydney had been met with hoots of laughter (and the over-riding feeling that a quick couple of spanks would send him reeling). Until he left Sydney, his name was almost totally unknown outside Australia. When he came to London he was 'an Australian buying into Fleet Street'. When he arrived in American he was no longer thought of only as an Australian, but rather as an international publisher who had a tough Fleet Street background behind him.

It is difficult to say how much he had learned in Fleet Street but it must have been considerable. He combined his talent for learning (Adelaide) with his battling instincts (Sydney) to meet the whole broader spectrum of Fleet Street life, politics and diplomacy. Had he arrived in Fleet Street any sooner he might well have failed. It is irrelevant to say that, had he stayed in London any longer, he might have got complacent, because it is now evident he never planned to do so. Once again his timing was perfect. He had stayed just long enough to further his reputation, both journalistically and financially; consolidate the whole company under one flag; choose his executives so the company could, in the main, run without him; find others to take with him; find the cash for a daring new venture; and get the organization, once again, geared up to expansion. He didn't stop in London a day longer than he had to. When the place was set up to look after itself his eyes cast about hungrily for new horizons.

But the higher he gets the harder it becomes to assess the motivation behind it all. In Adelaide, the beginning, he decided he must have a broader platform from which to operate because with only one newspaper his news sources were so strangled. His expansion motive, if he is to be believed, was that with three or four papers he could afford to buy syndication rights, have his own foreign coverage, and so on. This was obviously very logical. His foray into Sydney was understandable and highly successful. It was the most logical step he could have taken at the time.

With the move to London, however, we are dealing with something completely different. The motivation was no longer to produce bigger, better newspapers. It was self-ambition and challenge. The fact that his successful bid for the News of the World Organization was quickly followed by a fabulous Fleet Street success story, is great in itself. But by then all the original motives must have changed.

Was he sincere in his first efforts to produce better newspapers? If he was, when did that particular ambition begin to be taken over by purely expansionist ambitions? (By this I am not particularly trying to say ambition in a newspaper owner is a bad thing. But I *am* trying to establish Murdoch's real motives. Mainly because the most unanswerable thing about him, now epitomized by his furious attack on America, is exactly *what* drives the man on.) Is he now on a spiral from which he can simply not get off? Going higher and higher to the top of mountain after mountain merely because there is another one on the horizon? Is he doped on getting bigger? *Could* he stop if he wanted to?

I think it is now too late. Murdoch will not be satisfied until he has conquered America and when he has done that he will not be satisfied until he has conquered the world. Whatever the original motives were, they are now no longer only a matter of having better newspapers, but of having *more* newspapers. The fundamental Murdoch dream of a family dynasty has ceased to be an Australian concept but one of world proportions.

Essentially Murdoch is still playing two-up. He is on a winning streak of heads. And while the coins fall down his way he will find it hard to stop. His real danger in the future will be that, if the breakneck expansion continues, the corporation will get too big for him, or any single person for that matter, to handle. The story of the future will be to see whether Murdoch is gambler enough to stop before the coins start showing their tails.

Index